Charlotte Perkins Gilman
The Woman and Her Work

Charlotte Perkins Gilman
The Woman and Her Work

Edited by
Sheryl L. Meyering

With a Foreword by
Cathy N. Davidson

UNIVERSITY OF ROCHESTER PRESS

Originally produced and distributed 1989 by
UMI Research Press
an imprint of
University Microfilms Inc.
Ann Arbor, Michigan 48106

Reprinted in paperback and transferred to digital printing 2010

University of Rochester Press
668 Mt. Hope Avenue, Rochester, NY 14620, USA
www.urpress.com
and Boydell & Brewer Limited
PO Box 9, Woodbridge, Suffolk IP12 3DF, UK
www.boydellandbrewer.com

Cloth ISBN-10: 0-8357-1931-6
Cloth ISBN-13: 978-0-83571-931-5
Paperback ISBN-13: 978-1-58046-389-8

Library of Congress Cataloging-in-Publication Data

　　Charlotte Perkins Gilman : the woman and her work / edited by
　　　Sheryl L. Meyering
　　　　p. cm. — (Challenging the literary canon)
　　　Includes bibliographical references and index.
　　　ISBN 0-8357-1931-6 (hardcover: alk. paper)
　　　　1. Gilman, Charlotte Perkins, 1860-1935. 2. Authors, American — 19th
　　century — Biography. 3. Authors, American — 20th century — Biography.
　　4. Feminists — United States — Biography. I. Meyering, Sheryl L., 1948-.
　　II. Series.
　　PS1744.G57Z63 1989
　　818'.409 — dc19
　　[B]　　　　　　　　　　　　　　　　　　　　　　　　　88-27771
　　　　　　　　　　　　　　　　　　　　　　　　　　　　　　CIP

A catalogue record for this title is available from the British Library.

This publication is printed on acid-free paper.
Printed in the United States of America

To Linda and Cathy,
superior scholars, mentors, and friends

Contents

Foreword

Charlotte Perkins Gilman was a woman ahead of *our* time. To rediscover her as a woman merely for our time renders her a harmless cliché (too out of touch with her own world's reality to change it), and, at the same time, consigns her to certain oblivion once our time passes. Gilman is too important, too good to be rediscovered simply because she is relevant. More to the point, the whole concept of "relevance" perpetuates a simplistic view of history as progress, as if the present era is intrinsically superior to the past and we have now realized the society Gilman merely envisioned. No one would find that self-satisfied view further from the truth than Gilman herself. She was master of pointing out the pomposities and hypocrisies of the various eras that came and went during her lengthy writing career. In fact, many of her essays and stories offer up solutions to problems just now being addressed by the most recent of America's women's movements. Long before the "Me Decade," Charlotte Perkins Gilman wrote about the delusive nature of "having it all," perceptively analyzing the pitfalls of that female variation on the ages-old American dream of collective progress through individual self-fulfillment.

What makes this collection of essays so vital is that it shows how Gilman herself, as a woman and as an author, probed the most basic and *unchanged* conditions under which women—now and, no doubt, a hundred years from now—live out the contradictions of modern existence. These essays do not treat Gilman as an antiquarian curiosity nor as some lifeless icon untouched by the indecisions that inevitably plague the life of a thinking woman. Instead, they acknowledge Gilman's contribution as one of America's premier social philosophers, as an important fiction writer, and as an activist whose ideas can still threaten the status quo.

There is something timeless (or perpetually timely) about Gilman's work, and yet she suffered the cruelest fate of any artist—she outlived her own popularity, saw her work dismissed, watched herself be forgotten, like a silent bystander at her own literary funeral. But precisely when she began to seem most "unnecessary," her work was most needed. Winning the vote hardly changed the lives of American women, something Gilman predicted before passage of the Nineteenth Amendment and lamented thereafter. A suffragist herself, she yet warned that suffrage alone would not be enough. And she eloquently articulated the obstacles to woman's individual aspirations in a society where employment opportunities and remuneration were not equal for men and women and where not even such basics as childcare or shared domestic duties could be taken for granted. She understood that nothing, substantively, would change for women until everything did. And she demanded nothing short of the massive revamping of the gender values and priorities of her society.

As Sheryl Meyering shows in her fine Introduction to this collection, Gilman articulated the contradictory nature of women's roles both in her public and private writings. She is perhaps the most eloquent on the subject in the voluminous letters she wrote to the man who would become her first husband, Charles Walter Stetson, letters copied in Stetson's own hand into his own diary (an appropriate metaphor for his appropriating designs towards Gilman herself). One is struck over and over by the genius of this woman who understood the implications of the culturally oxymoronic designation "woman writer." Stetson recounts numerous instances of Gilman's ambivalence toward the role he would assign her, as submissive, domestic helpmeet to the great artist. He notes in his diary:

> While [Charlotte] was sitting in my lap she said, "When I am with you I feel '*little*,' you hurt my pride over & over, I don't feel half so powerful or think that I am of half as much need to the world in general. I shrink from it—my pride cries out. I feel so with no one else." The dear woman's pride *has* been touched: if I mistake not it is the beginning of a womanhood sweet beyond words.[1]

No one familiar with Gilman's later writings would be surprised to learn that this marriage was brief and disastrous. "Pride" had different meanings for the woman and the man, one of whom felt she had to fight for what the other felt it his duty to destroy. This dilemma, for Gilman, was at the heart of the tragic relations between the sexes. Her marriage to Stetson, with its debilitating assumptions about the nature of women and men, became the material for *The Yellow Wallpaper*, certainly among the most harrowing portraits of stultifying, self-destroying marriage ever written.

Like the wife and mother trapped in the yellow room, Gilman learned (and have we yet begun to master this lesson?) that, in larger political and psychological terms, "having it all" meant having nothing. In biographical terms, her nervous breakdown followed upon the birth of her child and the increasing realization of the destruction of pride—of her writing, revolutionary self—that being Stetson's wife and the mother of his child would require. In literary terms, the catastrophe of that marriage fueled her lifelong attempt to rewrite a society where all women were allowed to be creative, intelligent, and maternal. But for this new kind of woman to emerge, Gilman argued, there would have to be profound social restructuring of work, leisure, the "separate spheres" of male and female activity, collective child-rearing and domestic responsibilities, as well as a transvaluation of male and female values.

Gilman's largest concern, in all her work, is with *economy* (literally "household managing") in its fullest sense. She demanded reform in the "legal and social, mental and physical" arrangements of the world, reforms that would "mark the advance of the mother of the world toward her full place."[2] Our own generation has also raised these concerns, but few, in Gilman's time or ours, have explored them so thoroughly. There were inconsistencies in Gilman's theories (notably, vacillations between essentialist and environmentalist explanations for male and female personality differences); there were shortcomings in her personal vision (including bigoted racial and ethnic stereotypes); there were discrepancies between the life she aspired to and the one she led. This collection does not ignore those faults. But it also pays homage to one of America's most challenging and inventive writers. And it should make us humble to realize that we've not come such a very long way, baby, after all.

CATHY N. DAVIDSON

Notes

1. Mary Armfield Hill, ed., *Endure: The Diaries of Charles Walter Stetson,* (Philadelphia: Temple University Press, 1985), pp. 162–63.

2. Charlotte Perkins Stetson [Gilman], *Women and Economics. A Study of the Economic Relation between Men and Women as a Factor in Social Evolution,* 2nd ed. (Boston: Small, Maynard & Co., 1899), p. 148.

Introduction

Sheryl L. Meyering

When she died in 1935, Charlotte Perkins Gilman left behind a legacy of imaginative writing that includes a volume of poetry (and hundreds of uncollected poems), nearly two hundred short stories, and nine novels, among which are three utopian romances and one detective story. Only one of these novels was never published in its entirety. All the others were first serialized in Gilman's magazine, *The Forerunner,* and four of them were eventually published in book form.[1] Despite such a prolific career, however, the scope of Gilman's work was virtually forgotten for several decades after her death. When she was mentioned, it was usually in connection with her theoretical work, especially *Women and Economics,* the most famous of her six books of essays.

In 1956, Carl Degler published the first critical assessment of Gilman's work since her death, and as a result the long overdue rediscovery of Gilman as an important turn-of-the-century American writer was underway. In his essay, Degler decries the unjustified neglect Gilman suffered, observing that "if, as most would agree, America in the last fifty years has altered its attitude toward the working woman, then Charlotte Perkins Gilman must be assigned a significant part in the accomplishment of that change."[2]

The women's movement of the 1960s and the emergence of feminist criticism fueled the interest begun by Degler. All of Gilman's major works have now been reprinted, and in 1971 the Schlesinger Library at Radcliffe College acquired her papers. In 1973, the Feminist Press published an edition of "The Yellow Wallpaper" with its now well-known afterword by Elaine Hedges. Since that time "The Yellow Wallpaper," and to a lesser extent *Herland,* a utopian romance, have been widely anthologized and frequently taught in both nineteenth-century and twentieth-century literature courses, as well as in women's literature and women's studies courses. In 1980, Pantheon Books published *The Charlotte Perkins Gilman Reader,* a collection of eleven short stories and excerpts from seven novels, edited and introduced by Ann J. Lane. In addition, the number of Ph.D. dissertations being produced on Gilman is increasing dramatically.

Although critical articles on Gilman's lesser-known imaginative works are beginning to appear in leading literary journals, most analyses produced since the early 1970s have focused on "The Yellow Wallpaper" and, less often, *Herland*. Often feminist in approach, these articles have explored the stultifying oppression of the woman artist within a patriarchal culture and literary tradition. Creative women were trapped inside the rigid nineteenth-century ideology of the "woman's sphere," a world defined by domestic concerns. A woman fulfilled her life's calling by providing succor and a peaceful haven–home for her husband, enabling him to conduct the important business of the world. To fail in this calling was to fail as a woman.

As Sandra M. Gilbert and Susan Gubar have pointed out, "a society where women are warned that if they do not behave like angels they must be monsters" is crippling to all women, but especially to those women who strive for "literary self-creation."[3] Gilbert and Gubar read "The Yellow Wallpaper" as a "striking story of female confinement and escape, a paradigmatic tale, which . . . seems to tell *the* story that all literary women would tell if they could speak their 'speechless woe.' "[4]

In her afterword to the 1973 Feminist Press edition of "The Yellow Wallpaper," Elaine Hedges discussed the story's images of suffocation and confinement: "Woman as prisoner; woman as child or cripple; woman, even, as a fungus growth. . . . These images permeate Gilman's story. If they are images men had of women, and hence that women had of themselves, it is not surprising that madness and suicide bulk large in the work of late nineteenth-century women writers."[5] Comparing Gilman to Emily Dickinson, Edith Wharton, and Kate Chopin, Hedges goes on to point out that Gilman was just one of several women writers of her century whose characters served as "dramatic indictments . . . of the crippling social pressures imposed on women . . . and the sufferings they thereby endured."[6]

One particularly revealing record of Gilman's personal experience of the conflict produced by these "crippling social pressures" is the recently published diaries of the artist Charles Walter Stetson, Gilman's first husband.[7] Because Stetson inserted the complete texts of many of Gilman's letters to him, the reader is allowed a kind of panoramic view of their romantic relationship as it unfolded. We are given a clear picture of the ways Stetson's opinions and assumptions influenced Gilman and exacerbated the inner discord she suffered.

By the time she met Stetson in January 1882, Charlotte Perkins had already decided that her life would be one of independence and work. Her "mission" was to improve the world. On the occasion of their second meeting, she greeted Stetson "at the door with a pen in her mouth and her hand thrust out to be grasped" (26). In her second letter to him, written shortly after this meeting, she is adamant about her goals and aspirations:

> Let me tell you . . . that I am not the combining sort. I *don't* combine and I don't want to. My nature is the polliest of polygons, whose happiness it is true depends on the contact of its many faces . . . but which keeps its own unchanging shape. . . . My life is one of private aspiration and development, and of public service. . . . I will give and give and give you *of* myself, but never give myself to you or any man. (28–30)

Very soon, however, cracks begin to appear in her resolve. Less than a week later, Stetson records the following conversation:

> Said I: "Why do you not wish to be loved by me—to love me?"
>
> "I think that you know nothing would be me more joy than to know that you love me. But—you know of my plans: you know of the work I have set about doing."
>
> "How would my love hinder you? I can think of no good plans which true love ought to or would hinder."
>
> "Oh, on the simplest of physiological grounds I know that a love begun should be consummated: and consummation would mean relinquishment of all my plans—and it would feed the side of my nature which I am holding in check. I am pretty evenly balanced, animal & spiritual. Were I to give up—I fear I should give all up and become of no more use than other women." (33)

So began a tumultuous, anxiety-filled courtship that lasted nearly two-and-a-half years. Charlotte, of course, is split right down the middle. The prospect of marriage, home, and family appeals to her not only because society expects her to desire that life, but also because she is sexually and emotionally drawn to Stetson: "He was quite the greatest man . . . I had ever known," she says in her autobiography.[8] At the same time, however, she was certain that marriage and motherhood would sap her strength and steal her time, making work outside the home impossible for her. She articulates her distress with amazing clarity. A long section of her March 29, 1883, letter to Stetson bears quoting here:

> There will be times when this frenzy for freedom boils up with force, which ungratified, would bring misery to myself and those around me; and there will be times when the woman's heart will wake and cry with heart-rending loneliness.
>
> Then shall I seek for you like a dream—the tired child that wakes and feels for its mother, and if I do not find you there is nothing but a great blackness and despair, a deep remorseful agony, the unending horror of feeling that I myself have thrust you from me and woven my own shroud. That my love for you is strong you are yourself witness. You have yourself said that it was all you could even ask, more than you had hoped or dreamed. That the other me is strong witness the present trial, when a year's flourishing tenderness has vanished in a week or two; and the delight in your love is lost entirely in the horrified shrinking at confinement, restricting possession.
>
> Now these things are before me: I give myself to you and honorably fulfill all my duties at whatever cost: subduing my deep-rooted desires and crushing out this Doppelgänger of mine

whenever it appears. In due time I should reach content I doubt not; and should only suffer at intervals.

And *if* the glorious sweetness of our love held its own in both of us should know joy enough to overweigh all pain.

Or: I leave you, and strengthen myself at all points, subduing in turn fierce heartache when it rose. In due time I should reach content, I doubt not, and should only suffer at intervals. And *if* my promise of energy and power hold its own, my sense of duty and place fulfilled would counterbalance heartaches. (153)

These were the alternatives she herself envisioned. Stetson had not presented them to her as a kind of ultimatum. He did not need to. She was aware that her own inner torment was a result of having to *choose* between two equally painful options. Rejecting marriage meant "blackness and despair"; marriage itself meant "shrinking confinement." The violent emotional upheaval experienced as a result of this kind of double-bind has been poured onto countless pages of women's fiction, poetry, letters, and diaries, but never more forcefully than Gilman does it here.

Stetson himself sees the two Charlottes only too clearly, and throughout the entire painful courtship he tried to encourage the one who wanted marriage, home, and children, and to discourage the "Doppelgänger":

[Charlotte] had one of those spasms of wanting to make a name for herself in the world by doing good work: wanting to have people know her as Charlotte Perkins, not the wife of me. She drew back with her old time feeling of independence from the prospect of sinking herself in our community. God alone knows how the terrible mood came again to her, for one could scarce find a happier being than she has been for months, or one more desirous of making me happy and of having a home & husband, & children & undying love. And she changed—changed—changed—and who knows how? . . . I had been lifted away up by her masterful passion & caresses and it brought me low and stabbed me with a rugged edged knife. (144)

Stetson is convinced that the only way Charlotte can find fulfillment and peace of mind is to devote herself to him, their children, their home. Female energy is naturally ordained to be directed toward home and family. Thus, he sees Charlotte's desires as unnatural—they are "spasms." When they come over her, she is not "in a fit state to marry: there must be something very morbid in her brain . . ." (144–45). This morbidity, in turn, gives rise to what in Stetson's opinion are very bizarre, freakish ideas: "She had a wild theory about living in one place—a home of her 'own' and having me come and see her when the erotic tendency was at a maximum. Of course I would not do that: and I would not think much of a man who would do it. The sweetest of marriage is cooperation towards advancement: close communion at all times, and the founding of a hearth. I will accept nothing else" (144).

Stetson states his case openly to Charlotte, who vacillates from one side of the conflict to the other with increasing regularity and intensity. When she can bear it no longer, she proposes a postponement of the marriage plans and a separation from Stetson as a way to help her make a decision. He quotes the P.S. of a letter in which she tries to convince him that a separation is for the best: "It may be if I were once married, and a mother, I should stay so forever in glad content. I cannot tell." Then he comments on it: "The bearing of a lusty pair of twins would weed her of her folly. . . . That [P.S.], from 'The Princess' I think, to my mind has much truth in it" (154). He assesses her multiple personalities, and, of course, "The Princess" is the one he wants to marry. She would be a boon to his art: "My work is not done as well as it would be if I had a fond wife for my arms" (160). All the while, however, Charlotte worries that wifehood will block the path to her own self-fulfillment.

By the summer of 1883, Charlotte had made her choice. She would try to come around to Stetson's view: "that her work is to be done if done well and to purpose by getting into harmony with that 'woman' [inside her] instead of trying to murder it" (149). She agreed to marry him and steadfastly attempted to let "The Princess" prevail. She complied with his request that she not read Whitman, for Stetson believed Whitman's poetry was too indelicate for feminine sensibilities. She lavished on Stetson her appreciation for his helping her to see the light of truth about herself. He had changed her nature completely from the time of their early courtship: ". . . I had not this nature then. You have made me what I am. *Your love—* . . . hindered by every force of my resistant nature . . . *—Your love* has conquered, as Good always does at last; and by its steady pouring flood of gentle light and tenderest fire has won its one desire" (215).

Charlotte Perkins and Walter Stetson married in May 1884, and for a short time the bride immersed herself in a flurry of wifely activities, her Doppelgänger successfully kept at bay. But the price was heavy, for "getting into harmony with the 'woman'" within her required the repression of its double— the monstrously unnatural nonwoman. Liberating the former meant confining the latter, the Doppelgänger who eventually appeared behind the bars of the yellow wallpaper in her most famous story.

In addition to being imprisoned within a male-defined gender role, Gilman and her contemporaries were also trapped, or, more accurately, locked out of, an exclusively male literary tradition. In 1980, Annette Kolodny examined "The Yellow Wallpaper" as one example of women's fiction initially judged unfit for publication because it did not conform to "accepted norms of women's fiction."[9] Just as there were separate spheres for women in society, there were also separate spheres for women in literature, and any merging of the two was impossible, or at least unacceptable. In fact, Gilman had trouble publishing "The Yellow Wallpaper" less because it deviated from accepted standards for women's fiction, than because, as Kolodny explains:

. . . [T]he story located itself . . . as a continuation of a genre popularized by Poe. And insofar as Americans had earlier learned to follow the fictive processes of aberrant perception and mental breakdown in *his* work, they should have provided Gilman, one would imagine, with a ready-made audience for *her* protagonist's progressively debilitating fantasies of entrapment and liberation. As they had entered popular fiction by the end of the nineteenth century, however, the linguistic markers for those processes were . . . heavily male-gendered. . . . As a result, it would appear that the reading strategies by which cracks in ancestral walls and suggestions of unchecked masculine willfulness were immediately noted as both symbolically and semantically relevant did not . . . necessarily *carry over* to "the nursery at the top of the house" with its windows barred, nor even less to the forced submission of the woman who must "take great pains to control myself before" her physician husband.[10]

As Kolodny goes on to argue, Gilman was denied access to the formula that meant eventual literary legitimacy and success for Poe. Female writers were not to overstep their bounds.

One of the most frequent and easily identifiable responses nineteenth-century women writers made to this exclusion was simply to deny that they had any intention of writing "literatures" in the first place. Sometimes this denial took the form of frequent assertions that their narratives were truth, not fiction, and that they were bumbling and inept at relating them, not really equal to the task. Harriet Brent Jacobs, for example, in the preface to her *Incidents in the Life of a Slave Girl,* apologizes for her incompetence:

Reader, be assured this narrative is no fiction. I am aware that some of my adventures may seem incredible; but they are, nevertheless, strictly true. . . .

I wish I were more competent to the task I have undertaken. But I trust my readers will excuse deficiencies in consideration of circumstances . . . I trust my motives will excuse what might otherwise seem presumptuous.[11]

Harriet E. Wilson adopts the same method to introduce *Our Nig:* "In offering to the public the following pages, the writer confesses her inability to minister to the refined and cultivated, the pleasure supplied by abler pens. It is not for such these crude narrations appear. . . ."[12]

Some of the extreme self-deprecation in the above examples may be attributed to the writers' race. Both were black. Both based their stories on their personal experiences as slaves. Admittedly, their sense of self-worth and place within a white male-defined literary canon was even shakier than that of white women writers. However, the tendency of women writers to apologize for their work or in some other way to step from beneath the umbrella of "literature" so as to avoid censure and/or harsh criticism is not by any means unique to black women. In her study of nineteenth-century women's novels, Nina Baym discusses Fanny Fern's use of this same strategy of "disavow[ing] membership in an artistic fraternity." In the dedication of her novel *Rose Clark,* Fern says that her "unpretending story [should] be read" only in leisure time, as a quiet diversion. She goes on to give her readers a pointed warning: "Should any *dictionary on legs* rap inopportunely at the door for admittance, send him away to the groaning shelves of some musty library, where 'literature' lies embalmed, with its stony eyes, fleshless joints, and ossified heart, in faultless preservation."[13] Clearly, these women had internalized the message that serious literature was both written and appraised only by and only for men.

Considering the self-appraisal Gilman gives her work in her autobiography, she can be seen as standing in this same tradition: "I have written enough to make a set of twenty-five volumes of stories, plays, verse, and miscellany. . . . But this was all the natural expression of thought, except in the stories, which called for composition and were more difficult—especially the novels, which are poor."[14] She attributes her inadequate ability to the nervous breakdown chronicled in "The Yellow Wallpaper." She maintains that her "real purpose" in writing that story was to instruct S. Wier Mitchell, the doctor who treated her and prescribed the "rest cure." She was "put to bed and kept there, . . . was fed, bathed, and rubbed." She followed Mitchell's curt advice to the letter: "Live as domestic a life as possible. . . . Lie down an hour after each meal. Have but two hours' intellectual life a day. And never touch pen, brush, or pencil as long as you live."[15] Later, she came to believe that the good doctor needed to be shown the error of his ways, and one way of showing him was by presenting a portrait of the catastrophic results of his treatment. The story itself, however, she judged as something other than (although not necessarily less than) literature: "A few years ago Mr. Howells asked leave to include this story in a collection he was arranging. . . . I was more than willing, but assured him that it was no more 'literature' than my other stuff, being definitely written 'with a purpose.' In my judgment it is a pretty poor thing to write, to talk, without a purpose."[16]

Gilman's self-criticism here is less an attempt to escape the reproach of "literary" critics than an indictment of "literature" in general. If the literature of the time—that revered and mostly male body of work, sanctioned by critics and approved by the intelligentsia, also male—has no "purpose," then perhaps Gilman would agree with Fanny Fern that it is "fleshless" and "ossified," perfect but dead.

Whatever her true feelings about writing as an artist, Gilman continued to insist that that was not what *she* was doing. When Theodore Dreiser advised her to "consider more what the editors want," she replied that she certainly would consider it if she were "a competent professional writer." But because she is not a real artist but is merely writing "to express important truths," she expects the market for her work to be small.[17]

During the last twenty years, most critics have vigorously disagreed with Gilman's appraisal of "The Yellow Wallpaper." Concerning much of her other imaginative work, however, a tacit agreement with Gilman seems to have existed. Gary Scharnhorst, for example, has said of Gilman that "her literary theory was, fundamentally, an unapologetic defense of didacticism."[18] Ann J. Lane, in her introduction to *The Charlotte Perkins Gilman Reader,* also addresses the issue: "Gilman gave little attention to her writing as literature, and neither will the reader, I am afraid. . . . She wrote to engage an audience in her ideas, not in her literary accomplishments."[19] Traditionally, didacticism in literature has been treated with condescension at best. However, neither of these critics means to diminish Gilman's significant contribution to society and to the world of letters by mentioning her devotion to writing with a purpose. Ann J. Lane, for example, goes on to legitimize all of Gilman's fiction, and in so doing essentially contradicts Gilman herself: "[I]n the entire body of published and unpublished fiction from which [the stories in this collection] were selected, Gilman examines, clearly and pointedly, a variety of problems women share and a variety of proposed ways of dealing with those problems."[20] Here is an unambivalent recommendation of all Gilman's imaginative writing as vital and relevant to the society in which it was written and to which it was addressed.

Yet the *immensity* of Gilman's contribution has not been recognized partly *because* the mere mention of didacticism relegates such fiction to categories like "interesting and historically significant, but not really literature."

It is time to stop taking Gilman at her word. Had Hawthorne still been living, he surely would have included her in his "damn mob of scribbling women." She was compelled to protest that she was not writing literature in the same way her scribbling sisters were compelled to apologize for their lack of talent.

In her study *The Female Imagination,* Patricia Meyer Spacks takes the explanation of Gilman's subordination of desire one step further:

> Mrs. Gilman, in another recognizable feminine pattern, struggles to avoid asserting [an identity]. Believing herself a psychic cripple, she subordinates her desire for distinction to her commitment to large causes and achieves greatly as a mysterious corollary to self-deprecation. . . . Facing the world courageously, she insisted on her inability to really face it at all.[21]

Gilman insists that she never fully recovered from the "nervous prostration" she suffered in 1885, that she was left with a "lasting loss of power," "a crippled life."[22] Spacks interprets this insistence as a kind of solution to the problems created by society's definition of woman-as-artist. Gilman knows, says Spacks, that *real* women "devote [themselves] to [their] child[ren], give up . . . claims to artistry, limit [their] intellectual pretensions."[23] But Gilman's breakdown disallows that prescription, and it also makes becoming a self-actualized artist, a writer of literature, impossible. It allows her to choose a middle path. Because of her sickness, society must forgive her for not being the wife-mother. At the same time, she cannot be castigated for her work because, after all, she is not writing literature, or because, as Spacks points out, "she permits herself to do what she wants because her enjoyment of it is never complete. . . . [S]he exemplifies the remarkably devious relationship between a woman and her work."[24]

Regardless of their ambivalence or tentativeness toward their work, women have always written *literature*. If they were compelled to deny it, they were nonetheless compelled to continue to produce it. In Gilman's case, behind all the strategies and the naysaying, she has left us with the evidence that at least one of her assertions was undeniably true: "Think I must and write I must. . . ." How many variations on that declaration have been written by other women, before and since Gilman? One of the most famous was penned by Sylvia Plath over fifty years later: "The blood jet is poetry, / There is no stopping it."

In this first edition of critical essays on Gilman, I have tried to collect the most perceptive, convincing, and helpful studies in an effort to do justice to the enormous range and amount of imaginative work Gilman left us. Each article maps a way for readers to approach such a large body of fiction and poetry. In addition to providing a necessary biological background, this collection treats the seminal ideas Gilman developed throughout her work: the absolute necessity for women to do "meaningful work" outside the home; the stultifying oppression of patriarchal culture; the suffocating effects of the nineteenth-century doctrine of the "woman's sphere"; the impossible "double-bind" experience by the woman artist, and the depression and emotional breakdown which often result. These concerns are the hallmarks of contemporary women's literature as well. In other words, Charlotte Perkins Gilman marks an early part of the tradition in which such writers as Marge Piercy, Margaret Atwood, Toni Morrison, Margaret Drabble, Alice Walker, Adrienne Rich, Sylvia Plath, and countless others now stand. This collection is meant to provide the recognition such an important writer and literary foremother deserves.

Notes

1. For a complete and very helpful Gilman bibliography, see Gary Scharnhorst's *Charlotte Perkins Gilman: A Bibliography* (Metuchen, NJ: The Scarecrow Press, 1985). Also includes a list of selected criticism of Gilman's work.

2. Carl N. Degler, "Charlotte Perkins Gilman on the Theory and Practice of Feminism," *American Quarterly* 8 (Spring 1956): 21–39. Included in this collection.

3. Sandra M. Gilbert and Susan Gubar, *The Madwoman in the Attic* (New Haven: Yale University Press, 1979), pp. 51, 53.

4. Ibid., p. 89.

5. Elaine R. Hedges, "Afterword," to *The Yellow Wallpaper* (Old Westbury, N.Y.: The Feminist Press, 1973), pp. 54–55.

6. Ibid., pp. 54–55.

7. Mary Armfield Hill, ed., *Endure: The Diaries of Charles Walter Stetson* (Philadelphia: Temple University Press, 1985). Subsequent page references to this is edition will be included in the text.

8. Charlotte Perkins Gilman, *The Living of Charlotte Perkins Gilman* (New York: Arno Press, 1972), p. 82.

9. Annette Kolodny, "A Map for Rereading: Or, Gender and the Interpretation of Literary Texts," *New Literary History,* 11 (Spring 1980): 455.

10. Ibid., p. 455.

11. Harriet Brent Jacobs, *Incidents in the Life of a Slave Girl,* ed. L. Maria Child (New York: Harcourt Brace Jovanovich, 1973), p. xiii.

12. Harriet E. Wilson, *Our Nig* (New York: Vintage Books, 1983), preface.

13. Nina Baym, *Woman's Fiction: A Guide to Novels By and About Women in America, 1820–1870* (Ithaca, N.Y.: Cornell University Press, 1978), pp. 32–33.

14. Gilman, *Living,* p. 100.

15. Ibid., p. 96.

16. Ibid., p. 121.

17. Ibid., p. 304.

18. Gary Scharnhorst, *Charlotte Perkins Gilman* (Boston: Twayne, 1985), p. 11.

19. Ann J. Lane, "Introduction" in *The Charlotte Perkins Gilman Reader* (New York: Pantheon Books, 1980), p. xvi.

20. Ibid., p. xvii.

21. Patricia Meyer Spacks, *The Female Imagination* (New York: Alfred A. Knopf, 1975), pp. 208–9.

22. Gilman, *Living,* p. 98.

23. Spacks, p. 213.

24. Ibid., p. 214.

1

Charlotte Perkins Gilman on the
Theory and Practice of Feminism

Carl N. Degler

When Charlotte Perkins Gilman[1] published *Women and Economics* in 1898, the feminist movement in America gained an advocate of uncommon intellectual power and insight. Quickly acclaimed on both sides of the Atlantic for having written "the most significant utterance" on the women's questions since Mill,[2] she became the idol of radical feminists and was later judged "the most original and challenging mind which the woman [*sic*] movement produced."[3] Despite this recognition of her abilities, however, she has suffered a neglect in American intellectual history difficult to explain.[4] The neglect becomes especially regrettable when one reads her truly thought-provoking analyses of woman's position in a man's world—in remarkable anticipation of modern writers on the subject like Simone de Beauvoir, Margaret Mead, and Ashley Montagu.

Though Gilman's versatile and probing mind roamed over many subjects in the course of her forty years of active writing and lecturing, the focus here is on her thought relating to the position and nature of woman. It is hardly an exaggeration to speak of her as the major intellectual leader of the struggle for women's rights, in the broadest sense, during the first two decades of the twentieth century.[5] A confirmed suffragist, she never confined her attention to that limited goal but considered the whole large question of women in society as her province. Progress for women, she wrote in *Women and Economics,* is not to be measured only by the number of states granting suffrage to women, but rather is to be seen "in the changes legal and social, mental and physical, which mark the advance of the mother of the world toward her full place."[6]

The question of women's rights, to Gilman, was not the simple one of the democratic demand of women for equal prerogatives with men, though this,

---

This article originally appeared in *American Quarterly* 8 (Spring 1956): 21–39.

too, was a part of her well-stocked arsenal of argument. Her concern in all her writings[7] was essentially twofold: to show the disastrous and all-pervasive effects upon women and upon society of the continued suppression of her sex; and to demonstrate in theory and practice means whereby women could assume their rightful place in society. But in doing so her arguments were never shrilll or ill-tempered. The words of a modern feminist aptly describe Gilman's attitude toward the question of woman: "animated less by a wish to demand our rights than by an effort toward clarity and understanding."[8] One might add that, to Gilman, service to society was also an ingredient of her purpose.

The subjection of women originated, Gilman began, in prehistoric times[9] when the males first monopolized all social activity and women were confined to motherhood and domestic duties. Thus began the dependence of women upon men for their very food and shelter. Once this took place woman's livelihood, in the most basic sense, was a function of her ability to hold a man. "From the odalisque with the most bracelets," Gilman wrote, "to the debutante with the most bouquets, the relation still holds good, woman's economic profit comes through the power of sex-attraction."[10] In vain did she search the animal world for analogies to this relationship between the human sexes. For human beings, she found, were the only animal species "in which the female depends on the male for food, the only animal species in which the sex-relation is also an economic relation. . . . In no other animal species is the sex-relation for sale."[11]

Since woman's livelihood is received from men, her sexual attributes, the major attraction for men, are obviously highly developed and carefully nurtured. (Gilman compared this abnormal development in women with the overdevelopment of the horns of a stag or the milk-giving ability of a modern milch cow: both are sexual characteristics developed to excess.) The result is that "the male human being is thousands of years in advance of the female in economic status." Whereas "men produce and distribute wealth . . . women receive it at their hands."[12] This relegating of woman to roles associated only with sexual activity—and this was Gilman's thesis—is "disadvantageous to our progress as individuals and as a race."[13] In essence, it was to the proof and illustration of this conclusion that she devoted all her public efforts between 1898 and the middle of the twenties.

This dichotomy of the sexes, initiated in the beginnings of human society has prevailed into modern times; the man the worker in the world, the woman a parasite, beholden for every morsel of food, stitch of protective clothing, and even a bed at night, to some man—husband or father. Nor, can it be claimed, Gilman showed, that actually woman is economically independent because the husband's support is remuneration for her household labors. The very fact that each woman labors a different amount for that support—the rich as compared with the poor, for example—demonstrates that something more than a simple economic *quid pro quo* is operative. It is woman's duty to work in the home regardless of the compensation; the economic return to her bears no relation, in quantity or in quality, to the work performed.[14] No, the woman lives because the man suffers her to do so.

In other words, Gilman concluded, sex and economics go hand in hand in our world. To the young man entering the world the doors stand wide; failures only mean a new start; mistakes can be righted; all that he desires he can work to attain. To the young woman the same world is there, "but all that she may wish to have, all that she may wish to do, must come through a single channel and a single choice. Wealth, power, social distinction, fame—not only these, but home and happiness, reputation, ease and pleasure, her bread and butter—all, must come to her through a small gold ring."[15]

Even to have amusement, a girl must be sexually attractive. "The fun and pleasure of the world are so interwound with the sex-dependence of women upon men that women are forced to court 'attentions,' when not really desirous of anything but amusement." Association between men and women is always on a strictly sexual basis, "friendship between man and woman being a common laughing-stock." If a single man seeks feminine company there are two kinds: married and single. To see the former causes talk; to visit the latter frequently causes speculations of intentions; so he distributes his favors and knows none very well. Even after marriage the sexes enjoy little contact which does not have sexual overtones.[16]

Up until the nineteenth century rarely was woman allowed to break out of the restrictions imposed upon her by the economic dependence upon the male, even though "the ever-growing human impulse to create, the power and will to make, to do, to express one's new spirit in new forms" was in her as much as in man. For her there were only the ancient, simple duties of the home to be performed "in private and alone."[17] Always "the smothering 'no'" of the male's world held her back from realizing her human characteristics as well as her female ones.[18]

The disabilities imposed upon women were the basic explanations in Charlotte Gilman's mind for the feminine character itself. Since, for long generations, most women have spent their whole lives in contemplation of their own family affairs "they are near-sighted, or near-minded rather; the trouble is not with the nature of their minds, but with the use of them." Men, too, if they have been confined to be home would be "unlikely to manifest a high order of political intelligence."[19] Similarly, courage is not wanted in women, so they do not evidence it. "Women are not ashamed of being cowards. . . . As a man is not ashamed of licentiousness, which would be ruin to a woman, so a woman is not ashamed of cowardice which would utterly disgrace a man."[20] Woman demonstrates certain typically "feminine" traits because she occupies a special, narrow position in society: "she is merely working for her own family—in the sex-relation—not the economic relation; as a servant to the family instead of servant to the world."[21] So long as "all women have to be house servants from day to day, we are still a servile world."[22] In her capacity of family worker the woman is isolated from the rest of society, yet "social intercourse . . . is the essential condition of civilization. It is not merely a pleasure or an indulgence; it is the human necessity."[23]

The diverse material roles of the two sexes produce wholly different worlds and even outlooks for the man and the woman. "The home-bred brain of the woman continually puzzles and baffles the world-bred brain of the man. . . ."[24] "Men meet one another freely in their work, while women work alone."[25] This has the effect of producing more enduring friendships among men and explains "why they associate so much more easily and freely," for "they are further developed in race functions and . . . they *work together*."[26] On the other hand, "every sign of weakness, timidity, inability to understand, to do, is deemed feminine and admired."[27] It is not that "women are really smaller-minded, more timid and vacillating," Gilman maintained, displaying her basic environmentalistic approach, "but the whosoever, man or woman, lives always in a small dark place, is always guarded, protected, directed and restrained, will become inevitably narrowed and weakened by it."[28] Basically, she continued, "the facts are that women are people, and act very much like other people under the same conditions. . . ."[29] Being a servant has played its role in determining the character of women. The woman as a servant "was denied the moral freedom of being mistress of her own action and of learning by the merciful law of consequences what was right and what was wrong: and she has remained, perforce, undeveloped in the larger judgment of ethics."[30]

Gilman saw in woman's consuming interest in fashion a reflection of the female's part in the sexuoeconomic relation. Because of the woman's dependence on sexual attraction for a livelihood, she bears the sex decoration of the species—the reverse of that obtaining in the lower animals. Once sexual attraction is not longer the basis for woman's securing a living, then the feminine sex would be emancipated from its preternatural concern for sex decoration, i.e., fashion.[31]

To perpetuate these environmentally induced differences between the sexes, our man-dominated culture has compelled children to bear the indicia and limitations of the adult sexual world. Boys and girls are dressed differently "not on account of their personal needs, which are exactly similar at this period," but so that neither they nor anyone else "may for a moment forget the distinction of sex."[32] Girls' toys are mainly restricted to those associated with the future occupations of mother and housekeeper; the boys have a wide range of toys and games. "The little girl is kept forever within the limitations of her mother's 'sphere' of action; while the boy learns life, and fancies that new growth is due to his superior sex."[33]

We even expect the maternal feelings to bud in little girls, though we do not expect the boy to feel paternal. Children should not, Gilman contended, any more than kittens, be expected to be precocious in their feelings."[34] The so-called "tom-boy" is the "most normal girl . . . a healthy young creature, who is human through and through, not feminine until it is time to be."[35]

Terrible pressures, she pointed out, are exerted upon the young girl by the social fiat that marriage and the home be the sole occupation of woman. A man may expect to have home, family, love and companionship and still be an "active citizen of his age and country." The girl, on the other hand, "must 'choose'; must either live alone, unloved and uncompanied, uncared for, homeless, childless, with her work in the world for sole consolation; or give up all world service for the joys of love, motherhood and domestic service."[36] Social pressure further insures that she will favor marriage, for if she does not marry, then "the scorn of male and female alike falls on this sexless thing: she is a human failure." Yet—and this is the cruelest part—through all this the girl must act as if she were not interested. "Think of the strain on a highly sensitive nervous organism to have so much hang on one thing" and, at the same time, "to be forbidden to take any step toward securing it!"[37] Even the sexual ignorance of the young girl of her day Gilman saw as a consequence of the sexuoeconomic relationship. Since the husband "is the market" and he prefers her innocent of any sexual knowledge, the mother has no alternative but to preserve her daughter's ignorance in order successfully to prepare "her for the market."[38]

Unavoidably, of course, the man, too, suffers from this constriction of woman's place. "The boy with a servile mother, the man with a servile wife, cannot reach the sense of equal rights we need today."[39] Furthermore, the man has no competition in society when the woman is his inferior, his servant. He is tempted to cruelty, he becomes selfish from having a person devoted to his welfare, he is prideful of his false position of dominance.[40] The requirement that the man support a family puts a premium on money-getters. In a relation which compels a man to support a workless wife, money must be his goal, not service or ideals; his occupation cannot be freely chosen if he also desires a wife. Dedication to science or art or other financially unrewarding pursuits becomes either a hard choice or an impossibility.[41] The maintenance of the family "multiplies a man's desire for money; but in no way multiplies his ability. . . ."[42] Since the man realizes how dependent a wife is upon him for support "marriage is deferred and avoided, to the direct injury of both sexes and society at large."[43]

The home and family also feel the manifold effects of woman's subordinate and oversexed existence. The effort to isolate the home from the world—to enhance privacy—Gilman interpreted as a reflection of the sexually-oriented character of the family: "In our besotted exaggeration of the sex relation, we have cruelly supposed that a wish for a wider human relationship was a wish for wider sex-relationships and was therefore to be discouraged." Actually, when sex and economics are divorced, talk with mere relatives will not be enough and all members of the family will have the opportunity of interpersonal contacts so necessary to human development.[44] The genesis of frictions within the family often can be traced to the socially starved woman. The husband is her only world because he is her line of communication with the real world so she "wrings" all she can out of him to make the world she needs. She demands attention and love, but "it is not further love that she needs at all . . . it is not more man, but more world—more life—that she restlessly and dumbly craves. . . . Failing to get it, she pushes uneasily against this well-intentioned substitute for a world and racks him with her continual demands." Moreover, when the marriage is unhappy, the woman suffers more than the man just "because she has no other life from which to draw strength and practical consolation." He, at least, has his work, opportunity to gratify his ambition, to make money and so forth.[45]

When woman's world is bounded by the walls of the home, society—always Gilman's principal concern—has a high price to pay. To keep women in the home is an enormous social waste in an economic sense. "While every woman is expected to follow one trade the grade of efficiency must remain at the lowest possible average," Gilman argued.[46] All women cannot, any more than all men, be trained to do the same job efficiently because "specialization is necessary to develop skill. The domestic worker, wife or servant, is eternally unspecialized."[47] Much that society has gained in economic efficiency through specialization of man's labor has been lost in requiring women to perform nothing but the unskilled, undifferentiated labor of the home.[48] The very progress of the world has been retarded by excluding women. The housewife-mothered human race "has moved only half as fast and as far as it rightly should have done" and the heavy, time-consuming work of "the patient housewife . . . is pitifully behind the march of events."[49]

Prostitution and immorality Gilman attributed to this same "morbid excess in the exercise of" sex and the economic dependence of women. By requiring a man to support a wife before he may legitimately receive sexual gratification, he is driven to the prostitute as the cheaper alternative.[50] So long, she went on, as sex is emphasized in our society—as it is in our sexuoeconomic marriage—it will encourage the over-sexed man and the over-sexed woman and perpetuate the prostitute.[51]

The double standard, of course, stands forth as the most arrogant instance of male dominance, for chastity is a human, not an exclusively female virtue in Gilman's eyes: "Masculine ethics colored by masculine instincts, always dominated by sex, has at once recognized the value of chastity in women, which is right, punished its absence unfairly, which is wrong; and then reversed the whole matter when applied to men, which is ridiculous."[52]

In her description and analysis of the subtle and often unnoticed characteristics of a man-dominated culture, Gilman displayed both her incisive mind and her acute powers of observation. We have taken the male and his activities, she pointed out, as typical of *human* activities. Even the word virtue is derived from *"vir"*; "our human scheme of things," she wrote, "rests on the same tacit assumption; man being held the human type; woman a sort of accompaniment and subordinate assistant, merely essential to the making of people."[53] In popular speech when "we wish to praise the work of a woman, we say she has a 'masculine mind,' "[54] testimony in itself of the folk belief that to be a man is to be most human.[55] When females teach boys, the students, it is often said, "become 'effeminate.' " But when men teach girls the latter do not become the masculine equivalent. "Never has it occurred to the androcentric mind to conceive of such a thing as being *too* masculine. There is no such word!"[56] So habituated are men to thinking that maleness is humanness, that each step in the economic and social humanization of women has been termed "unfeminine."[57] Woman's exclusion from human activities has been justified on just these grounds—that she is pure sex and devoid of "humanness." Education offers an excellent example of this, where for centuries woman was denied schooling with men on the assumption she must be confined "exclusively to feminine interests."[58] In a word, we have created an androcentric culture,[59] treating women as merely extraneous, child-bearing females.

But to equate male sexual attributes with human nature results in harm to society from another direction. For, after all, the "manly" attributes of size, belligerence, aggressiveness, sportsmanship, and the like, are not the sum total of human virtues. All men, even, do not possess them. The artistic, the musical, the contemplative boy also fulfills a function in society, but he is pilloried in a culture identifying the masculine characteristics with the attributes of human beings. It is necessary to realize that "the advance of civilization calls for human qualities in both men and women."[60] Too often, from the standpoint of society, "the contradictions we have forcibly bred in women react injuriously upon men and are inherited by children."[61]

A culture dominated by men, Gilman believed, is inevitably permeated, on a variety of levels, by the peculiar sexual character of the male. In literature, for example, masculine interest—i.e., love, sex, combat—the interests which flow from man's sexual nature, has been apparent in the myriad stories concerned with such subjects, especially in popular fiction. Such literature ignores mother love—the more fundamental and considerably less transitory variety. Not all men wrote from this narrow viewpoint, of course, for writers like Balzac and Dickens had a truly broad, human outlook.[62] The large number of love poems, in like manner, Gilman explained by the dominance of the male and his primary interest.[63]

The dominance of man has influenced popular philosophy to accept the dictum that life is a struggle—which to man is congenial and preeminent in his existence. Actually life is also growth and a world dominated by women would, by contrast, stress that element.[64] The accent on death and the afterlife, so common in the great religions, similarly stems from the fact that man, the ancient hunter and killer, saw death, was concerned with it, and fitted it into the religions of his culture. To woman, on the other hand, birth and life are the crucial events of her existence.[65]

For all her exposure of the masculine influence molding our culture,[66] Gilman was no uncritical or misanthropic feminist. "There should be an end," she wrote, "to the bitterness of feeling which has arisen between the sexes in this century,"[67] Her evolutionary approach was too meaningful for her to denigrate man's historic activities in behalf of civilization. The economic dependence of women, she maintained, had been necessary so that man could forsake the role of hunter, fighter, and destroyer, and become the builder of civilization. The imprisonment of women had acted as a "coiled spring"—its "intense stimulus" enabling man to move mountains.[68] But, she emphasized, by the nineteenth century that stage in evolution was at an end; man alone could not longer advance civilization; the contribution of woman was required to continue the progress of humanity.[69]

As must be apparent to anyone even cursorily reading the strictures Gilman hurled against the domestic woman, the inevitable *sine qua non* for the final and complete emancipation of woman was economic independence. The working girl, the working wife and mother became the ideal which she preached.

Given the historical period in which she wrote, this solution was neither unexpected nor, in practice, even novel. Already, by the opening years of the twentieth century, millions of women, married and single, were finding places in the industrial system. To Gilman it seemed that these women, often struggling against the old restrictions and prejudices, were the heroines of the emancipation of their sex; indeed, they were taking the only path to true freedom. By their breaking of the age-old chains forged by the dependence of woman upon man for food, clothing, and shelter, they were free for the first time in modern history.[70] If women are to be anything, she proclaimed, they must cease to be merely domestic servants, nursemaids, and governesses in their own homes.[71]

In the last analysis, Gilman's insistence upon work outside the home as the liberating force for women rested on her fundamental assumption that women were human beings and that "a human creative must do human work; and all women are no more to be contented as house servants and housekeepers than all men would be."[72]

The word "all" in the statement contains, by implication, the two major justifications Gilman advanced for women's entering the labor market: not only was the restriction of woman to the home crippling individually to her as a human being, but, as noted earlier, it was socially inefficient. It was not that

Gilman thought that no woman would like housekeeping, for, as she said, "even cleaning, rightly understood and practised is a useful, that therefore honorable, profession."[73] The error lay in expecting all women to do it.

It is noteworthy that Gilman was basing her feminist arguments on higher ground than the mere demand for freedom, privilege, and power equal with men. She rested her case on the conviction that women were "heavily behindhand in their duty to the world; holding in their gift a mighty fund of Love and Service which we can no longer do without."[74] It was society which was losing as well as women, for women, even in their female capacity, had something to contribute to the world. Their very sexual nature fitted in, according to her view, with the overarching human needs of society. "To be a teacher and leader, to love and serve, to guard and guide and help," she pointed out, "are well in line with motherhood,"[75] all of which only "makes her exclusion from human function the more mischievous."[76] The altruism of motherhood, once it is allowed to influence the world, would be a force for good.[77] The very fact that the woman's "feminine functions" are "far more akin to human functions" than are those of the male means that freedom for women "will bring into human life a more normal influence."[78]

Charlotte Gilman, as the preceding paragraph illustrates, was prepared to admit that there were real character differences between the sexes, and further, that they were the consequence of the differing physiological structure and functions of the male and the female. She saw combativeness and desire, for example, as the most obvious male traits. Even "the little male"—the boy— "would be more given to fighting and destroying," she asserted; "the little female more to caring for and constructing things."[79] This, in turn, would lead to the male's being "progressive where the female is conservative by nature."[80] Nevertheless, the important point to Gilman, it should be emphasized, was not the differences, for they are minor compared to the characteristics held in common. But, insofar as the sexes do differ, they should utilize the differences to complement each other and not to subordinate one sex to the other:[81] "Women are human beings as much as men, by nature; and as women, are even more sympathetic with human processes. To develop human life in its true powers we need full equal citizenship for women."[82]

Motherhood for women and fatherhood for men are the only occupations decreed by Nature. Outside of these two: "Every handicraft, every profession, every science, every art, all normal amusements and recreations, all government, education, religion; the whole living world of human achievement: all this is human."[83]

And it should be open to women as human beings.[84] But Gilman was sufficiently perspicacious to realize that not all work would be done by women. For after all, she cautioned, "equality is not identity. There is work of all kinds and sizes—and half of it is woman's."[85] Presumably each sex would perform work congenial to its nature. But "we can make no safe assumption as to what, if any distinctions there will be in the free human work for men and women, until we have seen generation after generation grow up under absolutely equal conditions."[86]

Once elevated to the position of a human being, woman will, in the natural course of things, "develop social usefulness, becoming more efficient, intelligent, experienced."[87] Furthermore, the gainful employment of women would have beneficial effects upon men and the family. There would be greater family income and marriage would not have to be postponed in order to raise the man's income sufficiently to support a wife.[88] The husband would now have a worthy, intelligent partner who would "lift him up instead of pulling him heavily downward. . . ."[89] Even romance in marriage might increase, for it is difficult "to maintain the height of romantic devotion to one's house servant—or even one's housekeeper!"[90] "We shall live," she summed up, "in a world of men and women humanly related, as well as sexually related, working together, as they were meant to do, for the common good of all."[91]

To expect women to marry and to work at the same time, Gilman was well aware, created new problems. Almost contemptuously, however, she demolished the hoary argument that if women worked they would lose their charm in the eyes of men. "The respect of the male for the female," she clearly recognized, "is based on the distinction of sex, not on political or economic disability. Men respect women because they are females, not because they are weak and ignorant and defenseless." It is more likely that as they grow in humanness and lose nothing that is essential to womanhood, "they will win and hold a far larger, deeper reverence than that hitherto vouchsafed them."[92]

Gilman readily conceded that the record showed that as more and more women enjoyed economic independence, the divorce rate continued to rise and some women refused to marry at all. But this is only to be expected, she explained, when "the character of woman is changing faster than the character of matrimony."[93] More and more women are seeking companionship in marriage, now that they are free of the sexuoeconomic dependence; a "kind" husband and a good provider are not enough. After all, she wrote with a tinge of humor, when two young people love each other and spend long hours talking together, they do not "dwell in ecstatic forecast on the duties of housekeeping." They dream of "being alone, of *doing* things together."[94] The outstanding defect of the old marriage was its lack of equality—one partner out in the world, the other confined to the "smallest, oldest, lowest" work in the world.[95] Marriages will be happier and men and women happier when "both sexes realize that they are human, and that humanity has far wider duties and desires than those of the domestic relations."[96] In an age when more and more women are working, Gilman realized, we must "learn how to reconcile happy work with a happy marriage."[97] In some respects, in these passages, Charlotte Gilman was the prophet of the modern American marriage.

Even though some women who work never marry, this is not to be taken, she insisted, as a valid argument against gainful employment for women. How many illustrious men of the past, she asked, could have easily given up their work for marriage? Fortunately for them, they never had to make such a difficult choice, for as men in a man's world they could enjoy both. But some women, for a variety of reasons, cannot be both wives and workers in the world, and they choose the latter merely because they are human.[98]

Though Gilman viewed marriage as a desirable state for all human beings,[99] failure to marry was not a tragedy so long as women could work and thereby consecrate "their energies as human beings to mutual assistance and social service."[100] And on all sides there was evidence of the change in the direction she pointed; she was not a voice in the wilderness, but a leader of hosts.

Charlotte Perkins Gilman might be called a rationalistic radical, for lack of a more elegant term. Few considerations of tradition or sentiment inhibited her thinking. Recognizing this, we can understand better both the strength and weakness of Gilman's social thought. Her freedom from preconceptions and tradition allowed her to make fresh and often penetrating examinations of the human institutions around her. But that same attitude of mind also prevented her from appreciating the tenacious hold which prejudice, tradition, and sentiment had upon most of the men and women she was attempting to convince. Hence when she came to offer means to attain goals she set, her rationalism and radicalism, so incisive in analysis, merely served to vitiate her realism.

To all feminists, as to Gilman, the most stubborn obstacle to the equal participation of women in the affairs of the world was the ineluctable fact that women—or someone, at least—had to take care of the home. That someone, by that very fact, was thereby removed from the usual occupations of the world, and, to the conservative, this was justification enough for the confining of women to the kitchen, nursery, and cleaning closet. Since Gilman had called for women in the world, she had to offer a means to attain that objective. Unfortunately, the best she could devise was less than adequate.

Since the mother-centered home was the major obstacle to woman's employment, Gilman directed her intellectual artillery against that venerable institution. Though her view was foreshadowed in *Women and Economics,* her book *The Home,* published in 1903, was a full-scale, full battle-dress assault—a model of the completely rationalistic analysis of an ancient human institution—and a good example of her scorn for sentiment which had ceased to be functional. Her criticism was on two levels: first that the home crushed women—the argument we have followed; and second that the home as it existed was dirty, inefficient, uninteresting, and retrogressive. Entertaining and clever as her latter arguments and examples were, we need not go into them here.

In substance, of course, her critique of the home was closely related to her view of woman's need, for the functions of the home, too, should be specialized. Instead of having the cooking, sewing, child care, house cleaning done by a single woman—the mother-housewife—all these services would be professionalized and performed by outside, paid workers. So completely would this be carried out, according to Gilman, that there would be no kitchens in the new homes. This in itself, she envisaged, would greatly simplify cleaning, since the kitchen by its introduction of fire, cooking, grease, and smoke constituted one of the major creators of dirt in the home. Food would be professionally and nutritiously prepared in central kitchens and served either in the dining room of the home itself or in the central dining hall of the new apartments, which would become the accepted mode of living. At last the ancient handicraft of the kitchen would disappear: "we are going to lose our kitchens as we have lost our laundries and bakeries. The cook-stove will follow the loom and wheel, the wool-carder and shears."[101] While keenly aware of the esteem in which the haloed home was held, she boldly argued that the home was outmoded, and that its lack of specialization meant inefficiency and lack of development. The housewife, she wrote, is notoriously untrained and ignorant in the fields of nutrition and childcare, yet she is entrusted exclusively with these functions. With a mixture of truth and exaggeration Gilman ridiculed the ignorant mother: "Each mother slowly acquires some knowledge of her business by practising it upon the lives and health of her family and by observing its effect on the survivors."[102] Indeed, insofar as housekeeping has progressed through the application of new techniques and implements, she pointed out, it has been the result of outside, professionalized work not that of the woman in the home.[103] Under the new arrangements there would be "a clean, pretty, quiet home—not full of smell and steam and various messy industries, but simply a place to rest in . . . with a wife as glad to be home as the husband."[104] So often and so vehemently did Gilman offer her solution, that one periodical in 1913 could say, perhaps wearily, "Mrs. Gilman's ideas on this subject are well-known."[105]

Children, too, like the home itself, would be cared for by professionals. Alert to the contemporaneous educational trend of taking children under the care of society at an increasingly younger age, Gilman maintained her plan was merely the extension of this tendency to include babyhood. It is not possible, she argued, merely to train mothers to care for babies any more than they can be trained to supplant the grammar school.[106] Nevertheless, under her program, "the mother would not be excluded, but supplemented, as she is now, by the teacher and the school."[107]

Imagining all men were as rational as herself, Gilman pointed to no other social engine for the accomplishment of such a mighty domestic revolution other than its desirability.[108] This aspect of her thought, perhaps more than any other, is hopelessly tinged with utopianism.

Obviously Charlotte Perkins Gilman's insights into the position of women, and the consequences thereof for the two sexes and for society, are of much more interest to us today than her practical solutions, to the advocacy of which she devoted much of her energy. The kitchenless apartment, the beginnings of which were apparent in her time, is uninteresting to an America now wedded to the private house. Yet, in a sense, even the private home has eliminated, in part, at least, the deficiencies Gilman found in it: ignorance of nutrition and child care is no longer condoned in middle-class American families, particularly not when scientific cook books and authoritative baby books abound. She mistook a few kitchenless apartments for a trend, but she herself was part of a trend when she castigated ignorant motherhood and defended social education for the preschool child.

Increasing occupational opportunities for women, and the growing acceptance of the working wife by both husband and society today,[109] indicate that Gilman's major contribution—the requirement that women be *in* the world as well as *of* it, was essentially sound. The working wife is not as common as Gilman hoped or expected, but the practical reasons for that discrepancy are apparent. Unless some solution similar to that tendered by her, and rejected by society—professionalized home services—is developed, it is almost a superhuman task to be both a housekeeper, cook, and fulltime employee.[110] For as Simone de Beauvoir has observed in our own day, "for the most part it is still the woman who bears the cost of domestic harmony" when she works outside the home.[111] By the mid-twentieth century, the bulk of women in America have not found a means whereby they can both work and marry, but the opportunity is present, for society is now willing to condone that dual role if the woman is willing and capable of assuming the double burden. If, as most would agree, America in the last fifty years has basically altered its attitude toward the working woman, then Charlotte Perkins Gilman must be assigned a significant part in the accomplishment of that change.[112] As she prophesied, to utilize the labor and skills and nature of women as to enlarge the pool of human energy and to enhance human happiness.

Notes

1.   Mrs. Gilman was born Charlotte Perkins on July 3, 1860 and died by suicide August 17, 1935. She married Charles Walter Stetson in 1882, the union ending in separation and ultimate divorce, though not before the birth of a daughter. In 1900 she married her cousin George Houghton Gilman. After her marriage her contemporaries referred to her almost invariably by the three names she used, Charlotte Perkins Gilman. See her revealing, but uneven

autobiography, *The Living of Charlotte Perkins Gilman* (New York: D. Appleton Century Company, 1935) hereafter *The Living.* . . .

2. *Nation,* June 8, 1899, p. 443; *The London Chronicle* cited in A. Black, "The Woman Who Saw It First," *Century* (November, 1923), p. 39.

3. Mary Gray Peck, *Carrie Chapman Catt* (New York: The H.W. Wilson Company, 1944), p. 454. Mrs. Catt ranked Mrs. Gilman first in a list of the twelve greatest American women. *Ibid.,* p. 455.

4. She records in her autobiography that in the 1930s she found Connecticut College for Women uninterested in a lecture by her, though thirty years before her popularity was unsurpassed on a feminine campus like Vassar's. *The Living* . . . p. 333; Harriot Stanton Blatch and Anna Lutz, *Challenging Years; The Memoirs of Harriot Stanton Blatch* (New York: G. P. Putnam's Sons, 1940), p. 108.

5. Two historians, Charles and Mary Beard, have suggested she was just that. See their *Rise of American Civilization* (New York: The Macmillan Company, 1928), II, p. 431.

6. Charlotte Perkins Stetson [Gilman], *Women and Economics. A Study of the Economic Relation Between Men and Women as a Factor in Social Evolution,* 2nd ed. (Boston: Small, Maynard & Co., 1899) p. 148. Hereafter *Women.* In one place she admitted that suffragists considered her too radical and that she helped the cause only by making ordinary advocates of the ballot appear conservative. *Forerunner* (November, 1916), p. 287.

7. Beyond a doubt, her first prose work, *Women and Economics,* both announced her entrance into the field of social thought and brought her the greatest renown. Published originally in 1898, it ultimately was translated into German, Japanese, French, Dutch, Italian, Hungarian, and Russian, as well as running to seven English editions by 1911. But in the course of her busy, strenuous and often painful life, Gilman published five other books of nonfiction, a full-length utopian novel, a volume of poetry, two volumes of fiction, seven volumes of a monthly magazine, *The Forerunner,* the contents of which she wrote entirely herself, scores of articles, poems, and short stories in the popular and scholarly periodicals, and an autobiography published posthumously in 1935. For the purposes of this paper, her views have been drawn only from writings up to 1923, since after that date she was not so concerned with the question of women.

8. Quoted by the translator in Simone de Beauvoir, *The Second Sex* (New York: Knopf, 1953), p. v.

9. She was not concerned with the question of origins and as a result she had no really thought-out theory of the subjugation. See *Women,* pp. 60–61.

10. *Women,* p. 63.

11. Ibid., pp. 5, 95.

12. Ibid., p. 9.

13. Ibid., p. 33.

14. Ibid., p. 15.

15. Ibid., p. 71.

16. Ibid., pp. 308–11.

17. Ibid., pp. 66–67.

18. Ibid., p. 70.

19. *Forerunner*, October, 1910, p. 12.

20. Charlotte Perkins Gilman, *His Religion and Hers, A Study of the Faith of Our Fathers and the Work of Our Mothers* (New York: The Century Co., 1923), p. 133. Hereafter *Religion*.

21. Charlotte Perkins Gilman, *The Home, Its Work and Influence* (New York: Charlton Company, 1910), p. 92. This work was first published in 1903. Hereafter *Home*.

22. *Women*, p. 262.

23. Ibid., p. 295.

24. *Home*, p. 275.

25. *Women*, p. 307.

26. Ibid., p. 306.

27. *Home*, p. 277.

28. Ibid., p. 277.

29. Charlotte Perkins Gilman, "Woman, the Enigma," *Harper's Bazaar* (December, 1908), p. 1197.

30. *Women*, p. 335.

31. Charlotte Perkins Gilman, *The Man-Made World or, Our Androcentric Culture* (New York: Charlton Company, 1911), pp. 173–4. Hereafter *Man-Made*.

32. *Women*, p. 54.

33. *Man-Made*, p. 112. An interesting example of contrasting behavior bred into the two sexes during childhood is given by Gilman in the story of a boy and a girl on a railroad train. The mother holds the girl in her seat; the boy roams the train, talks with the conductor, asks questions, "learning all the time. The boy gets five times as much out of life as the girl and he knows it." *Home*, p. 279.

34. *Man-Made*, pp. 110–11.

35. *Women*, pp. 56–57.

36. Charlotte Perkins Gilman, "Passing of Matrimony," *Harper's Bazaar* (June, 1906), p. 496.

37. *Women*, p. 88.

38. Ibid., p. 86.

39. *Man-Made*, p. 42.

40. *Women*, pp. 337–38.

41. Ibid., pp. 112–14.

42. *Home*, p. 320.

43. *Women*, p. 93.

44. Ibid., pp. 304–5.

45. Charlotte Perkins Gilman, "All the World to Her," *Independent* (July 9, 1903), pp. 1615–16.

46. Charlotte Perkins Gilman, "Waste of Private Housekeeping," *Annals of the American Academy* (July, 1913), p. 91.

47. Gilman, "Waste of Private Housekeeping," p. 94. It should not be imagined that Gilman thought that women in the home did not work hard enough, for "the Housewife is one of the hardest workers on earth. She works unceasingly. . . ." She works harder than a man just because her work is so unspecialized. *Home*, pp. 290–1.

48. It is not out of place to observe that a few years later, in 1912, Wesley Clair Mitchell, the economist, was issuing the same complaint against the unspecialized home. See his title essay in the collection, *The Backward Art of Spending Money*, New York: McGraw-Hill Book Company, 1937).

49. *Home*, pp. 102–3.

50. *Women*, p. 30; Charlotte Perkins Gilman, "How Home Conditions React upon the Family," *American Journal of Sociology* (March, 1909), p. 601.

51. *Women*, pp. 96–97.

52. *Man-Made*, p. 134.

53. Ibid., p. 20.

54. Ibid., p. 21.

55. This was written almost fifty years before Mme. Simone de Beauvoir said the same thing: "A man is in the right in being a man; it is the woman who is in the wrong. It amounts to this: just as for the ancients there was an absolute vertical with reference to which the oblique was defined, so there is an absolute human type the masculine. . . . Thus humanity is male and man defines woman not in herself but as relative to him . . . ." *The Second Sex*, pp. xv–xvi.

56. *Man-Made*, pp. 149–50.

57. Ibid., p. 24.

58. Ibid., p. 147.

59. This term, a favorite of Gilman's, was taken from the writings of Lester Frank Ward, whose article in *Forum* for November 1888, "Our Better Halves," catalyzed her thinking on this subject. See *Living . . .* , p. 259.

60. *Man-Made*, p. 155.

61. Gilman, "Woman, the Enigma," p. 1197.

62. *Man-Made*, pp. 95–100. In an interesting and revealing analogy Gilman compares the kind of writing a drone and a worker bee would produce. The drone's work would be replete with sex and mating—his *raison d'etre;* the worker's with activity, labor and care—its life. *Man-Made*, p. 99.

63. Ibid., p. 84. Like so many reformers pushing favorite theses, Gilman often saw gold where only brass was present. At one point, for example, she contended that the trend in nineteenth-century historiography away from battles, wars, and statecraft in favor of social and economic affairs, was the consequence of the rise of women. Actually, of course, that historical movement began deep in the eighteenth century at least—hardly "the women's century." *Man-*

Made, p. 92. She even went so far as to lay the blame for the American party system and its
battles at the feet of our man-made world and its love of combat! *Man-Made*, pp. 221–22.

64. Charlotte Perkins Gilman, "Influence of Women on Public Life," *Public* (May 31, 1919), p.
572.

65. *Religion*, p. 42. In *Man-Made World*, p. 202, she gives her view of what the male has made
out of Christianity: "desire—to save one's soul. Combat—with the Devil. Self-Expression—
the whole gorgeous outpouring of pageant and display, from the jewels of the high priest's
breastplate to the choir of mutilated men to praise a male Deity no woman may so serve." It
is interesting, though Gilman did not make the point, that the one modern religion founded
by a woman, Christian Science, does deny the existence of death.

66. The great intellectual debt Charlotte Perkins Gilman owed to the Darwinian revolution of the
nineteenth century is apparent here in these repeated efforts to base her thinking on a kind of
biological certainty.

67. *Women*, p. 129.

68. Ibid., p. 133.

69. Ibid., p. 122.

70. It is true, as one of her critics, I. M. Rubinow, observed, that girls working in sweatshops
twelve hours a day did not feel as free as Gilman portrayed them. But the critic also lost sight
of the fact at which she was driving. Though many individuals, men as well as women, might
not be as free as the ideal, the real test was whether the opportunity was present or whether a
large segment of society was deliberately denied opportunities for free expression in labor.
Rubinow was correct, however, when he pointed out that historically the working class wife
who was gainfully employed was usually shamefully exploited rather than freer for her labor.
In this respect the middle-class bias of Gilman was as apparent as it was in much of the
women's rights movements as a whole. I. M. Rubinow, of the U.S. Bureau of Labor, made
his comments in the *American Journal of Sociology* (March 1909), pp. 614–19.

71. Beauvoir, p. 679, in our own day, still accepts Gilman's analysis: "It is through gainful
employment that woman has traversed most of the distance that separated her from the male;
and nothing else can guarantee her liberty in practice."

72. Gilman, "Passing of Matrimony," p. 498. Later she put her position into the slogan: "The
New Woman is Human first, last, and always. Incidentally she is female; as man is male."
Forerunner (January, 1910), p. 12.

73. *Women*, p. 246.

74. *Forerunner* (January, 1911), p. 29.

75. *Man-Made*, pp. 238–39.

76. Ibid., p. 235.

77. *Religion*, p. 47.

78. *Man-Made*, pp. 255–56. The modern anthropologist, M. F. Ashley Montague, in his *Natural
Superiority of Women* (New York: Macmillan Co., 1953), devotes a chapter, "The Genius
of Woman as the Genius of Humanity," to this very point. "What the world stands so much
in need of at the present . . . is more of the maternal spirit and less of the masculine," p. 147.

79. *Man-Made*, p. 112.

80. *Home*, pp. 88–89.

81. She thought she saw, as a result of this differentiation, diverse functions for men and women in some areas. For example, art "will perhaps always belong," she thought, "most to men. It would seem as if that ceaseless urge to self-expression, was at least originally, most congenial to the male." *Man-Made*, p. 250. Applied arts, on the other hand, would be an area in which women would do as well as men. It may not be coincidental that Gilman confessed to just this same latter division of talent in herself. See her autobiography, *The Living* . . . , p. 46. Certain sports, those involving the throwing of a ball, she conjectured, "will never appeal to women"—not because they are wrong, but because "they are only masculine" not human. *Man-Made*, p. 114. Modern feminist writers have also subscribed to this conception of limited differentiation between the sexes. See Beauvoir, p. 731; Margaret Mead, *Male and Female* (New York: W. Morrow, 1949), chap. xviii.

82. *Man-Made*, p. 260.

83. Ibid., p. 25.

84. Compare this statement with Margaret Mead, p. 378: "There is likewise the very simple consideration that when we have no indication that intelligence is limited to one sex, any occupational restriction that prevents gifted women from exercising their gifts leaves them, and also the world that is sorely in need of every gift, the poorer."

85. *Forerunner* (January, 1910), p. 13.

86. *Man-Made*, p. 250.

87. Gilman, "How Home Conditions React upon the Family," *American Journal of Sociology* (March, 1909), p. 605.

88. Charlotte Perkins Gilman, "What He Craved," *The Critic* (February, 1906), p. 188. It is appropriate to observe that since Gilman's time the proportion of working women has increased while the average age of marriage has fallen. The median ages for first marriages for men and women respectively in 1890 were 26.1 and 22.0. In 1949 the ages were: 22.7 and 20.3. L. I. Dublin, *Facts of Life* (New York: Macmillan Co., 1951), p. 42. In 1900, 13.4 percent of the women in the United States were gainfully employed; in 1954 the figure was 30.6 percent.

89. *Women*, p. 315.

90. *Home*, p. 281.

91. *Women*, p. 313.

92. Charlotte Perkins Gilman, "Are Women Human Beings?" *Harper's Weekly* (May 25, 1912), p. 11. In another place she put this in environmental, relativistic terms: "A woman is a woman and attractive to men of her place and times, whether she be a beaded Hottentot, a rosy milkmaid, a pretty school ma'am, or a veiled beauty of the Zenana." *Home*, p. 280.

93. Gilman, "The Passing of Matrimony," op. cit., p. 497.

94. *Women*, pp. 218–19.

95. Ibid., pp. 219–220.

96. Gilman, "All the World to Her," op. cit., p. 1616.

97. Charlotte Perkins Gilman, "Light on the Single Woman's Problem," *American Magazine* (August, 1906), p. 428.

98. Gilman, "Passing of Matrimony," op. cit., pp. 496–98.

99. "There is no real reason," she argued, "why women should not be women, wives and mothers, and also members of society, performing that social service which is our first duty as human beings." Charlotte Perkins Gilman, "Social Darwinism," *American Journal of Sociology* (March, 1907), p. 714. "Motherhood," she said elsewhere,—"if anything, is woman's business." Charlotte Perkins Gilman, "Good Tidings of Women—the World's Best Hope," *Woman's Home Companion* (February, 1906), p. 5.

100. *Forerunner* (July, 1916), p. 173.

101. *Women*, p. 267. It should be clearly understood that she was not advocating cooperative kitchens—a development of her time which she abominated—but rather individually purchased maid and cooking service like medical care.

102. Ibid., p. 229.

103. Gilman, "Waste of Private Housekeeping," op. cit., p. 91; *Home*, op. cit., p. 94.

104. *Home*, op. cit., p. 292.

105. Reply to Ellen Key, *Current Opinion*, op. cit. (March, 1913), p. 221.

106. *Woman*, pp. 283–84.

107. Ibid., p. 287.

108. See her utopian novel, *Moving the Mountain* (New York: Charlton Company, 1911).

109. In 1890, 13.9 percent of working women were married; fifty years later the figure was 36.4 percent.

110. See chapter 5 in Mirra Komarovsky, *Women in the Modern World; Their Education and Their Dilemmas* (Boston: Little, Brown, 1953), for a discussion, in concrete terms, of the problems facing the modern working wife and mother.

111. Beauvoir, pp. 694–95.

112. "So stirring was her analysis" of the home, Charles and Mary Beard have written, "and so clarion was her call for freedom in mind and labor that a new school of feminist thinkers was raised up in America and Europe which sent reverberations as far afield as awakening Japan." *The Rise of American Civilization*, II, p. 431.

2

Charlotte Perkins Gilman:
A Feminist's Struggle with Womanhood

Mary A. Hill

In a letter written from Belmont, New Hampshire, September 2, 1897, Charlotte Perkins Stetson exclaimed, "Thirty-five hundred words I wrote this morning, in three hours!" A book's chapter in one sitting; a successive six-week dizzy pace of morning writing; elaborate consultations with her closest critic, Houghton Gilman, soon to be her second husband; and thus was *Women and Economics* dashed into print. Jane Addams, already emerging as one of America's foremost social reformers, expressed her gratitude to Charlotte, her "pleasure and satisfaction," her "greatest admiration" for the "Masterpiece." Florence Kelly, another pioneer of social settlement reform viewed it as "the first real, substantial contribution made by a woman to the science of economics." According to *The Nation*, "Since John Stuart Mill's essays on *The Subjection of Women*, there has been no book dealing with the whole position of women to approach it in originality of conception and brilliancy of exposition."[1]

Charlotte Gilman quite naturally felt increasingly elated as positive reviews rolled in, despite the societal distortions her book both reflected and described. A flamboyant speaker, a writer with a penetrating wit, she was rapidly emerging as a major theorist and popularizer for the woman's movement in turn-of-the-century America. Publicly she attempted to analyze and expose the ubiquitous effects of sex-based inequalities and the sources of female strength; and privately she acknowledged that many of her perceptions emerged as well from agonizing conflicts of her life. "We ourselves," she publicly and sweepingly asserted, "have preserved in our own character the confusion and contradiction which is our greatest difficulty in life."[2] And privately she acknowledged the

This article originally appeared in *The Massachusetts Review* 21 (Fall 1980): 503–26.

war between contending factions in herself. To Houghton Gilman she described a major challenge of her life: "To prove that a woman can love and work too. To resist this dragging weight of the old swollen woman-heart, and force it into place—the world's Life first—my own life next. Work first—love next. Perhaps this is simply the burden of our common womanhood which is weighing on me so."[3]

The seeds of Charlotte's radical feminism were rooted in an early struggle for independence, self-assertion, and self-respect. Raised primarily within a female kinship network necessitated by her father's absence, and deprived from early infancy of the motherly affection for which she yearned, Charlotte nonetheless disclosed in her diaries and notebooks a growing strength of character, a playful, lively, independent personality. Rebellious against the model of repressive discipline her unhappy mother, Mary Perkins, attempted to impose, she was active in physical fitness programs, lecture clubs, and language classes. Armed with books and reading lists provided by her librarian father, Frederick Perkins, Charlotte was well-read in contemporary philosophical, historical, and anthropological thought. She delighted in her physical as well as her mental agility; her effort to control her body was maintained within her larger program to control her life. By the age of 21, she was self-supporting, busy from 6 A.M. to 10 P.M., and thriving in the process.

Despite the limitations imposed in her mother's prudish discipline, Charlotte constantly had calls, visitors, and stimulating friendships with males as well as females. She enjoyed hiking, sleighing, rowing, playing whist, and was exhilarated in her triumphs at the chess board. She enjoyed inspiring evening talks with Ada Blake and Augusta Gladding, and many long walks with Grace Channing, who became her lifelong friend. Also, she developed an intimate relationship with Martha Luther, a relationship of mutual trust and shared interests. They delighted in each other's company. "With Martha I knew perfect happiness," she later wrote. "Four years of satisfying happiness with Martha, then she married and moved away."[4]

Charlotte's friendship with Martha provided the kind of support, encouragement, and mutual affection historians currently believe was central to the experience of most nineteenth-century women. The reality of Charlotte's love was quite apparent, her grief at the impending separation was intense and disruptive. In 1881, Charlotte noted that "some swain" was threatening her relationship with Martha, that because of marriage she might lose her "most intimate friend." On November 5th she wrote: "Pleasant, to ring at the door where you've always been greeted with gladness; to be met by the smile that you value all other above—to see that smile flicker and vanish and change into sadness because she was met by *your* presence instead of her love." On November 16th she noted, "Walk in the dark streets for an hour or so in dumb misery."

In December, she summarized: "A year of steady work. A quiet year, and a hard one. . . . A year in which I knew the sweetness of perfect friendship, and have lost it forever."[5] After a typical self-scourging, she became more stoic, striving to submerge her grief by helping others. But the vacuum left by Martha's absence heightened Charlotte's longings for affection, and may have paved the way for her acceptance of the comforting protection of a man.

On January 12, 1882, Charlotte met an aspiring artist, Walter Stetson. Within seventeen days of their first meeting he proposed. Her diary entry reads: "I have this day been asked the one great question in a womans [*sic*] life and have refused." Two days later she wrote:

> Now that my head is cool and clear, now before I give myself any sense to another; let me write down my Reasons for living single.
> In the first place, I am fonder of freedom than anything else—. . . .
> I like to be *able* and *free* to help any and everyone, as I never could be if my time and thoughts were taken up by that extended self—a family. . . .
> I am cool, fearless, and strong. . . .
> For reasons many and good, reasons of slow growth and careful consideration, more reasons that I now can remember; I decide to Live—Alone.
> God help me![6]

For a time at least, Charlotte remained committed to her rationale for spinsterhood: "if I were to try the path you open to me I could never try my own," she wrote. "I know of course that the time would come when I must choose between two lives, but never did I dream that it would come so soon, and that the struggle would be so terrible." It was, as she put it directly to Walter, "a trial which in very truth *does* try me like fire."[7]

Despite her misgivings, Charlotte began to express increasing affection for Walter—"I am beginning to wonder how I ever lived through this winter, before you—; . . . You want to give me something! You are giving me back myself." By 1883, she was engaged to Walter and began to accept his sympathy, his comforting, his advice, even when it was constricting. For example, when a close friend gave her a new copy of Walt Whitman's *Leaves of Grass* she noted, "I am obliged to decline, as I had promised Walter I would not read it." She now resolved, first and foremost, to be *"Absolutely unselfish . . .* To find my happiness in the pleasurable sensations of others rather than in my own. To consider others, think of others, think first 'will he or she like it?' rather than shall I."[8]

As Charlotte's expressions of affection and self-sacrifice intensified, so also did her gloom. She experienced a loss of strength, discipline, and courage which she had worked so consciously to acquire. In December, 1883, she wrote: "Let me not forget to be grateful for what I have. Some strength, some purpose, some design, some progress, some esteem, respect—and affection. And some Love. Which I can neither feel, see, nor believe in when the darkness comes."

She continued: "I mean this year to try hard for somewhat of my former poise and courage. As I remember it was got by practice." Nonetheless, a severe depression began to take its toll:

> I would more gladly die than ever yet; saving for the bitter agony I should leave in the heart of him who loves me. And mother's pain.
> But O! God knows I am tired, tired, tired of life!
> If I could only know that I was doing right.[9]

Charlotte's expressed attitudes toward marriage and motherhood were fiercely ambivalent. Rationally aware of possible conflicts between self-development and love, she was largely unprepared to meet the complex unconscious as well as deliberate patterns of socialization which forced most women to accept self-sacrificing love as natural, inevitable, and right. Drawing from conflicting signals of her mother, Mary Perkins, Charlotte knew that women could achieve a modicum of independence, but always at a price. Mary Perkins was a divorced and eventually self-supporting woman, nourished and sustained by a female network of friends and relatives; her nonconformity strengthened Charlotte's capacity for independence. But suffering from the stigma of divorce, from economic hardship, from the guilt and emotional insecurity of her single lifestyle caused her, Mary quickened Charlotte's fear of spinsterhood. Both parents had also unwittingly encouraged Charlotte's independence by withholding their affection. Mary Perkins had denied caresses to her daughter: "I used to put away your little hand from my cheek when you were a nursing baby," Mary told Charlotte in her later years. "I did not want you to suffer as I had suffered." Likewise her librarian father, Frederick Perkins, kept his distance: "the word Father, in the sense of love, care, one to go to in trouble, means nothing to me," Charlotte wrote, "save indeed in advice about books and the care of them—which seems more the librarian than the father."[10]

A contemporary psychologist, Alexandra Symonds, discussed symptoms in her recent patients quite similar to those that Charlotte was beginning to exhibit. The women Symonds treated were active, vital, and self-assured before their marriages. Yet they were also often women who had to "grow up in a hurry." Denied experiences of warmth in childhood, they were encouraged to control their feelings and give the impression of strength and self-sufficiency. Symonds suggests a frequent pattern: "They repressed their healthy needs to be taken care of and repressed the child in them as well." Perhaps Charlotte's difficulties were rooted in the discipline and loneliness of youth, the loss of her friend Martha Luther serving only to exacerbate her thirst for love. Perhaps, as Symonds puts it, she desired "to put down a tremendous burden which she had been carrying all her life, and be the dependent little girl she had never been before."[11]

On May 2, 1884 Charles Walter Stetson and Charlotte Anna Perkins were married in Providence, Rhode Island. "O my God! I thank thee for this heavenly happiness!" she wrote in her diary the evening of the wedding.[12]

There were commonly expected roles of men and women in marriage that both Charlotte and Walter accepted. As a man, Walter was expected to provide for his family. He did not have to choose between marriage and his work. In fact, marriage lent further purpose to his artistic growth and creative efforts. Charlotte, by contrast, felt a momentous change occurring in her life. Formerly self-supporting, independent, and career-oriented, she found herself involved with time-consuming domestic chores which conflicted with the work she loved—painting and writing. Within a week, some spontaneous rebellion seemed to be occurring. She wrote in her diary, "I suggest he [Walter] pay me for my services; and he much dislikes the idea. I am grieved at offending him; mutual misery. Bed and cry." She was beginning to experience firsthand what later she would depict to trenchantly: "the home which is so far from beautiful, so wearing to the nerves and dulling to the heart, the home life that means care and labour and disappointment, the quiet, unnoticed whirlpool that sucks down youth and beauty and enthusiasm, man's long labour and woman's longer love."[13]

Although the personal dynamics of Charlotte's relationship with Walter remain elusive, sexual experiences may have contributed to her growing discontent. At times Charlotte viewed sexuality with traditional Victorian prudery: "Purity," she wrote in 1883, "is that state in which no evil impulse, no base thought can come in; or if forced in dies of shame in the white light. Purity may be gained by persistent and long continued refusal to entertain low ideas." Yet it is also clear that she was by no means always cold or unapproachable in early marriage. On June 15, 1884, she noted: "Am sad: last night and this morning. Because I find myself too—affectionately expressive. I must keep more to myself and be asked—not borne with." And on June 25 the same year she wrote, "Get miserable over my old woe—conviction of being too outwardly expressive of affection."[14]

Soon Charlotte was pregnant, a condition which lessened her physical and emotional stamina. Even after the birth of Katharine Stetson in 1885, Charlotte wrote in her diary, "Every morning the same hopeless waking . . . same weary drag." She appreciated her home, her healthy baby, the services of her mother and a competent domestic servant, yet was helpless and despondent: "and I lay all day on the lounge and cried."[15] A failure in her own eyes, she looked to Walter for protective love, and increasingly for pity. She was assuming what Carroll Smith-Rosenberg has referred to as those "character traits assigned to women in Victorian society and the characteristic symptoms of nineteenth-century hysteric: dependency, fragility, emotionality, narcissism."[16] Charlotte did not as yet attack the religion of maternity, the assumption that all mothers are "saintly givers." Instead, she resigned herself to misery. She wrote, Walter "would do everything in the world for me; but he cannot see how irrevocably bound I am, for life, for life. No, unless he die and the baby die, or he change or I change, there is no way out." She described her "hysteria" as follows:

> I could not read nor write nor paint nor sew nor talk nor listen to talking, nor anything. I lay on that lounge and wept all day. The tears ran down into my ears on either side. I went to bed crying, woke in the night crying, sat on the edge of the bed in the morning and cried—from sheet continuous pain. . . .
>
> I made a rag baby, hung it on a doorknob and played with it. I would crawl into remote closets and under beds—to hide from the grinding pressure of that profound distress. . . .[17]

In writing her autobiography, Charlotte described her "mental illness" as a disease beyond her understanding, an accidental misfortune. Suffering from recurrent depressions, she continued to believe that causes for her suffering lay not in the personal or political conflicts of her life, but in idiosyncratic weaknesses within herself. The price she paid for nonconformity was guilt, despite the fact that almost all of her feminist writings were inextricably related to her life, and despite the fact as well that her short story, "The Yellow Wallpaper" was itself a feminist-oriented autobiographical portrayal of insanity.

In "The Yellow Wallpaper," an "hysterical woman," overprotected by a loving husband, is taken to a summer home to recover from nervousness, and told to rest and sleep and try to use her "will and self-control" to overcome her miseries. The room her husband John assigns to her is covered with a yellow-patterned wallpaper. "The color is repellent, almost revolting; a smouldering unclean yellow, strangely faded by the slow-turning sunlight." Although the woman is quite ill, her husband, a physician, tells her that there is "no reason" for her suffering; she must dismiss those "silly fantasies." Of course, "it is only nervousness," she decides. But "it does weigh on me so not to do my duty in any way! . . . [and] such a dear baby! And yet I *cannot* be with him, it makes me so nervous." She tries to rest and do as she is told, but suffers doubly since her husband will not believe that she is ill. He "does not know how much I really suffer. He knows there is no *reason* to suffer, and that satisfies him." She thinks she should appreciate the protective love he offers. "He takes all care from me, and I feel so basely ungrateful not to value it more. . . . He took me in his arms and called me a blessed little goose." And yet it is impossible to talk to him "because he is so wise, and because he loves me so." Efforts to discuss the matter only bring a "stern reproachful look" and send her back to bed in shame.

John offers tender love, but enforces the inactivity which deepens her despair. I "am absolutely forbidden to 'work' until I am well again." Here he comes, "I must put this away—he hates to have me write a word." Rest is what her physician husband says is right, so "he started the habit by making me lie down for an hour after each meal."

The first stage of the breakdown is one of self-blame. The woman follows the doctor's orders and tries to stop the fantasies that people tell her are unreal. When a physician of "high standing" assures "friends and relatives that there is really nothing the matter with one but temporary nervous depression—a slight hysterical tendency—what is one to do?" Gradually, however, the woman starts to believe in her fantasies. "There are things in that [wall-]paper that nobody knows but me, or ever will. Behind that outside pattern the dim shapes get clearer every day. . . . I didn't realize for a long time what the thing was that showed behind that dim sub-pattern, but now I am quite sure it is a woman." Dramatically she trusts her perceptions and acts wildly but assertively. "I wasn't alone a bit! As soon as it was moonlight and that poor thing began to crawl and shake the pattern, I got up and ran to help her. I pulled and she shook, I shook and she pulled, and before morning we had peeled off yards of that paper." The protagonist begins to creep and crawl within her madness. She separates herself from the perception of others, and when in a climactic scene her husband faints, she crawls over his body and says, "I've got out at last . . . in spite of you!"[18]

"The Yellow Wallpaper" stands in dramatic contrast to Charlotte's autobiography, *The Living of Charlotte Perkins Gilman*. There, the separation from Walter Stetson is portrayed as resulting from her individual weaknesses, or equally simplistically, from a mismatched marriage. She was not inclined publicly or explicitly to indict loved ones in her life. Yet in "The Yellow Wallpaper," she presented insanity as a form of rebelion, a crucial turning point toward independence. Only in a fictional version of her illness would she publicly express her anger: "I've got out a last . . . in spite of you." Anger is also apparent in her diary. On April 18, 1887, she wrote:

> I am very sick with nervous prostration, and I think some brain disease as well. No one can ever know what I have suffered in these last five years. Pain pain pain, til my mind has given way. . . . You found me—you remember what I leave you—O remember what, and learn to doubt your judgment before it seeks to mould another life as it has mine.
>
> I asked you a few days only before our marriage if you would take the responsibility entirely on yourself. You said yes. Bear it then.[19]

Although Charlotte often faced uncontrollable depressions during the bleak years of 1884–87, fortunately a determination to trust her own abilities remained. In part, she benefited from a visit in California with Grace Channing and her family in the winter of 1885–1886. In this supportive atmosphere she regained a measure of her former self-confidence. She felt more well, of gayer disposition, when she was separated from her family, a primary source of her guilt-induced anxiety. Moreover, the diaries indicate an emerging feminist consciousness during these same years; her reading, lecturing, and writing on women's issues predated and possibly contributed to her separation from Walter in 1888. For example, in 1883 she argued with a close friend, Jim Simmons, "till 11:45 nearly talking about Woman's Rights." He was a "man far from broad," she noted. In 1884 she read John Stuart Mill's *The Subjection of Women* (she also read it to her mother), and then began to lecture and to write on women's issues. She attended her first Woman's Suffrage Convention in 1886. In January 1887, she read Margaret Fuller's *Woman in the Nineteenth Century* and "started a course of reading about women," although as she noted in her diary she stopped it temporarily to "oblige" Walter. By February she had accepted an offer from Alice Stone Blackwell to manage a suffrage column for a Providence weekly newspaper, *The People*.[20]

Many days Charlotte complained of weakness and exhaustion from domestic obligations yet found strength when she worked on articles or verse. Incensed by the situation of other women, she was depressed when she reflected on her own. On February 20, 1887 she had a "good talk" with a neighbor, Mrs. Smythe, who was "another victim" with a "sickly child" and an ignorant husband who was "using his marital rights at her vital expense." And a month later: "Getting back to the edge of insanity again . . . feel desperate. Write my 'column' though." She also returned to her physical fitness program. For example, on February 7, after getting "discouraged by Walter," she delighted in her "jolly time at the gym in the evening. I seem to slip into my old position of inspirer very easily. And the girls like it."[21]

What is most striking about Charlotte's life, particularly from 1884–1887, is that she had the energy to pursue any of the activities she found most satisfying. She was "ill," yet stubbornly ignored the admonitions of her family, refused their well-intentioned offers of "security," and proceeded to develop an indetendent plan of action. She rejected the advice of a nerve specialist, Dr. S. Weir Mitchell: "Live as domestic a life as possible. Have your child with you all the time. . . . And never touch pen, brush or pencil as long as you live."[22] Instead, she decided to try new alternatives. She believed that self-assertion, in her case the need to read, write, exercise, and enjoy the companionship of other women was crucial to her mental health. Lacking the support, or even the understanding of friends and relatives in Providence, Rhode Island, and with no income or well-defined plans for work, she determined to move herself and child to California in the fall of 1888. There, in Pasadena, the Channing family provided a brief respite of economic and emotional security.

Gradually, Charlotte began to meet other women like herself who were alone, without means of satisfying work, or without adequate income. Still personally distraught, she nonetheless moved toward a tactical involvement in the burgeoning feminist movement, began more seriously to analyze common problems women faced, and encouraged organizational and individual attacks on what she saw as pervasive social ills. Well-read in contemporary intellectual theory, and most particularly influenced by the writings of Lester Ward and Edward Bellamy, she became active in the lecture-writing circuit of the then highly politicized and often radical reform movements of the 1890s. Her expanding reputation brought her into close contact with socialist, nationalist, and Fabian thought. As a social theorist, she was eclectic rather than original. But in her partial adoption of socialist theory and in her continuing identification with oppressed groups, she was able to expand her feminist analysis beyond that of many of her contemporaries and to ground it in a broadly-based political perspective.

Turning now to the feminist analysis itself, I suggest that there were four major forces which Charlotte Gilman isolated as having created and perpetuated female inequality, or the "artificial" feminine personality. The underlying premise of her environmentalist analysis was the innate similarity of human potentials of males and females. As she put it:

> That is masculine which belongs to the male sex as such; to any and all males *without regard to species.* . . . That is feminine which belongs to the female sex, as such, *without regard to species.* . . . That is human which belongs to the human species, as such, *without regard to sex.* . . . Every step of social development, every art, craft, and science . . . these have to do with humanity, as such, and have nothing to do with sex.[23]

The first of the major factors impinging on the lives of women, she perceived, was their economic dependence on men. Women had become in effect property of men. Women's work, she argued, had a use value but not an exchange value. She wrote, "whatever the economic value of the domestic industry of women is, they do not get it. The women who do the most work get the least money, and the women who have the most money do the least work." She insisted that economic dependence, wherever it occurred, necessarily resulted in a loss of integrity and self-respect. Encouraging women to view the political dimensions of their situation, she declared, "We have not as a class awakened to the fact that we have no money of our own."[24]

Charlotte Gilman's economic struggles as a separated and subsequently divorced woman, and earlier the child of a divorced woman, made her especially sensitive to woman's economic plight. She knew from experience that economic security in the home was a mirage, that if deprived of the support of a male protector, women would invariably confront extremely limited work opportunities, and often tragic impoverishment. Yet she recognized that it was the family itself, as a social and economic institution, which perpetuated female enslavement and denied women opportunity for economic independence. Consequently, she differed from many feminists who believed that no "fundamental economic change would be necessary in home relationships for women to achieve equality."[25] For Charlotte Gilman, women's most essential goal was the building of an economic power base.

The second significant factor leading to "artificial" femininity, Gilman believed, was nonvoluntary alienating domestic servitude. She argued that inequality of women resulted from a division of labor along sex lines, further evidence of a causative relationship between the institution of the family and women's low level of achievement. Cooking, sewing, nursing, washing, caring for children—"not only do we undertake to have all these labors performed in one house, but by one person." Just consider, she wrote, "what any human business would be in which there was no faintest possibility of choice, of exceptional ability, of division of labor." She decried the fact that domestic industry had become a "sex function, . . . supposed to pertain to women by nature."[26]

Third, Gilman examined the effects of women's psychological dependence on men. An eclectic popularizer as well as a theorist, she reiterated and reshaped the theoretical arguments of her predecessors, Mary Wollstonecraft and John Stuart Mill, for example; but in the process she also anticipated the direction of some of the most recent and perceptive feminist theorists: the concentration on the politics of the family, for example, the recognition that the personal is political, the understanding that only by examining the daily lives of women and their experiences of submission to the demands of family life could an explanation of female "difference" ultimately be found.[27] Viewing women's powerlessness and dependence on men as both psychological and political phenomena, she argued that the female personality had become a slave personality. She wrote, "The position of women, after their long degradation is in many ways analogous to that of the freed slave. He is refused justice on account of his inferiority. To reply that inferiority is largely due to previous injustice does not alter the fact."[28] The female personality was likewise conditioned to submission. "Of women especially have been required the convenient virtues of a subject class: obedience, patience, endurance, contentment, humility, resignation, temperance, prudence, industry, kindness, cheerfulness, modesty, gratitude, thrift, and unselfishness."[29] Although the conditions of women's lives had important variations, Gilman believed there existed a common institutional experience—the home—which affected women whether rich or poor. The politics of the family crossed class lines.

Fourth, finally, and least persuasively, Gilman ventured beyond many of her socialist contemporaries in exploring the unique effects of sexual oppression on women. She believed that the sexual relationship had become an economic relationship, marriage very often itself being merely a legally enshrined version of prostitution. Forced to emphasize sexuality at the expense of humanity, woman had necessarily to give the impression of weakness, frailty, timidity, and passivity—in short to prove her capacity for submission, the male's for dominance and control. Gilman wrote:

We have been told so long that

"Love is of man's life a thing apart,
Tis woman's whole existence"

that we have believed it. . . . [O]ur whole existence was carefully limited to this field; we were dressed and educated to grace it; we were bloomed out into a brief and glorious career while under inspection and selection before our final surrender, and then we pursued the rest of our lives with varying devotion and satisfaction in this one department of life.[30]

She advocated the distribution of information on birth control and sex-related matters, the development of physical fitness programs for women, and an end to man-made fashion dictates. She called for human fulfillment, for women's full control of their bodies as well as their lives.[31]

However, Gilman's understanding of the causes for sexual oppression was far more impressive than her theoretical projections. In short, she could *attack* the "feminine" woman, but not *envision* an alternative of equal womanhood. Her life and writings were always inextricably related. Where she had achieved certain of her feminist goals—economic independence, physical fitness, and considerable psychological strength as well, she believed in woman's capacity for excellence. But because she could not interpret the conflicting loyalties which seemed to occur, both within herself and other independent women when they entered love relationships with men (and wavering herself between both strength and deference, self-righteousness, and self-sacrifice), Charlotte perhaps understandably concluded that certain stereotypes of "femininity" must some-how be innate.

The personal roots of Charlotte's theoretical contradictions are apparent in her early living, in her struggles with guilt as she faced her separation and divorce from Walter Stetson, and in her love relationship with Houghton Gilman, whom she married in 1900.[32] She wrote letters of passionate intensity to Gilman, but she seemd to fear him as a threat to her marginally established independence. A sensuous woman, she was also a well-trained warrior in the feminist campaign. Unintentionally and tragically, she created sexual and psychological barriers against an intimate male-female relationship.

Charlotte had known Houghton as a child, as an affectionate first cousin eight years her junior, whose companionship she very much enjoyed. After a hiatus of some seventeen years, Charlotte visited Houghton in his law office to obtain legal advice concerning royalties on a publication. Erroneously, she assumed the relationship was "safe" from "complications" because of kinship, though she expressed her preference for even safer grounds than that: "I only wish I was your grandma or great aunt or I have it! an invalid sister that you simply *had* to have around you all the time!!!" She was delighted with his friendship: "You seem very near somehow—a background to most of my thinking when I'm not at work." Or again, "It's astonishing how many times a day I incline to write you."[33] And write she did—twenty- or thirty-page letters, two or more times a week.

Nonetheless, expressions of increasing fondness for Houghton were interspersed with apologetic declarations of resistance:

> To most people . . . I can behave nicely. . . . But as soon as any one comes near me and takes hold, I wobble awfully. Now as you may have seen I am getting exceedingly fond of you. . . . And I don't like it. It makes me unreasonable. It makes me feel—where I don't want to feel; and think—where I don't want to think. It sort of wakes me up where I'm dead, or where, if I'm not dead I ought to be.
>
> Now I can't afford to be fond of anybody in that sort of way—man, woman, or child. I can't afford to want things. . . . But [your] being here . . . and being, to your sorrow—my "entire family"—why it brings out all that is worst and weakest in me, instead of what is strongest and best. It makes me unreasonable—sensitive—disagreeable—absurd. It makes me want to be petted and cared for—me! And then all this makes me very mad; and I say "go to! I'll get out of this in short order!"[34]

Charlotte seemed to vacillate wildly between feelings of strength and insecurity. She was "rich in the tricks and shifts of an old campaigner weatherbeaten and coarsened by long exposure." But also, she felt "bitterly depressed, often defeated, lonely, imprisoned, scared and wounded beyond recognition but not crippled past all usefulness. . . ." She seemed to need to ask for pity. She felt a "compelling desire . . . to complain and explain, to whimper . . . and seek for sympathy which don't do me any good if I get it." She extended her growing trust in Houghton with a "childish femininity":[35]

> I temporarily cuddle down and clutch you remorselessly. Later on I shall flop and wobble again. Later still soar off no doubt. But just for a little time—and with excellent reason that I can't help—behold me as it were a sleepy Newfoundland puppy in your overcoat pocket.[36]

Thus did a public advocate of woman's full equality privately reveal the anguish of her personal ambivalence. She wrote:

> I wish I could make a picture of the thing [herself] as I see it—sulky, frightened, discouraged, "rattled" to a degree; one foot forward and the other back; ready to rush forward in tumultuous devotion one minute, and run away shrieking the next—fingers in ears.[37]

However tentatively and indecisively, Charlotte began to break the barriers of her self-imposed lonely isolation. Insecurities sometimes reemerged in the form of uncontrollable depressions, the "grey fog" she had faced since 1884. But increasingly she felt a passionate happy love for Houghton which, characteristically, she had to formulate in writing. She left, therefore, abundant documentation of her sensuous yearnings, as well as of her apprehensions:

> I went to sleep with a smile on my lips and woke only to think again of the dear comfort that you are to me—of your unfailing loving kindness, your quiet strength, your patience and wisdom—and your tenderness. O it *does* feel so good! To have some one care for me enough to—well—to kiss me.[38]

She continued in December: "Everything is so different. I have a home now—in your heart." In February, 1898 she wrote: "Surely you can read it in my eyes—hear it in my voice, feel it in my arms about your neck—taste it on my lips that lean to you. You make me happy—so happy my darling. I love you—love you—love you!" And even more passionately for a supposedly "Victorian" lady, she wrote to him in May: "Sweetheart! You shall kiss me anywhere you want to and all you want to as soon as ever there is a chance. I will wait till you are exhausted and then begin operations on my own account."[39]

Despite such passionate declarations, Charlotte also delighted in the image of herself as cared-for child: "And it will be the wholesomest thing in the world to ... settle down to the definite and particular feeling of being your little girl."[40] Continuously she seemed to need protective reassurance; and when Houghton did not sufficiently comply, she responded angrily. So vulnerable did she feel, so intense was her level of hurt, that on one occasion in 1899, she threatened to break off the relationship entirely. She wrote: "When I think of what manner of letters I have written to you—of course I want to call them all back and burn them ... and never think of love again lest I die of shame."[41] She insisted that Houghton be strong and more assertive, and that she, as woman, should wait more passively:

> If you don't love me more than to make dutiful responses to my advances it won't do to marry on. . . .
> It is a woman's business to wait, not a man's.
> It is for a woman to be patient and still—not a man.
> If you are truly lover and husband—show it. If not—God bless you and good bye.[42]

Charlotte's outbursts were frequent but short-lived, her contests with self-hatred a recurring pattern of her life. She recovered from her anger, only to be tormented once again by uncontrollable anxiety. Back and forth she went: "I don't wholly like to be held—and yet I do!" She wanted protective love, yet despised herself for needing it. "Makes me kind of angry too," she later wrote. "Seems a weakness. To be so tangled up in another person."[43] Torn between her feminist convictions and her feelings, she expressed discontent with what she thought she had become—a non-womanly woman:

> Don't you see dear how much at a disadvantage I am beside you? Try and feel like a woman for a moment—put yourself in their place. You know what a woman wants to bring a man—a boundless whole-souled love, absolutely and primarily his own—all his own.
> I haven't that . . . I can only give you a divided love—I love God—the world—my work as I love you. I have so little to offer—so pathetically little. . . .
> O my dear—do you not see what poignant grief and shame it is to a woman to have no woman's gifts to give![44]

Charlotte apologized for having achieved many of her goals: "I'm sorry," she wrote Houghton, "that I can't add my life to yours—woman fashion . . . the usual style of immersion of the wife in the husband." Theoretically and practically she insisted on the right to satisfying work; emotionally she felt she should give it up to him. Come to my lectures, she had pleaded with Houghton in 1899. "Then you'd know—know me, know why I have felt as I do about marrying and all that. Why I so seriously fear lest the housekeeping part of it [marriage] should prove an injury to my health and a hindrance to my work." But hardly consistently for a radical feminist, she continued, "You see I am so afraid of my own long . . . instincts getting the better of me—and that, in my love for you and natural wish to make you comfortable I shall 'settle' too firmly."[45]

Ambiguities expressed in Charlotte's letters to Houghton were also apparent in her public writings. An advocate of women's full equality, she inconsistently, ironically, contrasted masculine work-instincts with "feminine" instincts of nurturance and service, male adult-like strength and courage with female childlike insecurity and fear. Thus this "militant madonna" portrayed woman's "natural" yearning for a male's protective love.

If to a degree the "instincts" argument served to undermine Gilman's environmentalist analysis of the origins of sexual inequality, it also provided crucial leverage in her fight for female self-respect. Perhaps defensively, Gilman attempted to reverse traditionally negative connotations of "femininity" by emphasizing the virtues of womanhood instead. Like most of her feminist contemporaries, proudly she proclaimed the primacy of womanhood: Woman's archetypal innocence was concomitant to her moral virtue; gentle kindness was a means of power, an antidote to assertive male combativeness. Woman's uniqueness was thus her strength and glory, her mother-love a countervailing force within the baneful androcentric culture.

The most explicit statement of Gilman's admiration and love for women was expressed in the novel *Herland* (1915). Utopia, she told her readers, was a land inhabited only by women and girl children, procreation occurring through parthenogenesis. Faithfully worshipping the "Goddess of mother love," and interacting cooperatively, respectfully, and affectionately, women demonstrated their capacity to build Utopia. Because they were not confined within the isolation of the private selfish home, women could use their nurturant capacities for social and community service. Trusting childcare only to the "highest artists," they developed the *true* "womanly" virtues: "Beauty, Health, Strength, Intellect, Goodness. . . ." In *Herland,* the "essential distinction of motherhood was the dominant note of their whole culture." Motherhood was the "great, tender, limitless uplifting force."[46]

Theoretically as well as fictionally, Gilman asserted the natural superiority of the female sex. Enthusiastically endorsing the "scientifically based" Gynaecocentric Theory of the sociologist Lester Ward, she elaborated extensively on the civilizing capacities of women, the destructive combativeness of men. She wrote: "The innate underlying difference [between the sexes] is one of principle. On the one hand, the principle of struggle, conflict, and competition. . . . On the other, the principle of growth, of culture, of applying services and nourishment in order to produce improvement."[47] Woman did not want to fight, to take, to oppress. Instead she exhibited "the growing altruism of work, founded in mother love, in the antiselfish instinct of reproduction."[48] Fundamental to the evolutionary process was woman's inherent responsibility for the preservation of the race, the selection of a mate, and the nurturance of children.

Charlotte Gilman presents us with a paradox. Having developed a multidimensional feminist theory based on the idea of the natural equality of the sexes, having challenged patriarchal norms dividing males and females into their respective public-private spheres, she also enthusiastically maintained that women were the saintly givers, men the warring beasts. When she glorified female "instincts" of love and service, her radical theory of feminism dissolved into a sometimes sentimental worship of the status quo. Compromising her environmentalist analysis, she alternately emphasized not female powerlessness, but woman's natural passivity; not artificially imposed dependence, but an innate desire to love and serve; not cowardice, but peacefulness and cooperation; not the oppressive restrictions of motherhood roles, but the glories of mother love. By proclaiming women's natural differences, Charlotte Gilman, like many of her contemporaries, "put to a test the entire ideology upon which arguments for the liberation of women had been based in the United States."[49]

Yet while claims to female nurturant superiority were ultimately dysfunctional, they were nonetheless, historically, a viable response to women's need for expanded decision-making power. A vital struggle for political autonomy lay beneath the mother-worship proclamations. Moreover, "suffragists were not blushing Victorians but seasoned politicians who had learned how to beat the male at his own game."[50] Charlotte Gilman refused to treat women purely as the victims—incompetents within the world of men. Instead, she urged women to develop self-respect on their own terms, not those exclusively defined by men.

Thus, when she emphasized woman's role as "the moral redeemer and culture bearer," she was acclaiming a philosophy which "actually permitted women to enhance their self-image as individuals and as a group and, ultimately to organize for action."[51] Whether tactically or ideologically, she seems to have understood that women might necessarily, if temporarily, expand their power by celebrating differences.

While Charlotte's dichotomous theories were in part an outgrowth of the intellectual and socioeconomic forces of her era, my purpose here has been to illustrate instead some private sources for her feminist perspectives. The existence of contradiction in her theories, her fiction, and her living by no means lessens the significance of her historical contribution. Her theoretical analyses were themselves impressive, but so also was her constant testing of those theories in the experimental laboratory of her life. Since she kept voluminous accounts of her private struggles, she unintentionally preserved in the panorama of her eccentricity and genius, a wealth of historical data which will enrich our understanding of the underlying dynamics of feminist theory and practice at the turn of the century.[52]

Notes

1. Quotations from private letters are made with the permission of The Arthur and Elizabeth Schlesinger Library on the History of Women in America, Radcliffe College, Cambridge, Massachusetts. Letters from Charlotte Stetson to Houghton Gilman, September 2, 1897; letter from Jane Addams to Charlotte Stetson, July 19, 1898; letter from Florence Kelley to Charlotte Stetson, July 26, 1898; *The Nation*, June 8, 1899.

2. Charlotte Perkins Gilman, *Women and Economics: A Study of the Economic Relation Between Men and Women as a Factor in Social Evolution* (New York: Harper ed., 1966), p. 331.

3. Letter from Charlotte Stetson to Houghton Gilman, July 26, 1899. My focus here is on the relationships and experiences most richly documented in the Charlotte Perkins Gilman collection, particularly the relationships with Walter Stetson and Houghton Gilman. Charlotte's relationships with her parents, with female friends, and with many significant others will receive further attention in a forthcoming biography—*Charlotte Perkins Gilman: The Birth of a Radical Feminist, 1860–1896*. For an interim biographical and theoretical analysis of the life and writings of Charlotte Gilman see Mary A. Porter (Hill-Peters), "Charlotte Perkins Gilman: A Feminist Paradox" (Ph.D. dissertation, McGill University, 1975).

4. Charlotte Gilman, *The Living of Charlotte Perkins Gilman* (New York: Appleton-Century Company, 1935), pp. 78, 80. Diaries, 1879–1883.

5. See particularly diary entries for October 12, October 30, November 5, November 16, December 16, 1881. Charlotte had many very close relationships with women during her lifetime, with Grace Channing, Adeline Knapp, Martha Luther, and Helen Campbell, for example. The data richly supports Carroll Smith-Rosenberg's suggestion that "women's sphere had an essential integrity and dignity that grew out of women's shared experiences and mutual affection." Carroll Smith-Rosenberg, "The Female World of Love and Ritual: Relations Between Women in Nineteenth-Century America." *Signs* 1:1 (Autumn, 1975), 9–10. As

historians increasingly appreciate the significance of female networks of support and companionship, we need also to consider the often painful feeling of rejection close female friends experienced with one another. Among Charlotte's most difficult emotional crises were the departure of Martha Luther and the disruption of the relationship with Adeline Knapp ("Dora" in *Living*, pp. 133, 141–44). See diary entries, 1892–1893.

6. "An Anchor to Windward," Diary, January 31, 1882.

7. Letters from Charlotte Perkins to Walter Stetson, February 20 and 21, 1882. According to the pre-1881 reading lists which Charlotte kept in her diaries, she was apparently unfamiliar with the rich feminist literature she might have drawn on. Moreover, it is striking that she did not mention her two successful great-aunts, Catharine Beecher and Harriet Beecher Stowe, as she described to Walter the seemingly irreconcilable conflict between marriage and career (letter to Walter Stetson, February 20, 1882):

    I am beset by my childhood's conscientiousness . . . the voice of all the ages sounds in my ears, saying that this [marriage] is noble, natural, and right; that no woman yet has ever attempted to stand alone as I intend but that she had to submit or else. . . .
    I have nothing to answer but the meek assertion that I am different from if not better than all these, and that my life is mine in spite of myriad lost sisters before me.

8. Letter to Walter Stetson, March 6, 1882; Diary, April 5, 1883; "Thoughts and Fingerings," November 3, 1883. Charlotte's acceptance in 1883 of Walter's authority contrasts strikingly with her self-confident assertions of February 13, 1882: "You are the first man I have met whom I recognize as an equal; and that is saying a good deal for me. I would call you grandly superior, but that I am fighting just now against a heart-touched woman's passion of abnegation." Letter to Walter Stetson, February 13, 1882.

9. Diary, December 31, 1883.

10. *Living*, pp. 10, 5.

11. "Phobias" emerge, according to the Symonds thesis, from a denial of self-expression that women often felt must be the price of love. "Marriage then becomes their 'declaration of dependence'. . . . [T]hey tend to become the paragons of Victorian femininity—helpless, housebound, and ineffectual." See Alexandra Symonds, M.D., "Phobias after Marriage: Women's Declaration of Dependence," in *Psychoanalysis and Women*, edited by Jean Baker Miller, M.D. (Middlesex, England: Penguin Books, 1973), pp. 288–303.

12. Diary, May 2, 1884.

13. Diary, May 9, 1884. Charlotte Gilman, *The Home: Its Work and Influence* (New York: McClure, Phillips and Company, 1903), p. 12.

14. "Thoughts and Fingerings," November 3, 1883; Diary, June 15, June 25, 1884.

15. Diary, August 30, 1885; *Living*, p. 89.

16. Carroll Smith-Rosenberg, "The Hysterical Woman: Sex Roles and Role Conflict in 19th-Century America," *Social Research* 39:4 (Winter, 1972), p. 671.

17. Diary, August 30, 1885; *Living*, pp. 91, 96.

18. Charlotte Perkins Gilman, "The Yellow Wallpaper," *New England Magazine* 5 (January, 1892), pp 647–56. I am taking the liberty of using "The Yellow Wallpaper" quite literally as autobiographical material. The names are different, but the fantasies symbolic; but when

asked to what extent "The Yellow Wallpaper" was based on fact, Charlotte replied, "I had been as far as one could go and get back." *Living,* p. 121.

19.   Diary, April 18, 1887.

20.   See diary entries November 16, 1883; February 24, October 6, 1886; January 5, January 19, February 5, 1887.

21.   Diary entries, February 20, March 20, February 7, 1887.

22.   *Living,* p. 96.

23.   Charlotte Gilman, "Masculine, Feminine, and Human," *Woman's Journal* 35 (January 16, 1904), 18.

24.   *The Home,* p. 22; *Women and Economics,* p. 14–15; Gilman, "Her Own Money: Is a Wife Entitled to the Money She Earns?" *Mother's Magazine* 7 (February 1912), 7.

25.   Aileen Kraditor, *Ideas of the Women's Suffrage Movement* (New York: Columbia University Press, 1965), p. 121.

26.   Gilman, "Domestic Economy," *Independent* 56 (June 16, 1904), 1359–60; Gilman, "The Normal Social Group Today," *The Forerunner* 4 (July 1913), 175; Gilman, *Women and Economics,* p. 226.

27.   See particularly Simone de Beauvoir, *The Second Sex.* Juliet Mitchell *Woman's Estate* (Vintage ed.; New York: Random House, 1973). Juliet Mitchell, *Psychoanalysis and Feminism* (New York: Pantheon, 1974). Kate Millet, *Sexual Politics* (New York: Doubleday and Company, 1970). Shulamith Firestone, *The Dialectic of Sex: The Case for Feminist Revolution* (Bantam ed.; New York: William Morrow, 1970). Sheila Rowbotham, *Women, Resistance, and Revolution* (Vintage ed.; New York: Random House, 1974). Sheila Rowbotham, *Woman's Consciousness* (Middlesex, England: Penguin Books, Ltd., 1973). Maria Della Costa, *The Power of Women and the Subversion of the Community* (2nd ed.; Bristol, England: Falling Wall Press, Ltd., 1973).

28.   Gilman, "Educated Bodies," *Woman's Journal* 35 (June 1904), p. 178.

29.   Gilman, *His Religion and Hers: A Study of the Faith of Our Fathers and the Work of Our Mothers* (New York: The Century Company, 1923), p. 134.

30.   Gilman, "Love Stories and Life Stories." *Woman's Journal* 35 (May 7, 1904), p. 146.

31.   Charlotte Gilman's support of Margaret Sanger's work in the birth control movement began roughly in 1915. Adopting the racist and ethnocentric attitudes all too common to her generation, however, Charlotte viewed birth control as an issue not only of personal importance for women; she also maintained that it could be used as a protection against the pressures of population expansion, particularly of the "unfit." See Gilman, "Birth Control, Religion, and the Unfit," *Nation,* 134 (January 27, 1932), p. 109; Gilman, "Birth Control," *The Forerunner,* 6 (July 1915), pp. 177–80.

32.   This discussion is limited to Charlotte's attitude toward Houghton Gilman between 1897 and 1900 and is not intended as an interpretation of their marriage relationship from 1900 to 1934.

33.   Letter from Charlotte Stetson to Houghton Gilman, September 11, September 2, September 5, 1897.

34.   Ibid., October 3, 1897.

35. Ibid., October 1, October 3, 1897; undated letter, October, 1897.

36. Ibid., November 4, 1897.

37. Ibid., November 7, 1897.

38. Ibid.

39. Ibid., February 20, May 6, 1898. On a number of occasions Charlotte mentioned her desire to have a child with Houghton, but when she thought that she might be unable, she expressed delight: "Happy thought—take no precautions—take no treatment—all runs smoothly and nothing happens!!! There's an easy way out of the difficulty!!!" Sex without fears of pregnancy seemed a grand relief. Letter from Charlotte Stetson to Houghton Gilman, May 16, 1900.

    Carl Degler argues that many nineteenth-century women may not have been so fearful of or opposed to the sexual experience as was formerly assumed. Historians have too frequently relied on prescriptive data, he maintains, thus distorting the actual attitudes and experiences of women themselves. See Carl Degler, "What Ought to be and What Was: Women's Sexuality in the Nineteenth Century," *American Historical Review* 79 (December 1974), pp. 1467–90. See also Charles E. Rosenberg, "Sexuality, Class, and Role in Nineteenth Century America," *American Quarterly* 25 (May 1973), pp. 131–53.

40. Letter from Charlotte Stetson to Houghton Gilman, January 9, 1898. Also referring to a letter he had written, she responded, "This is the letter that says I'm your darling little girl, which remark I have kissed many times." Ibid., November 14, 1899.

41. Ibid., January 22, 1899.

42. Ibid., January 25, 1899.

43. Ibid., June 2, November 6, 1898.

44. Ibid., November 14, 1899.

45. Ibid., March 14, 1900; February 28, 1899. On December 28, 1898 she wrote: "I quite envy those good women who really feel that the husband is their whole range of duty—it must be so sweet to have no call away from that dear love." In March she wrote, "Dear, it isn't fair! You ought to have a *whole* wife to give herself all to you." Although by November she more confidently asserted, "I want to carry out what I think is perfectly possible—a kind of married life that has both love and freedom. I see no need for the 'yoke.'" See letters, December 28, 1898; March 5, November 14, 1899.

46. Gilman, *Herland*, in *The Forerunner* 6 (May 1915), pp. 127–29; Ibid., *Forerunner* 6 (July 1915), p. 186.

47. Gilman, *His Religion and Hers: A Study of the Faith of Our Fathers and the Work of Our Mothers* (New York: The Century Company, 1923), p. 271. Lester Ward Projected a theory of sexual differentiation which he claimed proved "that in the economy of organic nature the female sex is the primary, and the male a secondary element." Clearly Darwinism could not be used as a justification for the subjection of the female sex, he argued, because in fact it was the female who was responsible for the preservation of the species. Since the first function of the male was simply to enable the female to reproduce, it was she who was the source of life and therefore of superior importance. Lester Ward, "Our Better Halves," *Forum* 6 (November 1888), p. 266. See also Lester Ward, *Dynamic Sociology* (New York: D. Appleton, 1883); Lester Ward, *Pure Sociology* (New York: Macmillan Co., 1903); Samuel Chugerman, *Lester F. Ward, The American Aristotle: A Summary and Interpretation of His Sociology*

(Durham, N.C.: Duke University Press, 1939). Of Ward's Gynaecocentric Theory, Charlotte Gilman wrote, "nothing so important to humanity has been advanced since the Theory of Evolution, and nothing so important to women has ever been given to the world." Gilman, *The Man-Made World: Our Androcentric Culture* (New York: Charlton Company, 1911), Dedication.

Charlotte Gilman's support of the woman-as-superior argument, side-by-side with her environmentalist feminist position can also be interpreted as yet another manifestation of Social Darwinist and Lamarckian thought. Characteristically, turn-of-the-century thinkers blurred the distinction between inherited and acquired characteristics. Again, however, the emphasis of this paper is on the personal more than the philosophical roots of Charlotte Gilman's feminist paradox.

48.   Gilman, *Human Work* (New York: McClure, Phillips and Company, 1903), pp. 211, 207.

49.   Jill Conway, "The Woman's Peace Party and the First World War," *War and Society in North America*, ed. J. L. Granatstein and R. D. Cuff (Toronto: Thomas Nelson and Sons, 1971), p. 52. See also Jill Conway, "Women Reformers and American Culture, 1870–1930," *Journal of Social History*, 5 (Winter 1971–72), pp. 164–77; Susan Hartman, "The Paradox of Women's Progress: 1820–1920" (St. Charles, Missouri: Forum Press); Mary Ryan, *Womanhood in America* (New York: Franklin Watts, Inc., 1975), pp. 139–248.

50.   Mary Ryan, *Womanhood in America*, p. 246.

51.   Barbara Sicherman, "American History: Review Essay," *Signs* 1:2 (Winter 1975), p. 470. Anthropologist Michelle Zimbalist Rosaldo argues "that the very symbolic and social conceptions that appear to set women apart and to circumscribe their activities may be used by women as a basis for female solidarity and worth." Michelle Zimbalist Rosaldo, "Woman, Culture, and Society: A Theoretical Overview," in *Woman, Culture, and Society*, p. 39.

52.   Because of the complexities of Gilman's private correspondence, and also because of the rich body of feminist materials that have become available in recent years, I am currently in the process if revising my perspectives on the implications of Gilman's private correspondence with Houghton Gilman. My two earlier volumes (*Charlotte Perkins Gilman: The Making of a Radical Feminist, 1860–1896* (1980) and *Endure: The Diaries of Walter Stetson* (1985)) cover the early origins of Gilman's feminist convictions. My forthcoming volume, however, will offer new interpretations of the rich correspondence with Houghton Gilman (1896–1900). It will not only show the depth of Gilman's anti-woman feelings but will also show her long-term struggle to attain a more positive affirmation of her womanhood. (*Charlotte Perkins Gilman: A Journey From Within*, Temple University Press, forthcoming.)

3

Gilman's "The Yellow Wallpaper": A Centenary

Linda Wagner-Martin

A friend is dead.
We cannot discount pain but the least bearable pain is the hus-
band's cry of anger: You cannot die. I need you. The children
need you. Your duty is to us.

The answer to that is silence.
Written by the author for a friend who died at the age of 39.

It seems no accident that important recent novels have been Toni Morrison's
Beloved, about the power of a sacrificed child over her mourning mother's life,
and Marilyn French's *Her Mother's Daughter,* a major fiction about four generations of women, linked together in their martyred and futile lives through the
mother-daughter bond. For at least these hundred years, since Charlotte Perkins
Gilman wrote her controversial and relentlessly accurate "The Yellow Wallpaper," women writers have confronted the basic conflicts of women's lives: how
to be both a person and a wife and mother; how to live with acceptable passivity
in a patriarchal culture while yet being aggressive enough to stay alive; and how
to be both "good" and sensual, supportive and necessarily selfish, and, above
all, sane.

Of these many conflicts inherent in women's trying to lead acceptable
female lives, perhaps the most troublesome is that of motherhood, its attendant
responsibilities, and its almost inevitable loss of self-identity. Women who care
for infants are almost literally used up in the process, the twenty-four-hour-a-
day surveillance subsuming their own mental and physical activities. No other
human situation demands the same level of inexorable attention. Yet of the
many controversies about women's roles, that of motherhood—and, as Dorothy

Dinnerstein emphasized, the care-giving during childhood as much as the actual birthing—has seldom been discussed. It is almost as if the role of mother is beyond discussion, beyond change: if one is a mother, one accepts its burdens with its joys, and does not in any way try to tailor its numerous givens.[1]

Recent studies have begun to question some of these assumptions. Marilyn Yalom in her important *Maternity, Mortality, and the Literature of Madness* questions "the extent to which maternity, as option or experience, serves as a catalyst for mental breakdown."[2] She discusses women's fear of childbirth, the guilt of not having children opposing the satisfaction (or, at times, dissatisfaction) with bearing a child, and other dimensions of women's psychology as it is affected by motherhood; and concludes, "The relationship between parenthood and madness seems to have no parallel in the lives of men."[3] Adrienne Rich's *Of Woman Born, Motherhood as Experience and Institution* confronts many of the same issues, using a more subjective model. That book opens with one of Rich's journal entries. "My children cause me the most exquisite suffering of which I have any experience. It is the suffering of ambivalence: the murderous alternation between bitter resentment and raw-edged nerves, and blissful gratification and tenderness. Sometimes I seem to myself, in my feelings toward these tiny guiltless beings, a monster of selfishness and intolerance."[4] The point, obviously, is that society expects women to be fulfilled through motherhood, and that women who question their roles as mothers, who complain or are angry about those roles, are suspect if not beyond human comprehension.[5]

A corollary to this attitude is the anger that greets the death of any woman who dies when her children are small. The case of Sylvia Plath's suicide—which was met with horror, largely because she had two children (one a year old, one nearly three), not because she was a promising young writer herself—is legendary, but it is equally clear that an almost automatic anger exists when any young mother dies of natural causes. People seem as likely to feel anger as sorrow, as if the mother—by dying—has purposely denied her responsibility for rearing her children.[6]

This tendency to judge, and often to condemn, women in their roles as mothers, is one reason Gilman's "The Yellow Wallpaper" remains moving and powerful even a hundred years after it was written. In its deft portrayal of women's roles, it attacks directly the most inimical stereotypes about wives and mothers—and, conversely, about husbands and fathers.

When Gilman wrote the short novella, she—married and a mother—had recently recovered from the trauma of a severe postpartum depression. And she had managed that recovery by defying the advice of one of the most respected of American physicians, S. Weir Mitchell. Mitchell was the physician of Jane Addams, Edith Wharton, and Winifred Howells, among other women who suffered from inexplicable Victorian "female" ailments such as hysteria and neurasthenia. Mitchell's treatment was a rest cure which depended upon seclusion, massage, electricity, immobility, and overfeeding. Isolated for up to six weeks, some women gained as much as fifty pounds on a milk-based diet. As a parallel to the rest and diet, most patients were forbidden to use their minds in any way. Gilman recalled in her autobiography that, because her "cure" added the almost constant presence of her infant daughter, Katharine, she "made a rag baby, hung it on a doorknob and played with it. I would crawl into remote closets and under beds—to hide from the grinding pressure of that profound distress."[7]

Closed out and away from any life other than that of feeding and sustaining their own bodies and those of their children, Mitchell's patients lost much sense of themselves as people. Two years later, Gilman left her husband, believing that she could not endure the role of wife. Several more years later, she sent Katharine to him and his new wife, Grace Channing, her own closest friend. Ann J. Lane recounts that when Charlotte sent Katharine back to her father—at least partly because she was lecturing and traveling a great deal in connection with woman suffrage and trade union issues, she was "promptly condemned by the press for 'abandoning' her child and being 'an unnatural mother.'" She had already affronted public opinion by divorcing a man for no apparant cause and, even more, by continuing a warm friendship with his new wife. However, placing her career above her responsibilities as a mother proved unforgivable, especially to a world that had locked women securely in their place—at home."[8]

The story as Gilman tells it in *The Living of Charlotte Perkins Gilman*, the autobiography published just after her death in 1935, is much more agonizing. Once she had taken Katharine and her mother to California to make a home, after separating from Stetson, she lived a weary existence, taking in sick boarders to make a living. "'It appears that I am sicker than I thought.' 'I am very weak.' 'Gave out in the morning. Sick—sicker. . . .'" "I did all the housework and nursed mother [who had cancer] till I broke down; then I hired a cook and did the nursing till I broke down; then I hired a nurse and did the cooking till I broke down. Dr. Kellog Lane said I must send mother to a hospital. This I could not bear to do. 'If you say definitely as a physician that I shall die, or go crazy,' I told her, 'I'll do as you say. But if I can possibly stand it I want to go on, I do not wish to have it said that I have failed in every relation in life.'"[9] Her omnipresent guilt at leaving her husband (even though, as her memoir also tells, poignantly, when she was with him, even before their child was born, "A sort of gray fog drifted across my mind, a cloud that grew and darkened")[10] colored all her interactions with people. She surely had done as much as any daughter could have done for her mother, who died at home in Gilman's care in 1893.

Gilman's love for her daughter Katharine shines through her autobiography. "We had happy years together, nine of them, the last four she was mine alone," she writes. Yet when the press censured her for sending Katharine to live with Stetson and Grace, Gilman was puzzled. "No one suffered from it but myself. . . . There were years, years, when I could never see a mother and child together without crying. . . . This, however, was entirely overlooked in the furious condemnation which followed. I had 'given up my child.' . . . To hear what was said and read what was printed one would think I had handed over a baby in a basket. In the years that followed she [Katharine] divided her time fairly equally between us, but in companionship with her beloved father she grew up to be the artist that she is, with advantages I could never have given her. I lived without her, temporarily, but why did they think I liked it? She was all I had."[11]

Gilman's autobiography makes clear her years of poverty and debt, her loneliness, and her arduous life. No wonder "The Yellow Wallpaper" portrays a spent woman so accurately. But it is not so much the truth of Gilman's presentation as the immediacy of her theme that attracts today's readers. "The Yellow Wallpaper" gives us the young married woman as mother.

In the narrative, the protagonist's baby appears infrequently, but at crucial times; his existence is clearly a key to his mother's problems. Gilman underscores the identity of the protagonist as wife-mother (a bewildered wife-mother, who sometimes becomes a child) by placing her in a room that was formerly a nursery—a nursery, however, with barred windows so that she cannot escape. The conflation of the roles of child and mother occurs as the narrator keeps her focus entirely on the enclosing walls of the sinister room. An infant would not be able to leave its nursery; neither is the mother (though Gilman makes clear that the protagonist does sometimes leave the house and walks in the garden or sits downstairs). For the purposes of our involvement with this narrative, however, the story's location is the nursery. And just as an infant would spend hours staring at walls and ceilings, kept in one place at the mercy of whatever authority was responsible for its care, so too does the protagonist. An infant would also have difficulty finding language to express its feelings. With a brilliance rare in nineteenth-century fiction, Gilman gives her suffering protagonist a restricted language that conveys her childlike frustration, even though it is not obviously childlike. For its effect, the protagonist's language works in tandem with the narrative's structure.

The narrative opens with the house which has been rented for the summer described an "ancestral hall."[12] The reader quickly thinks of the family line, with women the means of creating the children. Some baronial estate, some ancestor's place, all attention focused on the children of the family—implicitly the reader knows the true "place" and role of the unnamed protagonist. (Because she is never named, Gilman forces the reader to describe her as wife and, later, as mother, because the prominent characters in the story are John—who is named repeatedly, emphatically—and their child. Three of the paragraphs from the first page open with the husband's name, "John," and describe him in the act of either laughing at her, losing patience with her, or identifying himself as a physician, a tactic he chooses frequently to end arguments with his wife.)

In contrast to John's being named directly and often, the protagonist/writer refers to herself as "one." In the impersonal form (only later does she use *I*), she distances herself from the issues. She also creates a kind of prose poem on the second page of the text, which opens with the question "And what can *one* do?"and closes with the refrain, "But what is *one* to do?" Between these lines, Gilman writes a five-paragraph paradigm of the inequality possible between husbands and wives. The paradigm opens with the longest paragraph, stressing that John is a physician and using the pronoun *one* so often the reader nearly loses the sense of the passage: "If a physician of high standing, and one's own husband, assures friends and relatives that there is really nothing the matter with one but temporary nervous depression—a slight hysterical tendency—what is one to do?" Charged modifiers (*high, really, temporary*, and *slight*) undermine whatever complaint the depressed wife has, and by keeping the tone so impersonal, the narrator hides her anger and bewilderment.

The second paragraph links John with the protagonist's brother, another physician ("also of high standing") who agrees with John's diagnosis. The third has the protagonist using the wrong word for her medication, as if she is unable to understand medical terms, being female. But in the fourth and fifth segments, she speaks in the *I* persona for the first time—but in a heavily defensive construction:

> Personally, I disagreed with their ideas.
> Personally, I believe that congenial work, with excitement and change, would do me good.[13]

The force of these aggressive, sharp comments—the only arguments which are phrased directly in the novella—is undercut immediately as the reader comes to the closing refrain of the segment, "But what is one to do?" In giving up her authority, in trading her *I* for the *one,* the protagonist drops back into the posture of helplessness which her culture has helped her view as more acceptable than argumentation.

Admitting her frustration, the protagonist then begins to talk about the house. In fact, she calls the reader's attention to the strategy of talking "about the house" instead of about her anger. With this linguistic cue, the reader comes to see that whenever the protagonist makes a point of describing anything (description is rare in the story, except when the wallpaper begins to take over her consciousness), she is probably attempting—obliquely—to describe herself. In this passage, the house is beautiful as we assume she is or has been, but it is "quite alone . . . quite three miles from the village." The repetition of *quite* intensifies the distance between this location and that of other people, people who might help her. The rest of her description is of separation devices—walls, hedges, and gates that lock. These images of separation create the aura of emptiness that shadows the property, its greenhouses *broken*, its family *gone* through controversy and lawsuits.

Gilman repeats this pattern in later sections of the narrative: the protagonist uses details to describe some place or object, but the description also conveys the emotional tone of the narrative. This is most obvious when she describes the garden (with its imagery of rot and waste), the labyrinth of the wallpaper (which becomes the labyrinth of her life), and the wallpaper when it reflects her impression of herself as somehow sinning, dull, irritating, repellent, unclean, and suicidal. This powerful section of the text ends with the first admission of harsh feeling—hatred—she has allowed: "No wonder the children hated it! I should hate it myself if I had to live in this room long.//There comes John, and I must put this away,—he hates to have me write a word."[14] The juxtaposition of the hated room with John's appearance (John as responsible for her being kept in that particular room, as well as John responsible for her not being allowed to write) confirms her designating him her jailer, in several ways.

This section of suicidal thoughts and admitted hatred closes the first segment of the text. When the protagonist resumes her secret journal, two weeks have passed. The tone of the second section has changed: she has moved from anger to guilt. Early in this segment, the reader is told about the "dear baby," that the protagonist *"cannot* be with him, it makes me so nervous." The indefinite *him* suggests that she also cannot be with John (who is never nervous), who continues to laugh at her fears and her ailments. He has also begun to stay away overnight, claiming he must care for his "serious" cases. He has told her repeatedly that hers is *not* a serious case and Gilman suggests that she believes his words: his language tends to replace hers in the text from this point on.

The emphasis in this section is on the protagonist's guilt at not being able to do her "duty" as wife and mother. "I meant to be such a help to John, such a real rest and comfort, and here I am a comparative burden already!" The use of *already* suggests that her view is that women eventually become only burdens to their husbands, but that at first they are meant to play a supportive role. Elaine Showalter describes the high rate of increase in female insanity during the Victorian period as "one of history's self-fulfilling prophecies. In a society that not only perceived women as childlike, irrational, and sexually unstable but also rendered them legally powerless and economically marginal, it is not surprising that they should have formed the greater part of the residual categories of deviance from which doctors drew a lucrative practice and the asylum much of their population. Moreover, the medical belief that the instability of the female nervous and reproductive systems made women more vulnerable to derangement than men had extensive consequences for social policy. It was used as a reason to keep women out of the professions, to deny them political rights, and to keep them under male control in the family and the state. Thus medical and political policies were mutually reinforcing."[15] Gilman's protagonist acts out this scenario: she laments her failures, and couples them with the fact that she is by nature a "story-maker." Using the term in derogation rather than pride, she links that skill with whimsical thinking and fantasizing. One continuing struggle between John and his wife is his forcing her to think in a different way, to become "rational," to *know* with the same surety and dogmatism that her husband does. Anything other than this assertive knowledge is feminine whim, and is totally objectionable.

To show the metamorphosis of the wife into John's child, Gilman makes her more and more childlike. John calls her "a blessed little goose" as he hugs her, "takes all care from her," and laughs at her fears. She, accordingly and in response, remembers being afraid as a child in a dark room, identifying with a chair that seemed to be a "strong friend." She has this same response to the nursery bedroom, picking out friendly objects and fantasizing about them. A few days later, she writes that she is "fretful." She cries "at nothing"; she cries all the time. She cannot stand to be alone, yet she is alone much of the time. She takes cod liver oil and tonics, and when her depression seems unbearable, she "takes naps." A climactic scene in this second section of the narrative is John's carrying her to bed and reading to her, a scene Annette Kolodny and Judith Fetterley interpret as his assuming her language, stripping her of even that.[16]

The dishonest rhetoric of the comforting husband displays itself at this, the midpoint of the text. John says to reassure her "that I was his darling and his comfort and all he had, and that I must take care of myself for his sake."[17] The complete falsity of these comments (*all he had,* this highly regarded physician?) and his admonition to get well *for his sake* combine to emphasize the control he exerts, or tries to exert, over her. Even though she is told to do these things because she is *his,* rather than because she is herself, at the next moment he abandons her. The next paragraph states, "He says no one but myself can help me out of it, that I must use my will and self-control and not let any silly fancies run away with me." Since hers are only "silly" fancies, and since her illness is not serious at all, why must she be concerned with her condition—especially since he seems to care nothing for her health? (It is only for her *use* to him that she should recover.)

A three-paragraph meditation on the baby follows, as if to answer his admonition. Surely, the baby needs her as much as he does, yet *he* does not even mention the child. Her thoughts about the baby are selfless. She is glad the infant is not living in the "atrocious nusery": that is one benefit of her having the room. But then she refers to the baby as "a child of mine, an impressionable little thing."[18] Her wording claims the child, but also stresses its inferiority in its resemblance to herself: as *impressionable,* rather than rational, like its mother; as *little,* a female trait; and as inanimate as a *thing.*

Immediately following this identification, John calls the protagonist "little girl" and scolds her for walking in her bare feet during the night. (He discounts her insomnia as a symptom of her condition.) He insists that she is recovering, and when she argues with him—giving him facts—he hugs her rather than responding to what she has said. He answers her with meaningless rhetoric: "Bless her little heart! . . . she shall be as sick as she pleases! But now let's improve the shining hours by going to sleep, and talk about it in the morning!" There is no question that her illness is *her* creation, one more product of her willful imagination. She tries again to argue with him, only to receive the argument that he and their child need her; therefore, she must get well. "My darling . . . I beg of you, for my sake and for our child's sake, as well as for your own, that you will never for one instant let that idea [that she is mad] enter your mind! There is nothing so dangerous, so fascinating, to a temperament like yours. It is a false and foolish fancy. Can you not trust me as a physician when I tell you so?"[19]

Gilman chose to let the narrative's structure answer him in the negative. From this scene on, the protagonist hides her real feelings, pretends to get better, and moves into hallucinations of the bilious wallpaper and its trapped women. She has tried to reason with the authority figure—husband/physician— who guards and minimizes her life, but her words have no effect. She has before her the example of his sister, a woman content to be a perfect house-keeper and nothing else. She knows all too well that the qualities of creativity that she values are deprecated constantly by the learned physician. Without any positive response, Gilman's frustrated protagonist becomes mad.

"The Yellow Wallpaper" also shows clearly that without any way to use her own language, the protagonist adopts John's conception of what is appropriate for her to say. Once he has closed off her writing, so that she feels guilty for attempting to record her thoughts (in her own words), she speaks in a different language pattern—and she stops writing altogether. When she does try to talk with him, it is in monosyllables, plaintively, as if she were a child: "And you won't go away?" she asks the often-absent man. His all-too-practical an-swer, particularly heartless for the woman who fears being alone, is "It is only three weeks more and then we will take a nice trip of a few days." Juxtaposing three (long) weeks with a few days shows his insensitivity to her real concerns.

Once she has left John's province of control—real life—and escaped into the madness of her yellow wallpaper world, her comments are much more direct: "I thought seriously of burning the house," "It does not do to trust people too much." She is still caught in her role of "lady" of the manor and physician's wife, but she can find language to express her sense of contradiction: "I am getting angry enough to do something desperate. To jump out of the window would be admirable exercise, but the bars are too strong even to try.// Besides I wouldn't do it. Of course not. I know well enough that a step like that is improper and might be misconstrued. . . ."[20]

Gilman's protagonist may have found a more compatible world in her fantasy, but she still worries about her role as wife and mother. As the narrative ends—with her life as much in her own control as it has ever been—she is worried about wandering in this labyrinth, about physically losing her way. She is never to be the self-reliant, capable helpmeet of John's dreams.

And that is one of Gilman's points, that a woman reared to be a child, treated like a child by her husband (and, one supposes, a father) will respond in kind. No woman expects to be literally put to bed, or removed from all responsibility. Gilman's prose tells of the greatest indignity: the mother of the child becomes the child, the "little girl" of the household (though the mention of the double bed and the husband's presence at night suggests that a sexual role still dominates the relationship). And what is the role of the young daughter in a patriarchal household? To be Daddy's favorite. This is the anger that Sylvia Plath's poem "Daddy" bares—the rage that, once having been brought up to trust the father figure, in whatever guise it appears, then being abandoned by it, being misled by it, being misused by it is insufferable. Gilman's young unnamed wife thus shares in two kinds of anger: that at having her rightful responsibilities taken from her, and that at being misled and miscounseled by the father figures (husband as well as brother) in her life.

"The Yellow Wallpaper" shows what a frustrated woman does with anger. Repression cannot be healthful, and as the protagonist grows more and more quiet, she is becoming more and more mad. Her world has become the world of seething self-enclosure, sparked only by bright, jolting colors and the miasma of rotting odor. In the 1880s, as Carroll Smith-Rosenberg points out, a woman would probably have repressed her anger instead of showing it. If she had showed it, she might have been thought insane and institutionalized, a process which would probably have led only to deeper insanity. The ideal female would become the peaceful "good" girl, who does not cause trouble, does not want attention or help, but is content to wreak havoc in her own way—usually a silent, surreptitious, and vicious way.[21] Gilman's protagonist does just that. The defiance she comes to feel has finally been shed in favor of outright rebellion, yet what would have been more obvious rebellion (harming the baby or John, running away, destroying things important to the household instead of just the horrible wallpaper) does not occur. Instead, the well-behaved woman protagonist (the "good" girl even in her madness) stays within the room, although she has a house key and could easily leave, joining the imaginary women who creep through the wallpaper. (The whole tribe of rebelling women are moving as if they were infants just learning to crawl.) The pathos of the characteristically docile protagonist finally coming to rage, and action, but venting her anger in such a tentative and hidden way underscores Gilman's irony. Even coming to anger does not mean change or improvement. It certainly does not mean victory for the protagonist of this novella. Her escape into madness may have won her continuing argument with John, though he will not recognize that it has done that, but it is only a Pyrrhic victory because her present life is valueless to anyone, particularly to herself.

The larger question, once the literary merits of Gilman's text have been proved, is what significance does this trapped protagonist have for today's readers? What does it mean to write about a woman caught within these circles of male authority (and cultural reification of that authority), trapped within a sickening room and made, in effect, to lose her mind because of the disgust she feels for not only her culture and the roles it mandates for women, but for herself as a sexual, procreative woman? What is the mode of literature that results from such deep anger, such unrelieved depression, that the text itself is unrelieved, pointed inevitably toward an ending that only repeats—relentlessly—the text's theme?

In Gilman's "The Yellow Wallpaper," subtext becomes text, repressed discourse becomes visible. Gilman explained that in writing this novella, she had not intended "to drive people crazy, but to save people from being driven crazy."[22] Her didactic purpose, her intentional theme, was in some ways subverted by her own artistry. Unlike many of her shorter stories, "The Yellow Wallpaper" convinces less by its explicit content than by its metaphoric impression. As captured by the confines of the attic room as the protagonist is, the reader plots and charts, reads and worries as the story progresses. It is the Modernists' ideal of involving the reader to the fullest possible extent. In current narratological terms, according to Fetterley, the movement of the end of the story is precise and highly directional; the reader goes where Gilman takes him or her. "Increasingly, her behavior becomes flamboyant and outrageous. Getting out through the text of the wallpaper, she not surprisingly gets in to the subtext within the text that presents the story of a woman trying to get out."[23] She wins back her language, and vanquishes her husband—who has neither speech nor action by the end of the story. He lies as if dead in the path of her highly functional movement, and she simply crawls over him. The wallpaper has replaced the writing paper that he would have taken from her, and she has in some ways won back her right to speech and control.

By choosing to tell the protagonist's story from her perspective, complete with her changing psyche as she moves steadily into her madness, Gilman reverses the traditional plot of having an observer act as the narrator for the journey to insanity. In this choice, she has accomplished what Rachel Blau

DuPlessis might call telling "the untold story, the other side of a well-known tale."[24] To handle this narration in such a superbly ironic manner, with the protagonist's language first contradicting and then reifying that of her physician-husband, adds yet another valence to the complexity of such "telling." Even though the story ends with the protagonist's madness, it also suggests some ambivalence in the fact that—temporarily at least—her husband is silenced. He is no longer an obstacle to her doing what she intends, though she cannot behave with any constructive possibility at the present.

Perhaps setting the novella within the single restrictive room is also a kind of irony. Though it would be thirty years later that Virginia Woolf would write about the necessity for "a room of one's own," in "The Yellow Wallpaper" Gilman presents the perils of unsympathetic isolation. The protagonist has all too much of a room of her own, but she is isolated within it, and made to think that any artistic or intellectual activity is worthless. Rather than nurturing her efforts, the room suffocates them.

The contrary movement of the story, toward freedom from that oppression, does dominate the second half of Gilman's narrative, but it too takes the protagonist into only a false freedom. The woman is never "free": she does not dance or skip or fly, common images for the state of freedom. She only *creeps,* a derogation of the more positive word *crawls,* which is not in itself a very positive movement. Gilman's reliance on the word *creeps* almost silently reinforces the protagonist's role as mother. Just at the time when a mother would be eagerly charting her infant's progress by observing his physical skills, Gilman's protagonist is entirely removed from the charge of her child. Yet in her skewed vision, she asks for herself—and her trapped sisters behind the wallpaper—this stage of minimal physical prowess, to be able to creep. The ironic pathos of her "achievement" is intensified when the reader realizes that creeping is an accomplishment that most infants acquire naturally, and by themselves. It is only the first stage of a child's movement toward desires. Through her three-month incarceration in the nursery, a setting that customarily aids development, this adult woman has not "grown." She has regressed to a state where creeping is the height of her power.

"The Yellow Wallpaper" throughout is a splendid example of a gender-based narrative. Readers, especially male readers, may not see the importance of the word *creep,* or of the nursery with barred windows, or of the woman's speaking in a childlike language. The text may suffer because its full comprehension depends on the reader's understanding its codes, codes of language as well as codes of society and custom and world view. As Annette Kolodny has said so well, readers must come to a text with experience in both the literary traditions being used by the author and the real-life experiential contexts of the work: "as every good novelist knows, the meaning of any character's action or statement is inescapably a function of the specific situation in which it is embedded." Kolodny quotes Virginia Woolf as she comments that women writers might well alter established values in order to make serious what a male reader might think insignificant and then summarizes,

> Males ignorant of women's "values" or conceptions of the world will necessarily, thereby, be poor readers of works that in any sense recapitulate their codes.
> The problem is further exacerbated when the language of the literary text is largely dependent upon figuration . . . because figurative use can be inaccessible to all but those who share information about one another's knowledge, beliefs, intentions, and attitudes.[25]

Part of the difficulty with Gilman's "The Yellow Wallpaper" is that it is an elliptical, highly figurative narrative. Rather than being simple and direct, it is poemlike in its indirection: it creates a total fabric of meaning, the misreading of any part of which could change impact and intention. And because it is such an essential text, because its "meanings" are so central to the lives of millions of women readers both contemporary with it and existing in the hundred years since its publication, it deserves good readings. It is one powerful indictment of characteristic cultural position, that men control women, and that women are made to feel so guilty, and so dependent through their own roles as mothers, that male control becomes even more acceptable.

To judge "The Yellow Wallpaper" in light of criticism of the 1980s is difficult in many respects, because the reader has come to Gilman's text from reading Toni Morrison, Marge Piercy, Margaret Atwood, Marilyn French, Alice Walker, Gloria Naylor, and other contemporary women writers. 1980 texts are—happily—different from those written a hundred years earlier (though perhaps not so different as that amount of time might warrant). Many women characters in today's serious fiction stay sane, choose to lead their own lives, accomplish things, and pass on superior and practical values to their children. (The present concern with "ancestry" in both Morrison's and French's novels is a matriarchal emphasis, not a patriarchal.)

Not all women protagonists in contemporary fiction succeed, however, and as Linda Howe pointed out in a 1982 essay, "Narratives of Survival," many women protagonists are not fully achieving people. Unlike male characters in fiction, women seldom find success, happiness, or answers. They instead are content with mere survival. "Our heroine does not choose this struggle; it was given her along with her sex. She is the victim of society and accident, never of her own folly."[26] In what Howe calls the "narrative of survival," the heroine demonstrates that she possesses the courage, strength, inner resources, and power to stand alone, self-supporting and fulfilled, denying the need for parent, husband, lover or friend. Even though Gilman's protagonist did have some of these traits, she did not have enough—she was not allowed to understand enough, to cultivate enough skills—to save herself.

What she did accomplish, however, was a retreat into a world of her own making, a complete separation from the patriarchal existence that used her to be the mother of an ancestral line over which she had no control, and to which—subsequently—she had no value. Gilman did not think that such a retreat was an answer, nor did she see it as adequate in any way. Her own life proved what one frail but intelligent woman could accomplish, against many harsh odds. She therefore wrote her own narrative of survival, but the survival is not praised. Accordingly, "The Yellow Wallpaper" is—as Gilman intended—a cautionary and chilling experience.

Notes

1. Dorothy Dinnerstein, *The Mermaid and the Minotaur: Sexual Arrangements and Human Malaise* (New York: Harper Colophon, 1976); Nancy Chodorow, *The Reproduction of Mothering, Psychoanalysis and the Sociology of Gender* (Berkeley: University of California Press, 1978); Nancy Chodorow and Susan Contratto, "The Fantasy of the Perfect Mother" in *Rethinking the Family: Some Feminist Questions*, ed. Barrie Thorne with Marilyn Yalom (New York: Longman, 1982, 54–71).

2. Marilyn Yalom, *Maternity, Mortality, and the Literature of Madness* (University Park, PA: The Pennsylvania State University Press, 1985), p. 5.

3. Ibid., p. 8.

4. Adrienne Rich, *Of Women Born, Motherhood as Experience and Institution* (New York: W.W. Norton, 1976), p. 21.

5. Carroll Smith-Rosenberg, *Disorderly Conduct* (New York: Alfred A. Knopf, 1985); Eugenia Kaladin, *Mothers and More, American Women in the 1950s* (Boston: Twayne, 1984); Barbara E. Sang, "Women and the Creative Process," *The Arts in Psychotherapy* 8 (1981): 43–48; Paula Bennett, *My Life a Loaded Gun, Female Creativity and Feminist Poetics* (Boston: Beacon Press, 1986).

6. Edward Butscher, *Sylvia Plath: Method and Madness* (New York: Seabury, 1976); Elizabeth Hardwick, "Sylvia Plath," *Seduction and Betrayal: Women and Literature* (New York: Random House, 1974); Phyllis Chesler, *Women and Madness* (Garden City, New York: Doubleday & Co., 1972); Ellen L. Bassuk, "The Rest Cure: Repetition or Resolution of Victorian Women's Conflicts" in *The Female Body in Western Culture: Contemporary Perspectives*, ed. Susan Rubin Suleiman (Cambridge, MA: Harvard University Press, 1986), pp. 139–51.

7. Charlotte Perkins Gilman, *The Living of Charlotte Perkins Gilman, An Autobiography* (New York: D. Appleton-Century Co., 1935). p. 96; see also Barbara Ehrenreich and Deirdre English, *For Her Own Good, 150 Years of the Experts' Advice to Women* (Garden City, NY: Doubleday, 1979) and Diane Hunter, "Hysteria, Psychoanalysis, and Feminism: The Case of Anna O," in *The (M)other Tongue: Essays in Feminist Psychoanalytic Interpretation*, eds. Shirley Nelson Garner, Claire Kahane, and Madelon Sprengnether (Ithaca, NY: Cornell University Press, 1985), pp. 89–115.

8. Ann J. Lane, "The Fictional World of Charlotte Perkins Gilman," in *The Charlotte Perkins Gilman Reader* (New York: Pantheon Books, 1980), p. xii.

9. Gilman, *Living*, pp. 141, 140.

10. Ibid., p. 88.

11. Ibid., pp. 162–64.

12. Charlotte Perkins Gilman, *The Yellow Wallpaper*, Afterword by Elaine R. Hedges (Old Westbury, NY: The Feminist Press, 1973), p. 9. Because the text is so short, I will not use page numbers in the essay as a rule.

13. Ibid., p. 10.

14. Ibid., p. 13.

15. Elaine Showalter, *The Female Malady, Women, Madness, and English Culture 1830–1980* (New York: Pantheon Books, 1985), p. 73.

16. Annette Kolodny, "A Map for Rereading: Or, Gender and the Interpretation of Literary Texts," *New Literary History* 11 (1979–80), p. 457; Judith Fetterley, "Reading about Reading: 'A Jury of Her Peers,' 'The Murders in the Rue Morgue,' and 'The Yellow Wallpaper'" in *Gender and Reading, Essays on Readers, Texts, and Contexts*, eds. Elizabeth A. Flynn and Patrocinio P. Schweickart (Baltimore, Md.: Johns Hopkins, 1986), pp. 147–64.

17. Gilman, "Yellow Wallpaper," p. 22.

18. Ibid.

19. Ibid., p. 24.

20. Ibid., pp. 34–35.

21. Smith-Rosenberg, *Disorderly Conduct*.

22. Gilman, "Why I Wrote 'The Yellow Wallpaper'?" in *Gilman Reader*, p. 20.

23. Fetterley, "Reading about Reading."

24. Rachel Blau DuPlessis, *Writing Beyond the Ending, Narrative Strategies of Twentieth-Century Women Writers* (Bloomington: Indiana University Press, 1985), pp. 3–5.

25. Annette Kolodny, "Dancing Through the Minefield: Some Observations on the Theory, Practice and Politics of a Feminist Literary Criticism," *Feminist Studies* 6:1 (Spring 1980), pp. 12–13.

26. Linda Howe, "Narratives of Survival," *Literary Review* 26 (Fall 1982).

4

"Too Terribly Good to Be Printed": Charlotte Perkins Gilman's "The Yellow Wallpaper"

Conrad Shumaker

In 1890 William Dean Howells sent a copy of "The Yellow Wallpaper" to Horace Scudder, editor of the *Atlantic Monthly*. Scudder gave his reason for not publishing the story in a short letter to its author, Charlotte Perkins Stetson (later to become Charlotte Perkins Gilman): "Dear Madam, Mr. Howells has handed me this story. I could not forgive myself if I made others as miserable as I have made myself!"[1] Gilman persevered, however, and eventually the story, which depicts the mental collapse of a woman undergoing a "rest cure" at the hands of her physician husband, was printed in the *New England Magazine* and then later in Howells' own collection, *Great Modern American Stories,* where he introduces it as "terrible and too wholly dire," and "too terribly good to be printed."[2] Despite (or perhaps because of) such praise, the story was virtually ignored for over fifty years until Elaine Hedges called attention to its virtues, praising it as "a small literary masterpiece."[3] Today the work is highly spoken of by those who have read it, but it is not widely known and has been slow to appear in anthologies of American literature.

Some of the best criticism attempts to explain this neglect as a case of misinterpretation by audiences used to "traditional" literature. Annette Kolodny, for example, argues that though nineteenth-century readers had learned to "follow the fictive processes of aberrant perception and mental breakdown" by reading Poe's tales, they were not prepared to understand a tale of mental degeneration in a middle-class mother and wife. It took twentieth-century feminism to place the story in a "nondominant or subcultural" tradition which those steeped in the dominant tradition could not understand.[4] Jean F. Kennard suggests that the recent appearance of feminist novels has changed literary

Reprinted with the permission of the publisher from *American Literature* 57 (December 1985), 588–89. Copyright 1985 by Duke University Press.

conventions and led us to find in the story an exploration of women's role instead of the tale of horror or depiction of mental breakdown its original audience found.[5] Both arguments are persuasive, and the feminist readings of the story that accompany them are instructive. With its images of barred windows and sinister bedsteads, creeping women and domineering men, the story does indeed raise the issue of sex roles in an effective way, and thus anticipates later feminist literature.

Ultimately, however, both approaches tend to make the story seem more isolated from the concerns of the nineteenth-century "dominant tradition" than it really is, and since they focus most of our attention on the story's polemical aspect, they invite a further exploration of Gilman's artistry—the way in which she molds her feminist concerns into a strikingly effective work of literature. To be sure, the polemics are important. Gilman, an avowed reformer and a relative of Harriet Beecher Stowe, told Howells that she did not consider the work to be "literature" at all, that everything she wrote was for a purpose, in this case that of pointing out the dangers of a particular medical treatment. Unlike many of Gilman's other purposeful fictions, however, "The Yellow Wallpaper" transcends its author's expressed intent, and my experience teaching it suggests that both male and female students appreciate the story and generally understand that it raises questions about woman's role even when they know nothing about other feminist literature or the patriarchal biases of nineteenth-century medicine. I think the story has this effect for two reasons. First, the question of women's role in the nineteenth century is inextricably bound up with the more general questions of how one perceives the world. Woman is often seen as representing an imaginative or "poetic" view of things that conflicts with (or sometimes complements) the American male's "common sense" approach to reality. Through the characters of the "rational" doctor and the "imaginative" wife, Gilman explores a question that was—and in many ways still is—central both to American literature and to the place of women in American culture: What happens to the imagination when it is defined as feminine (and thus weak) and has to face a society that values the useful and the practical and rejects all else as nonsense? Secondly, this conflict and the related feminist message both arise naturally and effectively out of the action of the story because of the author's skillful handling of the narrative voice.

One of the most striking passages in Gilman's autobiography describes her development and abandonment of a dream world, a fantasy land to which she could escape from the rather harsh realities of her early life. When she was thirteen, a friend of her mother warned that such escape could be dangerous, and Charlotte, a good New England girl who considered absolute obedience a duty, "shut the door" on her "dear, bright, glittering dreams."[6] The narrator of "The Yellow Wallpaper" has a similar problem: from the beginning of the story she displays a vivid imagination. She wants to imagine that the house they have rented is haunted, and as she looks at the wallpaper, she is reminded of her childhood fancies about rooms, her ability to "get more entertainment and terror out of blank walls and plain furniture than most children could find in a toy store."[7] Her husband has to keep reminding her that she "must not give away to fancy in the least" as she comments on her new surroundings. Along with her vivid imagination she has the mind and eye of an artist. She begins to study the wallpaper in an attempt to make sense of its artistic design, and she objects to it for aesthetic reasons: it is "one of those sprawling, flamboyant patterns committing every artistic sin" (13). When her husband tries to suppress her imaginative and artistic impulses with his prescription of complete "rest," her mind turns to the wallpaper, and she begins to find in its tangled pattern the emotions and experiences she is forbidden to explore in other ways. John's fears about her imagination, in other words, become a self-fulfilling prophecy—her imaginative life becomes dangerous only when he forbids it.

Though he is clearly a domineering husband who wants to have absolute control over his wife, John also has other reasons for forbidding her to write or paint. As Gilman points out in her autobiography, the "rest cure" was designed for "the businessman exhausted from too much work, and the society woman exhausted from too much play."[8] The treatment is intended, in other words, to deal with physical symptoms of overwork and fatigue, and so is unsuited to the narrator's more complex case. But as a doctor and an empiricist who "scoffs openly at things not to be felt and seen and put down in figures," John wants to deal only with physical causes and effects: if his wife's symptoms are nervousness and weight loss, the treatment must be undisturbed tranquility and good nutrition. The very idea that her imaginative "work" might be beneficial to her disturbs him; indeed, he is both fearful and contemptuous of her imaginative and artistic powers, largely because he fails to understand them, or the view of the world they lead her to. The rest cure is a denial that her view has any validity, an affirmation that all human needs and problems are physical.

Two conversations in particular demonstrate his way of dealing with her imagination and his fear of it. The first occurs when the narrator asks him to change the wallpaper. He replies that to do so would be dangerous, for "nothing was worse for a nervous patient than to give way to such fancies." At this point, her "fancy" is simply an objection to the paper's ugliness, a point she makes clear when she suggests that they move to the "pretty rooms" downstairs. John replies by calling her a "little goose" and saying "he would go down to the cellar if she wished and have it whitewashed into the bargain" (15). Besides showing his obviously patriarchal stance, his reply is designed to make her aesthetic objections seem nonsense by fastening on concrete details—color and elevation—ignoring the real basis of her request. If she wants to go downstairs away from yellow walls, he will take her to the cellar and have it whitewashed. The effect is precisely what he intends: he trivializes her aesthetic concerns, making her see her objection to the paper's ugliness as "just a whim." The second conversation occurs after the narrator has begun to see a woman behind the surface pattern of the wallpaper. When John catches her getting out of bed to examine the paper more closely, she decides to ask him to take her away. He refuses, referring again to concrete details: "You are gaining flesh and color, your appetite is better, I feel really much better about you." When she implies that her physical condition isn't the real problem, he cuts her off in midsentence: "I beg of you, for my sake and for our child's sake, as well as for your own, that you will never for one instant let that idea enter your mind! There is nothing so dangerous, so fascinating, to a temperament like yours. It is a false and foolish fancy" (24). For John, mental illness is the inevitable result of using one's imagination, the creation of an attractive "fancy" which the mind then fails to distinguish from reality. He fears that because of her imaginative "temperament" she will create the fiction that she is mad and come to accept it despite the evidence—color, weight, appetite—that she is well. Imagination and art are subversive because they threaten to undermine his materialistic universe.

Ironically, despite his abhorrence of faith and superstition, John fails because of his own dogmatic faith in materialism and empiricism, a faith that will not allow him even to consider the possibility that his wife's imagination could be a positive force. In a way, John is like Aylmer in Hawthorne's "The Birthmark": each man chooses to interpret a characteristic of his wife as a defect because of his own failure of imagination, and each attempts to "cure" her through purely physical means, only to find he has destroyed her in the process. He also resembles the implied villain in many of Emerson's and Thoreau's lectures and essays, the man of convention who is so taken with "common sense" and traditional wisdom that he is blind to truth. Indeed, the narrator's lament that she might get well faster if John were not a doctor and her assertion that he cannot understand her "because he is so wise" remind one of Thoreau's question in the first chapter of *Walden:* "How can he remember his ignorance—which his growth requires—who has so often to use his knowledge?" John's role as a doctor and an American male requires that he use his "knowledge" continuously and doggedly, and he would abhor the appearance of imagination in his own mind even more vehemently than in his wife's.

The relationship between the two characters also offers an insight into how and why this fear of the imagination has been institutionalized through assigned gender roles. By defining his wife's artistic impulse as a potentially dangerous part of her feminine "temperament," John can control both his wife and a facet of human experience which threatens his comfortably materialistic view of the world. Fear can masquerade as calm authority when the thing feared is embodied in the "weaker sex." Quite fittingly, the story suggests that America is full of Johns: the narrator's brother is a doctor, and S. Weir Mitchell—"like John and my brother only more so!"—looms on the horizon if she does not recover.

As her comments suggest, the narrator understands John's problem, yet is unable to call it his problem, and in many ways it is this combination of insight and naiveté, of resistance and resignation, that makes her such a memorable character and gives such power to her narrative. The story is in the form of a journal which the writer knows no one will read—she says she would not criticize John to "a living soul, of course, but this is dead paper"—yet at the same time her occasional use of "you," her questions ("What is one to do?" she asks three times in the first two pages), and her confidential tone all suggest that she is attempting to reach or create the listener she cannot otherwise find. Her remarks reveal that her relationship with her husband is filled with deception on her part, not so much because she wants to hide things from him, but because it is impossible to tell him things he does not want to acknowledge. She reveals to the "dead paper" that she must pretend to sleep and have an appetite because that is what John assumes will happen as a result of his treatment, and if she tells him that she isn't sleeping or eating he will simply contradict her, calling attention to the physical details that prove him right. Thus the journal provides an opportunity not only to confess her deceit and explain its necessity but also to say the things she really wants to say to John and would say if his insistence on "truthfulness," i.e., saying what he wants to hear, did not prevent her. As both her greatest deception and her attempt to be honest, the journal embodies in its very form the absurd contradictions inherent in her role as wife.

At the same time, however, she cannot quite stop deceiving herself about her husband's treatment of her, and her descriptions create a powerful dramatic irony as the reader gradually puts together details, the meaning of which she does not quite understand. She says, for instance, that there is "something strange" about the house they have rented, but her description reveals bit by bit a room that has apparently been used to confine violent mental cases, with bars on the windows, a gate at the top of the stairs, steel rings on the walls, a nailed-down bedstead, and a floor that has been scratched and gouged. When she tries to explain her feelings about the house to John early in the story, her report of the conversation reveals her tendency to assume that he is always right despite her own reservations:

> There is something about the house—I can feel it.
> I even said so to John one moonlight evening, but he said what I felt was a *draught,* and shut the window.
> I get unreasonably angry with John sometimes. I'm sure I never used to be so sensitive. I think it is due to this nervous condition. (11)

As usual, John refuses to consider anything but physical details, but the narrator's reaction is particularly revealing here. Her anger, perfectly understandable to us, must be characterized, even privately, as "unreasonable," a sign of her condition. Whatever doubts she may have about John's methods, he represents reason, and it is her own "sensitivity" that must be at fault. Comments such as these reveal more powerfully than any direct statement could the way she is trapped by the conception of herself which she has accepted from John and the society whose values he represents. As Paula A. Treichler has pointed out, John's diagnosis is a "sentence," a "set of linguistic signs whose representational claims are authorized by society," and thus it can "control women's fate, whether or not those claims are valid." The narrator can object to the terms of the sentence, but she cannot question its authority, even in her own private discourse.[9]

To a great extent, the narrator's view of her husband is colored by the belief that he really does love her, a belief that provides some of the most striking and complex ironies in the story. When she says, "it is hard to talk to John about my case because he is so wise, and because he loves me so," it is tempting to take the whole sentence as an example of her naiveté. Obviously he is not wise, and his actions are not what we would call loving. Nevertheless, the sentence is in its way powerfully insightful. If John were not so wise—so sure of his own empirical knowledge and his expertise as a doctor—and so loving—so determined to make her better in the only way he knows—then he might be able to set aside his fear of her imagination and listen to her. The passage suggests strikingly the way both characters are doomed to act out their respective parts of loving husband and obedient wife right to the inevitably disastrous end.

Gilman's depiction of the narrator's decline into madness has been praised for the accuracy with which it captures the symptoms of mental breakdown and for its use of symbolism.[10] What hasn't been pointed out is the masterful use of associations, foreshadowing, and even humor. Once the narrator starts attempting to read the pattern of the wallpaper, the reader must become a kind of psychological detective in order to follow and appreciate the narrative. In a sense, he too is viewing a tangled pattern with a woman behind it, and he must learn to revise his interpretation of the pattern as he goes along if he is to make sense of it. For one thing, the narrator tells us from time to time about new details in the room. She notices a "smooch" on the wall "low down, near the mopboard," and later we learn that the bedstead is "fairly gnawed." It is only afterwards that we find out that she is herself the source of these new marks as she bites the bedstead and crawls around the room, shoulder to the walllpaper. If the reader has not caught on already, these details show clearly that the narrator is not always aware of her own actions or in control of her thoughts and so is not always reliable in reporting them. They also foreshadow her final separation from her wifely self, her belief that she is the woman who has escaped from behind the barred pattern of the wallpaper.

But the details also invite us to reread earlier passages, to see if the voice which we have taken to be a fairly reliable, though naive, reporter has not been giving us unsuspected hints of another reality all along. If we do backtrack we find foreshadowing everywhere, not only in the way the narrator reads the pattern on the wall, but in the pattern of her own narrative, the way in which one thought leads to another. One striking example occurs when she describes John's sister, Jennie, who is "a dear girl and so careful of me," and who therefore must not find out about the journal.

> She is a perfect and enthusiastic housekeeper, and hopes for no better profession. I verily believe she thinks it is the writing which made me sick!
>
> But I can write when she is out, and see her a long way off from these windows.
>
> There is one that commands the road, a lovely shaded winding road, and one that just looks off over the country. A lovely country, too, full of great elms and velvet meadows.
>
> This wallpaper has a kind of sub-pattern in a different shade, a particularly irritating one, for you can only see it in certain lights and not clearly then.
>
> But in the places where it isn't faded and where the sun is just so—I can see a strange, provoking, formless sort of figure, that seems to skulk about behind that silly and conspicuous front design.
>
> There's sister on the stairs! (17–18).

The "perfect and enthusiastic housekeeper" is, of course, the ideal sister for John, whose view of the imagination she shares. Thoughts of Jennie lead to the narrator's assertion that she can "see her a long way off from these windows," foreshadowing later passages in which the narrator will see a creeping woman, and then eventually many creeping women from the same windows, and the association suggests a connection between the "enthusiastic housekeeper" and those imaginary crawling women. The thought of the windows leads to a description of the open country and suggests the freedom that the narrator lacks in her barred room. This, in turn, leads her back to the wallpaper, and now she mentions for the first time the "sub-pattern," a pattern which will eventually become a woman creeping behind bars, a projection of her feelings about herself as she looks through the actual bars of the window and the metaphorical bars of her relationship to John. The train of associations ends when John's sister returns, but this time she's just "sister," as if now she's the narrator's sister as well, suggesting a subconscious recognition that they both share the same role, the same confinement behind the bars of a "silly and conspicuous" pattern, despite Jennie's apparent freedom and contentment. Taken in context, this passage prepares us to see the connection between the pattern of the wallpaper, the actual bars on the narrator's windows, and the "silly and conspicuous" surface pattern of the wifely role behind which both women lurk.

We can see just how Gilman develops the narrator's mental collapse if we compare the passage quoted above to the later one in which the narrator once again discusses the "sub-pattern," which by now has become a woman who manages to escape in the daytime.

I think that woman gets out in the daytime!

And I'll tell you why—privately—I've seen her!

I can see her out of every one of my windows!

It is the same woman, I know for she is always creeping, and most women do not creep by daylight.

I see her on that long road under the trees, creeping along, and when a carriage comes she hides under the blackberry vines.

I don't blame her a bit. It must be very humiliating to be caught creeping by daylight!

I always lock the door when I creep by daylight! (30–31)

Here again the view outside the window suggests a kind of freedom, but now it is only a freedom to creep outside the pattern, a freedom that humiliates and must be hidden. The dark humor that punctuates the last part of the story appears in the narrator's remark that she can recognize the woman because "most women do not creep by daylight," and the sense that the journal is an attempt to reach a listener, to reveal the creeping that goes on when no one is watching, becomes clear through her emphasis on "privately." Finally, the identification between the narrator and the woman is taken a step further and becomes more nearly conscious when the narrator reveals that she too creeps, but only behind a locked door. If we read the two passages in sequence, we can see just how masterfully Gilman uses her central images—the window, the barred pattern of the paper, and the woman—to create a web of associations which reveals the source of the narrator's malady yet allows the narrator herself to remain essentially unable to verbalize her problem. At some level, we see, she understands that John's treatment has taken away her humanity and made her crawl, yet she is so completely trapped in her role that she can express that knowledge only indirectly in a way that hides it from her conscious mind. She can reveal the source of her problem to the dead paper, but she cannot read what she has written on that paper because to make such knowledge conscious would destroy her identity, her view of herself and her husband as a loving couple.

In the terribly comic ending, she has finally destroyed both the wallpaper and her own identity: now she is the woman from behind the barred pattern, and not even Jane—the wife she once was—can put her back. Still unable to express her feelings directly, she acts out both her triumph and her humiliation symbolically, forcing John to listen to her in order to learn where she has hidden the key to the door and finally creeping around the room with her shoulder in the "smooch," passing over her fainting husband on every lap. Loralee MacPike suggests that the narrator has finally gained her freedom,[11] but that is true only in a very limited sense. She is still creeping, still inside the room with a rope around her waist. She has destroyed only the front pattern, the "silly and conspicuous" design that covers the real wife, the creeping one hidden behind the facade. As Treichler suggests, "her triumph is to have sharpened and articulated the nature of women's condition,"[12] but she is free only from the need to deceive herself and others about the true nature of her role. In a sense, she has discovered, bit by bit, and finally revealed to John, the wife he is attempting to create—the woman without illusions or imagination who spends all her time creeping.

The story, then, is a complex work of art as well as an effective indictment of the nineteenth-century view of the sexes and the materialism that underlies that view. It is hard to believe that readers familiar with the materialistic despots and feminine victims created by such writers as Hawthorne, Dickens, and Browning could fail to see the implications. Indeed, though Howells' comment that the story makes him "shiver" has been offered as evidence that he saw it as a more or less conventional horror story, I would assert that he understood quite clearly the source of the story's effect. He originally wrote to Gilman to congratulate her on her poem "Women of Today," a scathing indictment of women who fear changing sexual roles and fail to realize that their view of themselves as mothers, wives, and housekeepers is a self-deception. In fact, he praises that poem in terms that anticipate his praise of the story, calling it "dreadfully true."[13] Perhaps the story was unpopular because it was, at least on some level, understood all too clearly, because it struck too deeply and effectively at traditional ways of seeing the world and woman's place in it. Like Gilman's narrator, I would suggest, readers understood what the narrative says about the "silly and conspicuous" pattern of sexual relationships, but they could not make that understanding conscious or public without revealing the "subpattern" which threatened their identity and that of the society they lived in—without making themselves miserable, to use Horace Scudder's term. That, in any case, seems to be what Howells implies in his comment that the story is "too terribly good to be printed" and in his refusal to elaborate on what makes it terrible or why he is printing it despite the terrible nature of its goodness.

The clearest evidence that John's view of the imagination and art was all but sacred in Gilman's America comes, ironically, from the author's own pen. When she replied to Howells' request to reprint from the story by saying that she did not write "literature," she was, of course, denying that she was a mere imaginative artist, defending herself from the charge that Hawthorne imagines his Puritan ancestors would lay at his doorstep: "A writer of story-books!—what a mode of glorifying God, or being serviceable to mankind in his day and generation—may that be? Why, the degenerate fellow might as well have been a fiddler!"[14] It would, of course, be misguided to regret an impulse that led Gilman to produce such works as *Women and Economics,* but one can't help wondering what this later female scion of good Puritan stock might have done had she been able to set aside such objections and reconcile her belief in "work" with her considerable talent for writing "literature." In any case, one hopes that this work of imagination, art, and social criticism will be restored to the place that Howells so astutely assigned it, alongside stories by contemporaries such as Mark Twain, Henry James, and Edith Wharton.

Notes

1. Quoted in Charlotte Perkins Gilman, *The Living of Charlotte Perkins Gilman: An Autobiography* (1935; rpt. New York: Arno, 1972), p. 119.

2. *The Great Modern American Stories: An Anthology* (New York: Boni and Liveright, 1920), p. vii.

3. "Afterword," *The Yellow Wallpaper* (Old Westbury, NY: Feminist Press, 1973), p. 37.

4. "A Map for Rereading: Or, Gender and the Interpretation of Literary Texts," *New Literary History* 11 (1980), pp. 456–57.

5. "Convention Coverage or How to Read Your Own Life," *New Literary History* 13 (1981), pp. 73–74.

6. Gilman, *Living,* p. 24.

7. *The Yellow Wallpaper* (Old Westbury, NY: Feminist Press, 1973), p. 17. Page numbers in the text refer to this edition.

8. Gilman, *Living,* p. 95.

9. "Escaping the Sentence: Diagnosis and Discourse in 'The Yellow Wallpaper,'" *Tulsa Studies in Women's Literature* 3 (1984), p. 74.

10. See Beate Schopp-Schilling, "'The Yellow Wallpaper': A Rediscovered 'Realistic' Story," *American Literary Realism* 8 (1975), pp. 284–86; Loralee MacPike, "Environment as Psycho-pathological Symbolism in 'The Yellow Wallpaper,'" *American Literaty Realism* 8 (1975), pp. 286–88.

11. MacPike, p. 288.

12. Treichler, p. 74.

13. Quoted in Gilman, *Living,* p. 113.

14. *The Scarlet Letter* (Columbus: Ohio State University Press, 1962), p. 10.

5

Convention Coverage or How to Read Your Own Life

Jean E. Kennard

I must have reread Northrop Frye's *Anatomy of Criticism*—or at least many parts of it—several times since the first reading fifteen years ago. Yet despite this familiarity, when I looked at it again this spring, I found myself uncomfortable with a couple of sentences which had never troubled me before: "All humor demands agreement that certain things, such as a picture of a wife beating her husband in a comic strip, are conventionally funny. To introduce a comic strip in which a husband beats his wife would distress the reader, because it would mean learning a new convention."[1]

My objection had nothing to do with Frye's basic concept of a convention as an agreement which allows art to communicate. I agreed with this definition which he had developed more fully earlier: "The contract agreed on by the reader before he can start reading is the same thing as a convention."[2] I was also in sympathy with a critical approach based upon the response of the reader. Nor did my objection concern the question of humor, which, it is perhaps worth noting, I was quite able to ignore even though it was Frye's primary focus.

My distress as a reader was with his example. I was uncomfortable with a discussion of wife beating as an even potential acceptable source of humor. To talk about it as a new convention seemed insensitive. My discomfort extended, though more diffusely, to the idea of considering any form of violence amusing. I had a strong feeling that the picture of a wife beating her husband was no longer funny; in other words, that other people (that is, people I knew) would no longer find it funny. I granted, however, that it was at one time "conventionally funny" and realized that I had probably accepted it as such when I first read Frye. The indication of that acceptance was a failure to notice or remember the example.

This article originally appeared in *New Literary History* 13 (Autumn 1981): 69–88.

For me, obviously, a convention had changed, and some of the reasons at least seemed apparent. Such extraliterary experiences as talking with friends who worked with battered women, an increased awareness of violence in every city I visited, together with reading feminist scholarship, had led me to formulate values which resisted the convention Frye named. I no longer agreed to find it funny.

I start with this quotation from Frye and my response to it as a reader because, while providing a useful definition of convention (that is, one that I agree with), it raises some interesting questions (that is, the ones I want to consider here): How and when do literary conventions change? To what extent can the sources of these changes be other than literary?

These questions are, of course, part of the broader issue of the relationship between literary conventions and life. I am using the term *life* to mean any experience other than that of reading literature, realizing that the peculiarity of this exclusion is part of the question. As my discussion of Frye's quotation suggests, I believe the questions can be most usefully addressed through an approach which has been rather loosely defined as reader-response criticism. Since I am a feminist critic, my interest in these issues is to understand their usefulness, if any, to feminist literary criticism and to feminist concerns generally. In saying this I believe I am admitting to as much but to no more bias than that of any other critic.

It is against a naive equation of literature with life that Frye is arguing when he emphasizes the importance of the literary tradition: "Poetry can only be made out of other poems; novels out of other novels. Literature shapes itself, and is not shaped externally. . . . [I]t is possible for a story of the sea to be archetypal, to make a profound imaginative impact on a reader who has never been out of Saskatchewan."[3] While some contemporary critics might point out that the impact would no doubt be different on a reader who lived in Maine, many would agree with Frye's basic assumption that reading and writing involve an understanding of literary conventions and that in order to read (or write) one has to have read. This assumption lies behind Harold Bloom's work on influences,[4] for example, and behind Roland Barthes's discussion of the "intertextual."[5] Geoffrey Hartman points out that "we must read the writer as a reader";[6] Nelly Furman that "the writer's work can also be construed as the product of a prior reading."[7]

For Jonathan Culler the literary conventions we learn from reading are a set of expectations—of significance, of metaphorical coherence, of thematic unity—which we impose on the text; the ability to apply these conventional procedures in reading other works constitutes a reader's "literary competence": "To read a text as literature is not to make one's mind a *tabula rasa* and approach it without preconceptions; one must bring to it an implicit understanding of the operations of literary discourse which tells one what to look for."[8]

But Culler does not account for why readers who have learned the same literary strategies will read the same texts differently nor why the same readers will read the same texts differently at different times.

In an attempt to answer these questions, Stanley Fish introduces the notion of "interpretive communities," groups of readers who share certain interpretive strategies (who agree to apply particular literary conventions).[9] He gives as his examples psychoanalytic critics, Robertsonians, and numerologists. According to Fish, readers may move from one "interpretive community" to another and may belong to more than one at any one time. Fish believes that interpretive communities create the texts they read—write rather than read them[10]—by selectively applying certain conventional procedures, a position more radical than that of many other reader-response critics. He allows for the possibility of an endless series of interpretations of any one work.

Fish does not, however, examine the process of or the reasons for "ways of interpreting" being "forgotten or supplanted, or complicated or dropped from favor";[11] and although he certainly allows for extraliterary influences on changing conventions, he does not claim to be primarily interested in discussing them. His emphasis is on the lack of a fixed text: "When any of these things happens," he continues, "there is a corresponding change in texts, not because they are being read differently but because they are being written differently."[12] He does not examine what conditions are necessary to make "these things happen" nor what results from texts changing.

I suggest that any account of changes in literary conventions will have to consider nonliterary as well as literary influences. The fact that the word *convention* has meaning in both literary and nonliterary contexts alone suggests this connection. Raymond Williams, while agreeing with the definition of convention I have been employing so far,[13] begins his discussion of the term with a reminder of its origins in a nonliterary context: "The meaning of convention was originally an assembly and then, by derivation, an agreement. Later the sense of agreement was extended to tacit agreement and thence to custom. An adverse sense developed, in which a convention was seen as no more than an old rule, or somebody else's rule, which it was proper and often necessary to disregard."[14]

The interrelation of literary conventions and life is suggested also in the parallels between the history of the word in this nonliterary sense and the process of growth and decline literary conventions undergo. In 1899 readers of Kate Chopin's *The Awakening* reacted with bewilderment expressed as anger when Edna Pontellier rejected her husband, took a lover, and left the family house because they had at that point no agreement that (1) leaving her house and husband and taking a lover can indicate a woman is searching for self-fulfillment, and (2) this search for self-fulfillment should be approved. By the time Sue Kaufman published *Diary of a Mad Housewife* (1967), Joyce Carol

Oates *Do With Me What You Will* (1973), Erica Jong *Fear of Flying* (1974), and Doris Lessing *The Summer Before the Dark* (1974), agreement on these interpretations had taken place among a sufficient number of readers to make the novels readily understood. A convention had been established. Yet by 1977 when Marilyn French published *The Women's Room,* she talked of this convention as "an old rule," "a convention of the women's novel" which she intended to break.[15] When does bewilderment become boredom? When did we begin to talk of "just another mad housewife novel"? By what process does the convention become too conventional?

As my example suggests, when a convention is an agreement on the meaning of a symbolic gesture in a literary context rather than agreement to use a specific interpretive strategy, to seek metaphorical coherence, for example, the question of value is made more obvious. This is not to say that interpretive strategies are neutral and do not in themselves imply certain moral values, only that these values become clearer when we are considering what Frye has called "associative clusters" or archetypes. His example is a good illustration of this: "When we speak of 'symbolism' in ordinary life we usually think of such learned cultural archetypes as the cross or the crown, or of conventional associations, as of white with purity or green with jealousy."[16] When we consider changes in literary conventions, we are considering changes in our agreements on both how we shall interpret and how we shall evaluate that interpretation. These changes are certainly influenced, then, by aspects of our cultural context which are not specifically literary.

Norman Holland claims readers imprint every text with their own "identity themes";[17] and, although there may be limitations to his definition of identity,[18] in any consideration of changes in reading conventions some attention must be paid to the subjective judgment of the individual reader. Nelly Furman recognizes the reader as "a carrier of perceptual prejudices";[19] Annette Kolodny argues convincingly that gender often affects the ability to read specific texts.[20] "That which you are, that only can you read," claims Bloom.[21] And here we come full circle since "what we are" is compounded of our experiences, literary and nonliterary.

Let me sum up the assumptions I have been discussing so far and from which I shall be arguing in the latter part of this article. An interpretation/ reading of any text (whether or not the text is to any extent fixed) is dependent on two things: one, the literary conventions known to the reader at the time— these conventions include both reading strategies and associative clusters of meaning; two, the choices the reader makes to apply or not any one of these conventions—these choices are dependent on what the reader is at the time. It is a question, then, of what the individual reader chooses to notice or to ignore at the time of reading, and this idea raises the specter of a multiplicity of unchallengeable readings and the end of our discipline as we have known it. I shall attempt to exorcise the specter later.

If a convention is that which allows literature to be read, then readings of the same texts separated by many years should be instructive on the question of changes in conventions. It is here that the work of feminist scholars can be extremely helpful. This is partly because we see as one of our major tasks the rereading of earlier works, both those well established in the traditional literary canon and those previously excluded from it.[22] In the past ten years feminist scholarship has provided us with a large number of new readings which have resurrected such neglected works as Charlotte Perkins Gilman's "The Yellow Wallpaper" (1892) and Kate Chopin's *The Awakening* (1899) and radically changed our view of entire centuries. Sandra Gilbert and Susan Gubar's *The Madwoman in the Attic,* for example, has completely reinterpreted the women writers of the nineteenth century.[23] Feminist rereadings are also helpful in understanding changes in conventions for two other reasons: one, they are often unusually radical in their divergence from earlier readings;[24] two, they represent the views of a clearly defined "interpretive community."

Though feminist critics have successfully employed many different methodologies, the alliance between feminist criticism and reader-response criticism seems to have been particularly fruitful. In the past three years Judith Fetterley's *The Resisting Reader,*[25] Annette Kolodny's "A Map for Rereading: Or, Gender and the Interpretation of Literary Texts"[26] and "Dancing Through the Minefield: Some Observations on the Theory, Practice and Politics of Feminist Criticism," Gilbert and Gubar's *The Madwoman in the Attic,* and Nelly Furman's "Textual Feminism" have all demonstrated the usefulness of reader-response criticism to feminists.[27] In my own footnotes to this article I have already found reason to refer to four of these texts. This connection is not surprising, of course, since rereading is to such a large extent our enterprise, and we might be expected therefore to be concerned with many of the same questions about the process of reading and the nature of audiences.

Despite radical reinterpretations, feminist critics have on the whole remained on the conservative side with regard to the question of the "fixed text." If the implication is not always that a feminist rereading reveals the only "correct" meaning of a text, it is usually assumed that it reveals what has always been there but not previously seen. Elaine Showalter claims feminist criticism "has allowed us to see meaning in what has previously been empty space. The orthodox plot recedes, and another plot, hitherto submerged in the anonymity of the background, stands out in bold relief like a thumbprint."[28] Sandra Gilbert and Susan Gubar talk of "literary works that are in some sense palimpsestic, works whose surface designs conceal or obscure deeper, less accessible (and less socially acceptable) levels of meaning" (91). Annette Kolodny, in an article which discusses and allows for a plurality of interpretations, talks of a male critic's possible inability when reading women's writing "to completely decipher its intended meaning" (456).

It is perhaps because feminist critics have usually held to the notions of a fixed text and of discovering rather than of creating meaning that we have not examined the question of why our rereadings, our discoveries, took place when they did. I suggest that when we look at why it was possible for Elaine Hedges to read "The Yellow Wallpaper" as a feminist work in 1973, for this reading to become accepted, for Gilman's novella to find a place in a revised canon of American literature, we are looking at a series of conventions available to readers of the 1970s which were not available to those of 1892. It is an examination of these conventions that I intend to undertake here in order to see whether it allows us to hypothesize in any way about how literary conventions change.

My suggestion that it is the literary conventions of the 1970s that allowed feminist readings of "The Yellow Wallpaper" does not necessarily imply anything about Gilman's intention. It is essentially irrelevant to my concern here— though in other contexts important—whether or not this meaning was, as Gilbert and Gubar claim, "quite clear to Gilman herself" (91). I am using "The Yellow Wallpaper" as an example, realizing that other works would perhaps be equally fruitful,[29] because of the similarity in the readings which have taken place since 1973 and because of the vast discrepancy between these readings and previous ones. I shall draw on four feminist readings: Elaine Hedges's "Afterword" to the Feminist Press edition of the text; Annette Kolodny in "A Map for Rereading"; Sandra Gilbert and Susan Gubar in *The Madwoman in the Attic;* and my own. Although these interpretations emphasize different aspects of the text, they do not conflict with each other.

In its time and until the last eight years, "The Yellow Wallpaper" was read, when it was read at all, "as a Poesque tale of chilling horror,"[30] designed "to freeze our blood,"[31] praised, when it was praised, for the detail with which it recorded developing insanity. Even as late as 1971 Seon Manley and Gogo Lewis included it in a collection entitled *Ladies of Horror: Two Centuries of Supernatural Stories by the Gentle Sex* and introduced it with the following words: "There were new ideas afloat: perhaps some of the horrors were in our own minds, not in the outside world at all. This idea gave birth to the psychological horror story and 'The Yellow Wallpaper' by Charlotte Perkins Gilman shows she was a mistress of the art."[32]

No earlier reader saw the story as in any way positive. When Horace Scudder rejected it for publication in *The Atlantic Monthly,* he explained that he did not wish to make his readers as miserable as the story had made him. As Elaine Hedges points out, "No one seems to have made the connection between insanity and the sex, or sexual role of the victim, no one explored the story's implications for male-female relationships in the nineteenth century" (41).

Feminist critics approach "The Yellow Wallpaper" from the point of view of the narrator. "As she tells her story," says Hedges, "the reader has confidence in the reasonableness of her arguments and explanations" (49). The narrator is seen as the victim of an oppressive patriarchal social system which restricts women and prevents their functioning as full human beings. The restrictions on women are symbolized by the narrator's imprisonment in a room with bars on the window, an image the narrator sees echoed in the patterns of the room's yellow wallpaper. "The wallpaper," claims Hedges, symbolizes "the morbid social situation" (52). Gilbert and Gubar talk of "the anxiety-inducing connections between what women writers tend to see as their parallel confinements in texts, houses and maternal female bodies" and describe the wallpaper as "ancient, smoldering, 'unclean' as the oppressive structures of the society in which she finds herself" (90). The women the narrator "sees" in the wallpaper and wants to liberate are perceived to be "creeping." "Women must creep," says Hedges, "the narrator knows this" (53). I see the indoor images of imprisonment echoed in the natural world of the garden with its "walls and gates that lock, and lots of separate little houses for the gardeners and people" (11). Like so many other women in literature, the only access to nature the narrator has is to a carefully cultivated and confined garden. Gilbert and Gubar point out that in contrast the idea of "open country" is the place of freedom (91).

The representative of the repressive patriarchal society is the narrator's husband John, "a censorious and paternalistic physician" (89), as Gilbert and Gubar call him. John has "a doubly authoritative role as both husband and doctor" (457), Kolodny points out. The description of John as rational rather than emotional, as a man who laughs at what cannot be put down in figures, emphasizes his position as representative of a male power which excludes feeling and imagination. Indeed, the first sentence in the story which suggests a feminist reading to me is a comment on John's character: "John laughs at me, of course, but one expects that in marriage" (9).

John's treatment of his wife's mental illness is isolation and the removal of all intellectual stimulation, "a cure worse than the disease" (89), as Gilbert and Gubar call it. Feminist critics see the narrator's being deprived of an opportunity to write, the opportunity for self-expression, as particularly significant. Kolodny (457) and Gilbert and Gubar (89) remind us that the narrator thinks of writing as a relief. Hedges sees the narrator as someone who "wants very much to work" (49). By keeping her underemployed and isolated, John effectively ensures his wife's dependence on him. She must remain the child he treats her as. Hedges draws attention to the fact that he calls her "blessed little goose" and his "little girl" and that the room she stays in was once a nursery (50). For Hedges, John is "an important source of her afflictions" (49).

The narrator experiences her victimization as a conflict between her own personal feelings, perceived by feminist critics as healthy and positive, and the patriarchal society's view of what is proper behavior for women. Since, like so many women up to the present day, she has internalized society's expectations of women, this conflict is felt as a split within herself. Early in the story the words "Personally, I" (10) are twice set against the views of John and her brother. Nevertheless, she also continues to judge her own behavior as John does. "I get unreasonably angry with John sometimes" (11), she explains; "I cry at nothing, and cry most of the time" (19). As Hedges points out, this split is symbolized by the woman behind the wallpaper: "By rejecting that woman, she might free the other imprisoned woman within herself" (53). The narrator's madness is perceived by Hedges and others as a direct result of societally induced confusion over personal identity. If the images of women as child or cripple, as prisoner, even as fungus growth in Gilman's story are "the images men had of women, and hence that women had of themselves," Hedges writes, "it is not surprising that madness and suicide bulk large in the work of late nineteenth-century women writers" (54).

The most radical aspect of the feminist reading of "The Yellow Wallpaper" lies in the interpretation of the narrator's descent into madness as a way to health, as a rejection of and escape from an insane society. Gilbert and Gubar describe her as sinking "more and more deeply into what the world calls madness" (90). They see her "imaginings and creations" as "mirages of health and freedom" (91). Hedges stresses this aspect of the story. She describes the narrator as "ultimately mad and yet, throughout her descent into madness, in many ways more sensible than the people who surround and cripple her" (49). "In her mad-sane way she has seen the situation of women for what it is," Hedges continues, and so "madness is her only freedom" (53).

It is the interpretation of madness as a higher form of sanity that allows feminist critics finally to read this story as a woman's quest for her own identity. Deprived of reading material, she begins to read the wallpaper. "Fighting for her identity, for some sense of independent self, she observes the wallpaper" (50–51), writes Hedges. More sophisticatedly, Kolodny claims the narrator "comes more and more to experience herself as a text which can neither get read nor recorded" (457). Both Kolodny and Gilbert and Gubar emphasize that the narrator creates meaning in the wallpaper in her need to find an image of herself which will affirm the truth of her own situation and hence her identity. Kolodny writes: "Selectively emphasizing one section of the pattern while repressing others, reorganizing and regrouping past impressions into newer, more fully realized configurations—as one might with any formal text—the speaking voice becomes obsessed with her quest for meaning" (458). Gilbert and Gubar describe the narrator's creation of meaning as a reversal of the wallpaper's implications: "Inevitably she studies its suicidal implications—and inevitably, because of her 'imaginative power and habit of story-making,' she revises it, projecting her own passion for escape into its otherwise incomprehensible hieroglyphics" (90). Although the narrator is not seen to emerge either from madness or marriage at the end of the novella, her understanding of her own situation and, by extension, the situation of all women can be read as a sort of triumph. This triumph is symbolized by the overcoming of John, who is last seen fainting on the floor as his wife creeps over him.

In order to read the story this way, much must be assumed that is not directly stated, much must be ignored that is. There is no overt statement, for example, that invites us to find a socially induced cause for the narrator's madness, to assume that her situation is that of all women. There is perhaps even a certain perversity in claiming that a mentally deranged woman crawling around an attic floor is experiencing some sort of victory. It is also true that if the narrator claims she thinks writing would relieve her mind, she also says it tires her when she tries (16). Since she so often contradicts herself, we are free to believe her only when her comments support our reading. Much is made of the color yellow; feminist readings do little with this. Despite all these objections, which could probably be continued indefinitely, it is the feminist reading I teach my students and which I believe is the most fruitful. In pointing out the "weaknesses" in my own reading, I am only providing the sort of evidence that could be used to counter any interpretation of the story. I am interested in why we read it as we do, not whether we are correct in doing so.

In order to read/write the story or any story in a feminist or in any other way, we are, of course, dependent on some interpretive strategies, some reading conventions, which, if not fixed, have remained relatively so for a long period of time. The ability to see the narrator's confinement in a room as symbolic, for example, comes from other reading; we have learned to symbolize. We have come to the text as to any text, as Culler says, with certain expectations based on our previous literary experience.

But the ability to read the narrator's confinement in a room as symbolic of the situation of women in a patriarchal society depends on an agreement, on a literary convention, which, I suggest, was formed from contemporary experience—both literary and extraliterary. The feminist reading of "The Yellow Wallpaper" depends on the knowledge of a series of "associative clusters" of meaning which have been employed sufficiently frequently in contemporary literature for us to accept them as conventions. The existence of these conventions in the 1970s accounts both for the new reading and for its widespread acceptance. In saying this I am not claiming that any one reader had read any particular works or been exposed to specific experiences.

The conventions I refer to overlap each other but are associated with four basic concepts: patriarchy, madness, space, quest. The concept of patriarchy or of male power appears most frequently in contemporary fiction in the characters of men, often husbands, who are unimaginative, compartmentalized, obsessively rational and unable to express their feelings. The prototype for these figures—like so much else in contemporary feminist thought—comes from Virginia Woolf, from the character of Mr. Ramsay in *To The Lighthouse* (1927). These men are to be found everywhere in contemporary fiction by women, particularly in the fiction of the seventies. Norm in French's *The Women's Room*, Brooke Skelton in Margaret Laurence's *The Diviners* (1974), and the narrator's father in *Surfacing* are three examples of the type. As husbands they are unquestioning representatives of the status quo. As a result their wives, usually the protagonists of the novels, begin to feel they are being treated as children or as dolls. Ibsen's image of a wife as doll is conventional in this fiction—for example, Joyce Carol Oates's *Do with Me What You Will*—and occurs also in poetry. In Margaret Atwood's "After I Fell Apart" the speaker talks of herself as a broken doll gradually being mended;[33] in Sylvia Plath's "The Applicant" the speaker, as a doll, applies for a position as wife.[34]

In fiction the female protagonist gradually learns to recognize the universality of her experience, conceives in some fashion of the notion of patriarchy, and "slams the door" on her past. In such "early" feminist works as Erica Jong's *Fear of Flying* or Doris Lessing's *The Summer before the Dark,* the agent of her freedom is another man, a lover. This is the contemporary version of the nineteenth-century convention of the two suitors which I explored in my book *Victims of Convention*.[35] In the older convention the maturity of the female protagonist is measured by her choice of a "right" suitor, one who represents the novelist's views, over a "wrong" suitor, one whose views parallel the heroine's own initial weaknesses. She marries the right suitor and the novel ends. In the contemporary version the husband has become the "wrong" suitor, the representative of patriarchal restrictions; the lover represents freedom. It was the contemporary version of the convention that Marilyn French described herself as breaking when she set out to explore in *The Women's Room* what really happens after the heroine walks out.

John in "The Yellow Wallpaper" can easily be read as an example of the husband as patriarch; his well-meaning but misguided efforts to help his wife as the result of a view of women as less than adult. He is also a doctor and that compounds the situation. Recent nonfiction, both popular magazines and books, has challenged the conventional notion of the good doctor and emphasized the fact that the traditional treatment of women, particularly in childbirth, exists for the convenience of the medical profession, not for the health of their patients. Two highly influential feminist studies, Adrienne Rich's *Of Woman Born* (1976) and Mary Daly's *Gyn/Ecology* (1978), make this point. Traditional medicine is indicted for treating women as objects, for committing the basic sin of patriarchy. Just as the antidote for the compartmentalization of traditional medicine is seen to be holistic medicine, the values implied by the indictment of patriarchy are those considered implicit in matriarchy: nurturance, collaboration, emotion, unity. It is here that feminist values and those of the sixties counterculture overlap.

The concept of madness is related to patriarchy since female madness is read as a result of patriarchal oppression. Gilbert and Gubar point out that "recently, in fact, social historians like Jessie Bernard, Phyllis Chesler, Naomi Weisstein, and Pauline Bart have begun to study the ways in which patriarchal socialization literally makes women sick, both physically and mentally" (53). The observation that many women novelists and poets experienced mental breakdowns, that many of those who did commited suicide, has been made frequently in feminist scholarship since 1970. "Suicides and spinsters-/ all our kind!" writes Erica Jong in "Dear Collette," "Even decorous Jane Austen / never marrying, / & Sappho leaping, / & Sylvia in the oven, / & Anna Wickham, Tsvetaeva, Sara Teasdale, / & pale Virginia floating like Ophelia, / & Emily alone, alone, alone."[36]

In seventies' fiction by women, madness or some form of mental distur-bance became a conventional representation of the situation of women in a patriarchal society. Kate Brown, in Lessing's *The Summer before the Dark,* looks back on her married life and decides she has acquired not virtues but a form of dementia. In Sue Kaufman's *Diary of a Mad Housewife,* Tina Balser subscribes to the notion that her failure to perform as the perfect wife means she is going mad. In Joyce Carol Oates's *Do with Me What You Will,* Elena's total passivity so well fulfills the desires of her husband that he does not consider her, as the reader (this reader at least) does, mentally ill. Again, the same convention occurs in the poetry—for example, Jong's "Why I Died"[37] or Carol Cox's "From the Direction of the Mental Institution."[38]

The appropriateness of this convention (our willingness to agree to it) is probably a coalescence of two aspects of experience. First, women frequently feel mad because their own reality/feeling is in conflict with society's expecta-tions. This is often expressed in literature as the sense of being "split." The protagonists of Sylvia Plath's *The Bell Jar* (1963), Margaret Laurence's *The Diviners,* Margaret Atwood's *Surfacing,* and Rita Mae Brown's *Rubyfruit Jun-gle* (1973) are among many who describe this sensation. The nameless narrator of *Surfacing* says, "I'd allowed myself to be cut in two";[39] her head (her rationality) is no longer attached to her body (her emotions). Morag Gunn in *The Diviners* experiences an increased sense of "being separated from herself."[40] So feminist critics can readily identify Gilman's narrator's division of herself as an example of this split. The need to assert the female personal voice as a way to reestablish wholeness or health results from an awareness of the split. When the narrator of "The Yellow Wallpaper" asserts "Personally, I," I person-ally read it with this knowledge in mind.[41]

Second, women who try to express difference (do not submit to patriarchal expectations) are frequently called "crazy." Alice Munro's short story "The Office," in which a woman who rents an office to write in is considered mad, is a good illustration of this,[42] as is Ellen Goodman's column in the *Boston Globe* on the occasion of Martha Mitchell's death, "Here's To All the Crazy Ladies."

Another aspect of this "associated cluster" of meanings is the Laingian notion of madness as a form of higher sanity, as an indication of a capacity to see truths other than those available to the logical mind. An extension of the tradition of the wise fool, this concept was reinforced by a vision-seeking drug culture in the sixties and occurs frequently in literature by both women and men. Such novels as Ken Kesey's *One Flew Over the Cuckoo's Nest* (1962), in which inhabitants of a mental institution are seen to be saner than their doctors, and Doris Lessing's *Briefing for a Descent into Hell* (1971), in which the reader must choose between the reality of the institutionalized protagonist and that of his doctors, are typical examples. The work of Doris Lessing is perhaps the best illustration of the use of this concept, which is first fully developed in her novel *The Four-Gated City* (1969). Here Martha Quest identifies herself with the apparently mad wife of her lover Mark and comes to hear voices from a world validated as superior at the end of the novel. Carol P. Christ describes Lynda, the wife, as being "destroyed by psychologists who called her powers madness."[43] Especially useful to feminist writers since it defines the established society as less perceptive than she who is called deviant, the concept is conventional enough by 1973 for Elaine Hedges to talk of "her mad-sane way" and speak volumes (particularly those of Doris Lessing) to her readers.

It is significant that the central experience of *The Four-Gated City* takes place during two weeks in which Martha and Lynda remain enclosed in Lynda's room and, like the narrator of "The Yellow Wallpaper," crawl around its perimeter. The conventions associated with space, particularly with rooms, are central to a feminist reading of "The Yellow Wallpaper." Although still indicative in contemporary fiction by women of the limitations of women's sphere, a convention French employs in the first—the toilet—scene of *The Women's Room*, rooms are also claimed as independent space (with or without the five hundred pounds a year Woolf told us was also necessary). "You keep me in" has become "I keep you out." This dual use of the conventions associated with rooms, which as Gilbert and Gubar remind us are also representative of female bodies, can be seen in two short stories: Doris Lessing's "To Room 19"[44] and the Munro story "The Office" I referred to earlier. In the former a woman rents a hotel room in which to be alone and is forced to invent a lover to protect her space; in the latter a woman is accused of sexual promiscuity when she rents an office in which to work. The association between independent space and women's creative work—a connection we make in reading "The Yellow Wallpaper"—is, of course, established clearly by Woolf in *A Room of One's Own* (1929).

The concept of space also includes the question of women in relationship to nature, too large a subject to fully explore here, and which only peripherally affects the reading of "The Yellow Wallpaper." It is interesting to note, though, that Gilbert and Gubar read the narrator's double's escape into open country as "not unlike the progress of nineteenth-century women out of the texts defined by patriarchal poetics into the open spaces of their own authority" (91). Traditionally women have been identified with nature, a convention which has effectively precluded, in American literature at least, the possibility of female protagonists interacting with nature in the way male protagonists have. This applies to the wilderness rather than to such tamed natural environments as gardens, and to the American wilderness rather than, for example, to the Canadian where female protagonists do not find the space already occupied by the heroes of Hemingway, Faulkner, and Steinbeck. The possibilities for the boy in Faulkner's "The Bear," who sees the woods as both mistress and wife, to find himself in nature by confronting a bear are simply not open to women. No American woman novelist has written a novel like Marian Engel's *Bear* (1976) in which a female character has her version of the same experience.

For this reason, perhaps, women on spiritual quests—I come to my final concept—do not journey horizontally in contemporary American literature, do not cross wildernesses like frontier heroes, despite the actualities of frontier history. We appear to quest vertically: we dive and surface or we fly. Carol P. Christ's recent book, *Diving Deep and Surfacing,* examines some of these motifs in the novels of Doris Lessing and Margaret Atwood and in Adrienne Rich's *Diving into the Wreck* (1973) and *The Dream of a Common Language* (1978). *Surfacing* is a particularly interesting example since the protagonist begins by searching for her father horizontally, which involves a long journey by road and an exploration of the woods, but she only finds him when she dives. Christ does not examine the flying metaphor, which is obvious in the titles of Erica Jong's *Fear of Flying* and Kate Millett's *Flying* (1974).

The aspect of the quest concept which we need to reread "The Yellow Wallpaper," however, has more to do with a different convention. To see the narrator as a quester for self-fulfillment is to agree to grant her our trust (to see her as the accurate perceiver of reality), which we do partly because she is female, partly because she speaks to us directly (though we have the choice here of opting for the unreliable narrator convention), and partly because we agree to read madness as sanity. Both Gilbert and Gubar and Kolodny see her as searching for her identity, her place, in the wallpaper and call this "reading." The convention we are using here is that suggested by Adrienne Rich in "Diving into the Wreck." We are aware of the "book of myths / in which our names do not appear," recognize the need for a literary past which reflects "the thing itself and not the myth,"[45] and examine our literary history with this in mind. Again, the convention has two aspects: one, literature is seen as lying about women, and our truths remain unwritten or suppressed, as Tillie Olsen explains in *Silences* (1978); two, the literature we have been given is seen as a quarry which must be mined to produce the truths we need. So Jane Clifford in Gail Godwin's *The Odd Woman* (1974) hunts fiction to find the character she most resembles; so Maxine Hong Kingston's narrator in *The Woman Warrior* (1976) translates the legends of her Chinese past into workable myths for her American present and learns to say "I" and "Here"; so Morag Gunn learns that whether or not her adopted father Christie's tales of her Scottish ancestors were true is unimportant since they have given her the "strength of conviction." So the narrator of "The Yellow Wallpaper" can be read as reading her own text in (into) the patterns of the wallpaper.

What does this examination of the contemporary conventions necessary for rereading "The Yellow Wallpaper" demonstrate about the way literary conventions change? I suggest that these conventions can all be seen as responses to, changes in, conventions which had become oppressive to the feminist "interpretive community." By oppressive I mean both dishonest, suggesting an idea contrary to the view of experience called reality by the interpretive community, and inadequate, not able to provide a form in which to express that view of experience. If a conventional view is seen as dishonest, then the convention is often reversed. So a gothic treatment of female madness which exploits the reader's sadistic impulses (pleasure in another's pain) and sees women as basically unstable (hysterical) is reversed in two ways in the contemporary conventions associated with madness: the woman's mental disease is seen to be the fault of society (patriarchy) rather than her own; madness is read as sanity. The conventional associations of space function in the same way. Reversal here takes the form of changing a negative evaluation to a positive one. In other literature by women we have seen women writers adopt the supposedly negative slurs directed at them: they have written poems which celebrate themselves as witches, lesbians, Amazons;[46] they have deliberately exploited the confessional mode for which their writing had been condemned;[47] they have emphasized the "insignificant" kitchen imagery of their own lives.[48] This is a tactic also used by other victims of discrimination: "Black is beautiful"; "gay is good."

Reversal may take the form of exposing the implications of an old convention by changing the point of view, often by changing the gender of the participants. Erica Jong's *Fear of Flying*, for example, was considered original at the time of publication because it made men rather than women sex objects. Similarly, in a recent film *Nine to Five*, a male is held captive by his female employees. Poems in which male poets are rewritten from the female point of view employ this same procedure. See, for example, Mona Van Duyn's "Leda" and "Leda Reconsidered,"[49] Julie Randall's "To William Wordsworth from Virginia,"[50] Judith Rechter's "From Faye Wray to the King."[51]

When experience cannot be expressed in the available literary conventions, new conventions appear to develop. I say "appear" because these new conventions could perhaps be described as occupying the gaps left by the old. At all events they are not totally unrelated to what has gone before. So the conventions associated with diving, surfacing, and flying as forms of quest may seem to be new until they are recognized as vertical alternatives to a traffic jam on the horizontal. Woman's search for her own story, which ends in its creation, is a response to the absence of that story in literary history.

To fully test my hypothesis that literary conventions change when their implications conflict with the vision of experience of a new "interpretive community" would require going beyond the feminist rereading I have examined here, and more space than I have. It can certainly be demonstrated, though, that changes in literary conventions are frequently justified in the name of a greater truth to present reality, to "life." "Is life like this? Must novels be like this?" asks Virginia Woolf as she builds her case against the fictional conventions of "realistic" novels in favor of a truth to the reality of the mind, to the stream of consciousness: "If he [a writer] could write what he chose and not what he must, if he could base his work upon his own feeling and not upon convention, there would be no plot, no comedy, no tragedy, no love interest or catastrophe in the accepted sense. . . . Life is not a series of gig lamps symmetrically arranged."[52] In Lessing's *A Proper Marriage* Martha Quest complains: "In the books, the young and idealistic girl gets married, has a baby—she at once turns into something quite different; and she is perfectly happy to spend her whole life bringing up children with a tedious husband."[53] This convention no longer represents life as Martha knows it; it has clearly become "someone else's rule" which it is now "necessary to disregard."

The appeal to "real life" is not limited to the twentieth century. In the sixteenth century Marguerite de Navarre is already concerned that the "flowers of rhetoric" not hide "the truth of history."[54] Nor is it limited to female writers. Ford Madox Ford appeals in the same way as Virginia Woolf to perceived experience as he explains why he and Conrad began changing a fictional convention: "It became very early evident to us that what was the matter with the Novel, and the British novel in particular, was that it went straight forward, whereas in your gradual making acquaintanceship with your fellows you never do go straight forward. . . . We agreed that the general effect of a novel must be the general effect that life makes on mankind."[55]

The problem with appealing to the "general effect life makes" is that we do not all agree on what is lifelike. When we talk about "reality," we are really talking about a writer's or a reader's vision of experience, the way s/he needs to see it. Conventions change according to our needs as readers or, if we accept

Fish's views, as groups of readers, as "interpretive communities." It follows, then, that conventions are always to some extent outmoded, always "old rules," lagging necessarily behind the vision they are designed to express. Once we can identify "a mad housewife novel," it is already too late to write another one successfully.

This view of literary conventions can prove useful to feminist critics. The fact that the conventions we use to reread the literary past are already dying should remind us that the remaking of the literary canon is a process and must remain ongoing; it is not a goal to be achieved. New texts will appear hidden in the old in answer to new needs, in response to new conventions. These texts in turn will affect that "real life" experience which forces changes in conventions.[56]

Like the narrators of "The Yellow Wallpaper" and *The Woman Warrior*, like Morag Gunn, we project ourselves into the text's "otherwise incomprehensible hieroglyphics." The value of our rereadings lies not in their "correctness" nor in our ability to demonstrate their intentionality but, like Christie's tales, in their ability to enrich our present by providing us with that book of myths in which our names do appear. To do this they do not need to be "true," merely satisfying. As Morag Gunn says to her daughter Pique when she asks whether the stories she was told as a child really happened, "'Some did and some didn't, I guess. It doesn't matter a damn, don't you see?'"[57]

The idea that we invent rather than discover new meanings does not lessen the importance of the rereading enterprise.[58] To remind ourselves that we all create the conventions that allow us to read the text is to grant our readings as much authority—or as little—as any other. Indeed, it provides us with an answer to those frequent accusations of bias. Feminists and other clearly defined interpretive communities are no more biased than any other readers; our biases are simply more readily identifiable and often more acknowledged.

Nor should this notion raise what Walter Benn Michaels has called "the fear of subjectivity" among Anglo-American literary critics, the fear that "if there were no determinate meanings, the interpreter's freedom could make a text anything it wanted."[59] In theory (some theories) we as individual readers can choose to make of the text anything we wish, but in practice we do not do so. This is not only because we read by means of the conventions shared by our interpretive communities and are, as Fish has pointed out, programmed by our experience: "To the list of made or constructed objects we must add ourselves, for we no less than the poems and assignments we see are the product of social and cultural patterns of thought."[60] It is equally, or perhaps alternatively, because we always surrender some part of the individual freedom we do have in order to seek affirmation for our reading from our interpretive community. If our reading is not accepted, it will not satisfy us, that is, comfort us by providing that sense of community we read for in the first place. In reading we seek a coming together, a convention.

Notes

1. Northrop Frye, *Anatomy of Criticism: Four Essays* (1957; rpt. Princeton, 1971), p. 225.

2. Frye, p. 76. Cf. p. 99: "The problem of convention is the problem of how art can be communicable."

3. Frye, pp. 97, 99.

4. See, e.g., Harold Bloom, "The Breaking of Form," in *Deconstruction and Criticism*, ed. Geoffrey Hartman (New York: Seabury Press, 1979), p. 3: "The truest sources, again necessarily, are in the powers of poems *already written,* or rather, *already read.*"

5. See, e.g., Roland Barthes, "From Work to Text," in *Image-Music-Text*, ed. and trans. Stephen Heath (New York: Hill & Wang, 1977), p. 160: "The citations which go to make up a text are anonymous, untraceable, and yet *already read:* they are quotations without inverted commas."

6. Geoffrey Hartman. "Words, Wish, Worth: Wordsworth," in *Deconstruction and Criticism*, p. 187.

7. Nelly Furman, "Textual Feminism," in *Woman and Language in Literature and Society*, ed. Sally McConnell-Ginet, Ruth Borker, and Nelly Furman (New York: Praeger, 1980), p. 49.

8. Jonathan Culler, "Literary Competence," in *Structuralist Poetics* (Ithaca: Cornell University Press, 1975). Rpt. in *Reader-Response Criticism: From Formalism to Post-Structuralism*, ed. Jane P. Tompkins (Baltimore: Johns Hopkins University Press, 1980), p. 102. Cf. Annette Kolodny, "Dancing Through the Minefield: Some Observations on the Theory, Practice and Politics of A Feminist Literary Criticism," *Feminist Studies*, 6:1 (Spring 1980), p. 10: "What we have really come to mean when we speak of competence in reading historical texts, therefore, is the ability to recognize literary conventions which have survived through time."

9. Stanley E. Fish, "Interpreting the *Variorum*," *Critical Inquiry* 2 (Spring 1976), pp. 465–85.

10. Fish, p. 483: "In other words these strategies exist prior to the act of reading and therefore determine the shape of what is read." Cf. Furman, p. 52: "Furthermore the reader is not a passive consumer, but an active producer of a new text."

11. Fish, p. 484.

12. Fish, p. 484.

13. Raymond Williams, *Marxism and Literature* (Oxford: Oxford University Press, 1977), p. 179: "For it is of the essence of a convention that it ratifies an assumption or a point of view so that the work can be made and received."

14. Williams, p. 173.

15. Quoted in "Breaking the Conventions of the Women's Novel," *Boston Globe*. 28 Nov. 1977, p. 15.

16. Frye, p. 102.

17. Norman Holland, "Unity Identity Text Self," *PMLA*, 90:5 (October 1975), p. 818: "All readers create from the fantasy seemingly 'in' the work fantasies to suit their several character structures. Each reader in effect, recreates the work in terms of his own identity theme."

18. Jonathan Culler points out that Holland is working with a simplified notion of personal identity, that people "are not harmonious wholes whose every action expresses personal identity, that people "are not harmonious wholes whose every action expresses their essence or is determined by their ruling 'identity theme.'" "Prolegomena to a Theory of Reading," in *The Reader in the Text: Essays on Audience and Interpretation,* eds. Susan R. Suleiman and Inge Crosman (Princeton: Princeton University Press, 1980), p. 53.

19. Furman, p. 52.

20. Kolodny, p. 12.

21. Harold Bloom, *Kabbalah and Criticism* (New York: Seabury Press, 1975), p. 76.

22. All feminist critics agree on the importance of this enterprise. The most frequently cited reference on the subject is Adrienne Rich's call for "re-visioning" our literary past in "When We Dead Awaken: Writing as Re-Vision," *College English* 34:1 (October 1978), p. 18.

23. Sandra Gilbert and Susan Gubar, *The Madwoman in the Attic: The Woman Writer and the Nineteenth-Century Literary Imagination* (New Haven: Yale University Press, 1979). Since this work will be cited regularly, all subsequent page references will be indicated in the text.

24. Hélène Cixous's comments provide the strongest explanation for this. See "The Laugh of Medusa," trans. Keith Cohen and Paula Cohen, *Signs* 1:4 (Summer 1976), pp. 875–93: "A feminine text cannot fail to be more than subversive. It is volcanic; as it is written it brings about an upheaval of the old property crust, carrier of masculine investments; there's no other way."

25. Judith Fetterley, *The Resisting Reader: A Feminist Approach to American Fiction* (Bloomington: Indiana University Press, 1978).

26. Annette Kolodny, "A Map for Rereading: Or, Gender and the Interpretation of Literary Texts," *New Literary History* 11:3 (Spring 1980), pp. 451–67. Since this article will be cited frequently, all subsequent page references will be indicated in the text.

27. What is surprising and annoying is that reader-response critics so rarely recognize the similarities or refer to the work of feminist critics. Even two recent collections, both with extensive bibliographies and both edited by women, make no mention of feminist criticism: Tompkins, ed., *Reader-Response Criticism,* and Suleiman and Crosman, eds., *The Reader in the Text.*

28. Elaine Showalter, "Review Essay," *Signs* 1:2 (Winter 1975), p. 435.

29. Kate Chopin's *The Awakening* is the obvious second choice. Conversations available to readers differ for other reasons than time, of course. An interesting illustration of the influence of geography is Margaret Atwood's novel *Surfacing* (New York: Simon & Schuster, 1972), which was read in the United States as a feminist statement and in Canada as a statement about Canadian nationalism.

30. Elaine R. Hedges, "Afterword," in Charlotte Perkins Gilman's *The Yellow Wallpaper* (Old Westbury, N.Y.: The Feminist Press, 1973), p. 39. Since this work will be cited frequently, all subsequent page references will be indicated in the text.

31. William Dean Howells, ed., *The Great Modern American Stories* (New York: Boni & Liveright, 1920), p. vii.

32. Interestingly, the work is classified as "Juvenile Literature" under the Library of Congress classification system.

33. Atwood, "After I fell Apart," in *The Animals in That Country* (Boston: Little, Brown, & Co., 1968).

34. Sylvia Plath, *Ariel* (New York: Harper & Row, 1966).

35. Jean E. Kennard, *Victims of Convention* (Hamden, Conn.: Archon Books, 1978).

36. Erica Jong, *Loveroot* (New York: Holt, Rinehart, & Winston, 1975).

37. Jong, *Half-Lives* (New York: Holt, Rinehart & Winston, 1973).

38. In *Mountain Moving Day,* ed. Elaine Gill (Trumansburg, N.Y.: Crossing Press, 1973).

39. *Surfacing,* p. 129.

40. *The Divines* (Toronto, 1974), p. 263.

41. The use of the first person in feminist criticism is related to this notion. See Suzanne Juhasz, "The Critic as Feminist: Reflections on Women's Poetry, Feminism and the Art of Criticism," *Women's Studies* 5 (1977), pp. 113–27; Sandra Gilbert, "Life Studies, or, Speech After Long Silence: Feminist Critics Today," *College English* 40 (1979), pp. 849–63; Jean E. Kennard, "Personally Speaking: Feminist Critics and the Community of Readers," *College English* 43 (1981), pp. 140–45.

42. Alice Munro, *Dance of the Happy Shades* (Toronto: Ryerson Press, 1968).

43. Carol P. Christ, *Diving Deep and Surfacing: Women Writers on Spiritual Quest* (Boston: Beacon Press, 1980), p. 64.

44. Doris Lessing, *A Man and Two Women and Other Stories* (New York: Simon & Schuster, 1963).

45. Adrienne Rich, *Diving into the Wreck* (New York: Norton, 1973), p. 24.

46. See, e.g., Susan Sutheim, "For Witches," and Jean Tepperman, "Witch," in *No More Masks,* eds. Florence Howe and Ellen Bass (Garden City, N.Y.: Anchor Books, 1973), pp. 297, 333. *Amazon Poetry,* eds. Elly Bulkin and Joan Larkin (Brooklyn, N.Y.: Out & Out Books, 1975).

47. See e.g., Kate Millett's *Flying* (New York: Knopf, 1974) and Kolodny's article on critical responses to it, "The Lady's Not for Spurning: Kate Millett and the Critics," *Contemporary Literature* 17:4 (1976), pp. 541–62.

48. See e.g., Tillie Olsen's "I Stand Here Ironing," in *Tell Me A Riddle* (Philadelphia: Lippincott, 1961). Also Jong's "The Woman Who Loved to Cook," in *Half-Lives;* Nikki Giovanni's "Woman Poem," in *Black Feeling, Black Talk/Black Judgement* (New York: W. Morrow, 1970).

49. Mona Van Duyn, *To See, To Take* (New York: Atheneum, 1970).

50. In *No More Masks,* p. 158.

51. *No More Masks,* p. 257.

52. Virginia Woolf, "Modern Fiction," in *The Common Reader* (London: Hogarth Press, 1951).

53. Doris Lessing, *A Proper Marriage* (1952; rpt. New York: New American Library, 1970), p. 206.

54. Marguerite de Navarre, *The Heptameron,* trans. Walter K. Kelly (London, n.d.), p. 9.

55. Quoted in Jocelyn Baines, *Joseph Conrad: A Critical Biography* (London: Weidenfeld & Nicolson, 1960), pp. 136–37.

56. Cf. Christ, pp. 4–5: "In a very real sense, there is no experience without stories. There is a dialectic between stories and experience. Stories give shape to experience, experience gives rise to stories."

57. *The Diviners,* p. 350.

58. Cf. Nelly Furman's discussion of textual criticism in "Textual Feminism."

59. Walter Benn Michaels, "The Interpreter's Self: Peirce on the Cartesian Subject," *Georgia Review* 1 (1977), pp. 383–402.

60. Fish, *Is There A Text in This Class? The Authority of Interpretive Communities* (Cambridge, Mass.: Harvard University Press, 1980), p. 332.

6

Monumental Feminism and Literature's Ancestral House: Another Look at "The Yellow Wallpaper"

Janice Haney-Peritz

In 1973, the Feminist Press brought forth a single volume edition of Charlotte Perkins Gilman's "The Yellow Wallpaper," a short story which had originally appeared in the May 1892 issue of *New England Magazine*. Since William Dean Howells included Gilman's story in his 1920 collection of *Great Modern American Short Stories,* it cannot be said that between 1892 and 1973 "The Yellow Wallpaper" was completely ignored. What can be said, however, is that until 1973, the story's feminist thrust had gone unremarked; even Howells, who was well aware not only of Gilman's involvement in the women's movement but also of her preference for writing "with a purpose," had nothing to say about the provocative feminism of Gilman's text.[1] In the introduction to his 1920 collection, Howells notes the story's chilling horror and then falls silent.[2]

Although brief, Howells's response does place him in a long line of male readers, a line that includes the following: M.D., the anonymous doctor who in an 1892 letter to the Boston *Transcript* complained about the story's morbidity and called for its censure; Horace Scudder, the editor of *The Atlantic Monthly* who in a letter to Gilman claimed to have been made so miserable by the story that he had no other choice than to reject it for publication; Walter Stetson, Gilman's first husband who informed her that he found the story utterly ghastly, more horrifying than even Poe's tales of terror;[3] John, the physician-husband of the story's narrator who in coming face to face with his mad wife is so astonished that he faints; and last but not least, Milton's Adam, the "first" man, who is represented as being both chilled and horrified by a woman's storytelling:

This article originally appeared in *Women's Studies* 12 (1986): pp. 113–28.

Thus *Eve* with Count'nance blithe her story told;
But in her Cheek distemper flushing glow'd.
On th'other side, *Adam,* soon as he heard
The fatal Trespass done by *Eve,* amaz'd,
Astonied stood and Blank, while horror chill
Ran through his veins, and all his joints relax'd.[4]

It is this male line of response that the 1973 edition of "The Yellow Wallpaper" seeks to disrupt and displace, implicitly by affixing to the text the imprint of the Feminist Press and explicitly by appending to the text an afterword in which Elaine Hedges reads the story as a "feminist document," as "one of the rare pieces of literature we have by a nineteenth-century woman which directly confronts the sexual politics of the male-female, husband-wife relationship."[5] So effective has this disruption and displacement been that it is not much of an exaggeration to say that during the last ten years, Gilman's short story has assumed monumental proportions, serving at one and the same time the purposes of a memorial and a boundary marker. As a memorial, "The Yellow Wallpaper" is used to remind contemporary readers of the enduring import of the feminist struggle against patriarchal domination; while as a boundary marker, it is used to demarcate the territory appropriate to a feminist literary criticism.[6] Although I am interested in pointing out some of the more troubling implications of a literary criticism in which Gilman's story functions as a feminist monument, before doing so, it is necessary to take another look at "The Yellow Wallpaper" itself.

From beginning to end, "The Yellow Wallpaper" presents itself as the writing of a woman who along with her physician-husband John and her sister-in-law Jennie is spending the summer in what she calls an "ancestral hall," a home away from home which has been secured in the hope that it will prove beneficial to the narrator's health and well-being. In ten diarylike entries that span her three-month stay in this ancestral hall, the narrator not only recounts her interactions with John and Jennie but also describes in detail the yellow wallpaper that covers the walls of a large upstairs room, a room which at one time seems to have been a nursery and, at another, a gymnasium; this summer, however, it has become the master bedroom, a place where the narrator spends much of her time, drawn in, it seems, by the very yellow wallpaper which so repels her.

However, before her attention becomes focused on the wallpaper, the narrator attempts to grasp her situation by naming the kind of place in which she finds herself as well as the kind of place she would like it to be. In the opening lines of her text, she refers to the place as both a "colonial mansion" and an "hereditary estate"; however, what she would like to believe is that the place is really a "haunted house."[7] According to the narrator, a haunted house would be "the height of romantic felicity," a place more promising than that which "fate" normally assigns to "mere ordinary people like John and [herself]" (9). Since haunted houses are a peculiarly literary kind of architecture, the narrator's desire for such a place may be associated not only with her desire for writing but also with her interest in the wallpaper; in all cases, what is at issue is the displacement of a colonial inheritance that fate seems to have decreed as her lot.

But even though a haunted house may be desired, the possibility of realizing that desire is seriously in doubt. Not only does John find his wife's desire laughable but in the beginning, the narrator also demurs, afraid that at this point she is demanding too much too soon of either fate or John. As the narrator sees it, the problem is that John scoffs at "talk of things not to be felt and seen and put down in figures" (9). To John, the narrator's haunted house is nothing; however, so too is her feeling that she is not well. Nevertheless, at the same time that he assures his wife that there is really nothing the matter with her, John also prescribes a regimen which will help her get well: she is not to think about haunted houses or her condition; nor, given her habit of fanciful story-making, is she to write. Instead, she is to eat well, exercise in moderation, and rest as much as she can in the airy upstairs room, the master bedroom.

Ironically, it is precisely because the narrator is patient enough to follow some of the doctor's orders that she finds it necessary to deal with the yellow wallpaper which covers the walls of the master bedroom. At first glance, that wallpaper appears to be nothing more than an error in taste—"one of those sprawling, flamboyant patterns committing every artistic sin" (13); at second glance, however, more troubling possibilities emerge, for as the narrator notes, the wallpaper's pattern "is dull enough to confuse the eye in following, *pronounced* enough to constantly irritate and provoke study, and when you follow the lame uncertain curves for a little distance they suddenly commit suicide— plunge off at outrageous angles, destroy themselves in *unheard-of contradictions*" (13, emphasis added). Although commentators have seen in this description of the wallpaper a general representation of "the oppressive structures of the society in which [the narrator] finds herself" (*Madwoman*, p. 90), the word "pronounced" as well as the phrase "unheard of contradictions" suggest that the specific oppressive structure at issue is discourse. Furthermore, since we have just been treated to an account of John's discourse on his wife's condition, a discourse based on the unspoken and therefore "unheard of contradiction" that somehow she is both well and ill, we may want to be even more specific and say that the oppressive structure at issue is a man's prescriptive discourse about a woman.

However, as it is described by the narrator, the yellow wallpaper also resembles the text we are reading—that is, it resembles the narrator's own writing. In part, this resemblance can be attributed to the fact that the narrator's writing not only recounts John's prescriptive discourse but also relies on the very binary oppositions which structure that discourse—oppositions like sick and well, the real and the fanciful, order and anarchy, self and other, and male and female. Thus, it is not surprising to find that the narrator's reflections produce a text in which one line of thinking after another "suddenly commits suicide—plung[ing] off at outrageous angles, [and] destroy[ing itself] in unheard of contradictions." For example, although the narrator claims that writing would do her good, she also says that it tires her out (21). Worse yet, at the very moment that she is writing, she expresses a wish that she were well enough to write (16). Such contradictions not only betray the narrator's dependence on the oppressive discursive structure we associate with John but also help us to understand why she jumps from one thing to another, producing paragraphs that are usually no more than a few lines in length. Since a discursive line of reasoning based on binary oppositions like sick and well is bound to "destroy" itself in "unheard-of contradictions,"[8] one way the narrator can continue to produce a text that has some pretence to being reasonable is quickly to change the subject, say from her condition to the house or from the wallpaper to John.

If the resemblance between the narrator's writing and John's discourse is disturbing—so much so that it often goes unremarked—it may be because what we want of a woman's writing is something different, a realization of that *écriture féminine* which figures so significantly in many contemporary attempts to specify what makes a woman's writing distinctive.[9] However, if we repress this resemblance, we may forget to pose what Luce Irigaray calls "the first question": that is, "how can women analyze their own exploitation, inscribe their own demands, within an order prescribed by the masculine?" Having posed this first question, Irigaray suggests that one answer might be for a woman "to play with mimesis," to deliberately "resubmit herself . . . to 'ideas,' in particular to ideas about herself, that are elaborated in/by a masculine logic." Although such miming runs the risk of reproducing a discursive system in which woman as Other is repressed, according to Irigaray, it may also have the uncanny effect of making "'visible' . . . what was supposed to remain invisible: the cover-up of a possible operation of the feminine in language."[10]

In "The Yellow Wallpaper," the narrator's labor of miming does seem to produce just some such uncanny effect, for not only does her writing expose the "unheard of contradictions" in a man's prescriptive logic but in dealing with those contradictory impasses by jumping from one thing to another, it also makes the reader aware of gaps in that discursive structure. Furthermore, since the narrator occasionally notes what she might have said but didn't, those gaps can also be read as "unheard of contradictions"; that is, they can be read as the places where the narrator might have contradicted John's prescriptions, if only the woman had a voice to do so. Lacking such a voice, the narrator partially recoups her loss in a writing that is punctuated by the "unsaid," by what remains muted in a discourse which at this point seems to be what matters most.

To the extent that the narrator's writing does indeed display discourse to be what is really the matter, then we cannot presume that the text's "hereditary estate" is built on or out of the bedrock of a real anatomical difference between the sexes. However, if the ancestral hall is not to be considered a real "hereditary estate," neither is it to be considered a real "colonial mansion," a place defined by the nondiscursive social relations between masters and slaves. Instead, the ancestral house must be thought of as in and of what Lacan has called the symbolic order, the order of Language.[11] By committing herself to a writing about discourse and by focusing her attention on the yellow wallpaper as a discursive structure, the narrator has turned what seemed to be a real hereditary and colonial estate into an uncanny place in which nobody is or can be at home—no matter what s/he might say to the contrary.

If "The Yellow Wallpaper" ended at this point, we might consider it a Poesque text, for as Joseph Riddel has convincingly argued, what Poe introduced into American literature was the theme of "de-constructed architecture," a them which later American writers obsessively repeat.[12] By locating man's ancestral house within the symbolic order, Poe produced a writing that disrupted all nontextual origins which might once have made the house of man seem sufficient to have stood its ground. "The Yellow Wallpaper," however, does not end at this point—the point of deconstructed architecture—for in the text's crucial third section, the narrator discerns something "like a woman stooping down and creeping about behind [the wallpaper's] pattern" (22) and with this vision, the register of the narrator's reading and writing begins to shift from the symbolic to the imaginary.

The possibility of such a shift was foreshadowed in the text's second movement wherein the narrator counterpointed her description of Jennie as the perfect housekeeper with a remark that the wallpaper had some kind of subpattern—a "formless sort of figure that seems to skulk about behind that silly and conspicuous front design" (18). However, at this point no explicit splitting of the subject occurred, for the narrator still appeared to be both willing and able to comprehend this nascent imaginary figure within the symbolic order. Instead of apprehending the formless figure as a really different body, the narrator merely noted that from one perspective, the paper's design seemed to be composed of "bloated curves and flourishes . . . [which] go waddling up and down in isolated columns of fatuity" (20).

By the end of the third movement, however, the imaginary does emerge as a distinctly different way of seeing and an explicit splitting of the subject does indeed take place. This crisis of sorts seems to be precipitated by a failure of intercourse; first, there is the narrator's unsuccessful attempt to have a "real ernest reasonable talk" with John; then, there is a prohibition—John's refusal to countenance his wife's proposed visit to Henry and Julia; and finally, there is a breakdown in the master bedroom itself as John reads to his wife until her head tires. The scene is now set for the emergence of something different; as the moonlight creeps into the darkened bedroom, something *"like* a woman" is seen "creeping about" behind the wallpaper's outer pattern. Although this vision initiates the shift in register from the symbolic to the imaginary, the explicit splitting of the subject only takes place after the awakened John resolutely dismisses his wife's apprehensions by reminding her that as a doctor, he is the one who really knows. From this point on, the narrator sees things otherwise; now the wallpaper's "outside pattern" is perceived to be bars, while its subpattern is perceived to *be* a woman rather than something *"like* a woman" (26).

With the emergence of the imaginary over the symbolic, the narrator's writing takes a different tack than that of a Poe text in which a haunted house is revealed to be nothing more nor less mysterious than a house of fiction. Unable to rest secure in the no-place of such a deconstructed architecture, the narrator of "The Yellow Wallpaper" turns a symbolic house into the haunted house she initially feared might be too much to demand of fate. But even though this haunted house may seem to promise "the height of romantic felicity"—that is, the realization of a self—we should not forget that it is located within and constituted by what Lacan calls the Imaginary.[13]

In Lacanian psychoanalysis, the Imaginary is specified not only by its assimilation to a dual relation between, on the one hand, a subject and an image, and, on the other, a subject and an other, but also by the absence or repression of a symbolic mediation between the subject and its doubles. Without mediation, a subject has no access to the symbolic dimension of his or her experience and is therefore driven to establish the imaginary in the real. As a result of this realization, a complicated interplay between the eroticism and aggression characteristic of unmediated dual relations surfaces, as does a childlike transitivism.

In "The Yellow Wallpaper," the emergence of the imaginary as well as its assimilation to an unmediated dual relation first produces a clarity of perception and purpose which temporarily obscures the transitivism the story's ending exposes. As the shadow-woman becomes as "plain as can be," the narrator finds that it is possible to distinguish clearly day from night, sleep from waking, and most importantly, "me" from them. Now the woman who had earlier wondered what one was to do when caught in a contradictory situation (10) knows exactly what she must do: she must free the shadow-woman from the paper-pattern that bars her full self-realization and through identification, bind that woman to herself. However, since this process of identification necessitates the alienation of the subject by and in an image, it engenders not only an implicitly ambivalent relation between the narrator and her imaginary double but also an explicit rivalry between the narrator and John. Perceiving John to be her other, the narrator acts as though she could only win a place for herself at his expense; hence, when she undertakes the realization of her imaginary double, she does so with the express intention of "astonish[ing]" John (34). Apparently, the narrator wants to amaze John as Eve did Adam and as the Medusa did many a man.

If at one level this desire seems aggressive, then at another it appears erotic, for what is involved is a transitivism in which it is unclear exactly who is doing what to whom. Indeed, if it can be said that by becoming another woman, the narrator realizes herself in spite of John, then it can also be said that the self she realizes is not "her" self but a self engenderd by John's demands and desires. On the one hand, the narrator seems to have become the child John has always demanded she be, for like a child, she crawls around the perimeter of the master bedroom, bound by an umbilical cord that keeps her firmly in place. On the other hand, however, the narrator's identification with the wallpaper's shadow-woman seems to have turned her into the woman of John's dreams, for not only did the shadow woman first appear while John was sleeping, but the narrator also suspects that when all is said and done, she is what John really desires, the secret he would reveal if he were given the opportunity to do so.

In the final words of "The Yellow Wallpaper," the narrator describes how she must crawl over John's astonished body. Like the transitivism of the narrator's 'self-realization,' this closing image displays a conjunction of erotic and aggressive impulses, a conjunction which once again suggests that by identifying herself with the wallpaper's shadow-woman, the narrator has firmly installed herself in the realm of the imaginary, the realm of haunted houses.

Although the text of "The Yellow Wallpaper" ends at this point, the story does not, for it has been repeated by a number of important feminist critics who have seen in "The Yellow Wallpaper" not only an accurate representation of the situation of woman in patriarchal culture but also a model of their own reading and writing practices. While Elaine Hedges can be said to have begun this repetition in her influential afterward to the Feminist Press's edition of the text, it is Sandra Gilbert and Susan Gubar who turn repetition into monumentalism. In their magesterial work, *The Madwoman in the Attic,* Gilbert and Gubar not only repeat the story but also present it as a paradigm, as *"the* story that all literary women would tell if they could speak their 'speechless woe'" (89). According to Gilbert and Gubar, that woe begins when like the narrator of "The Yellow Wallpaper," a woman writer senses her "parallel confinements" in patriarchal texts, paternal houses, and maternal bodies (89); and, it ends when like the narrator of "The Yellow Wallpaper," the woman writer "escape[s] from her textual/architectual confinement" (91). The way to this end, however, is fraught with difficulty for like the narrator of "The Yellow Wallpaper," the woman writer must engage in a revisionary reading of the handwriting on the wall; only then will she discover her double, the other woman whose passion for escape demands recognition. By identifying with this other woman, the writer effects her liberation from disease into health and thereby finds that she has entered a new space, "the open space of [her] own authority" (91).

Although my reading of "The Yellow Wallpaper" makes me doubt that an imaginary revision and identification can indeed free women from either textual or architectural confinement, at this point I am less interested in questioning the specifics of Gilbert and Gubar's interpretation and more interested in pointing out some of the side effects such a monumental reading may have on feminist literary criticism. These side effects are particularly evident in two recently published essays that attempt to delineate the nature and function of contemporary Anglo-American feminist literary criticism.

In her 1980 essay entitled "A Map for Re-Reading: Or, Gender and the Interpretation of Literary Texts," Annette Kolodny continues the story of "The Yellow Wallpaper" more or less along the feminist lines set down by Hedges, Gilbert and Gubar. However, since Kolodny is interested in explaining why this feminist story was not recognized as such in its own time, her essay can also help us toward an understanding of what is involved when "The Yellow Wallpaper" is turned into a feminist monument. According to Kolodny, "The Yellow Wallpaper" was unreadable in its own time because neither men nor women readers had access to a tradition or shared context which would have made the "female meaning" of the text clear. Men readers may have been familiar with Poe but Poe would not have prepared them for a woman narrator whose problems are sociocultural rather than idiosyncratic. On the other hand, women readers may have been familiar with domestic fiction but such fiction would not have prepared them for a narrator whose home life is psychologically disturbing. Although Kolodny contends that Gilman uses the breakdown in communication between the narrator and John to prefigure her story's unreadability, she also declares this unreadability to be historically contingent. Nowadays, it seems, we have the wherewithal to read the story "correctly," for nowadays we have the shared context, if not the tradition we need to identify what she calls the story's "female meaning."

In an attempt to be more precise about how we know what we now know about female meaning, Jean Kennard takes up the story of "The Yellow Wallpaper" once again in her 1981 essay entitled "Convention Coverage or How to Read Your Own Life." Linking the feminism of the 1970s and 1980s with a massive reversal of both literary and nonliterary conventions, Kennard claims that a new and explicitly feminist set of interpretive conventions has made it possible to agree on the following ideas: that the oppressive use of power by a male is an instance of patriarchy; that a patriarchal culture's socialization of women makes them ill; that a woman's discomfort in ancestral halls indicates a healthy desire for a room of her own; and that both a revisionary reading of texts and a descent into madness are creditable ways for a woman to find and therefore free herself. Although Kennard shows how all these ideas engender a reading of "The Yellow Wallpaper" as the story of woman's quest for identity within an oppressive patriarchal culture, what I find particularly valuable about her essay is its explicit linking of a certain kind of feminism, a certain kind of feminist literary criticism, and a certain reading of "The Yellow Wallpaper."

But what, we might wonder, accounts for this linking? Here too Kennard may be of assistance, for to some extent she realizes that even before new conventions can be used to engender this feminist reading of "The Yellow Wallpaper," the contemporary critic must recognize and accept the narrator as a double with whom she can identify. However, in so doing, the contemporary critic can be said to repeat the move the narrator of "The Yellow Wallpaper" makes when she discovers and identifies herself with an imaginary woman, the woman behind the wallpaper's pattern. As I see it, this repetition accounts for a number of similarities between the narrator's imaginary mode of conceiving and representing her situation and the seemingly 'new' conventions that support a certain kind of modern feminist literary criticism which might also be called imaginary. Like the narrator of "The Yellow Wallpaper," some contemporary feminist critics see in literature a really distinctive body which they seek to liberate through identification. Although this body goes by many names, including the woman's story, female meaning, *écriture féminine,* and the maternal subtext, it is usually presented as essential to a viable feminist literary criticism and celebrated as something so distinctive that it shakes, if it does not destroy, the very foundations of patriarchal literature's ancestral house.[14]

However, if it is at all accurate to say that in repeating the story of "The Yellow Wallpaper" this kind of modern feminist criticism displays itself as imaginary, then it seems to me that it behooves us to be more skeptical about what appears to be "the height of romantic felicity."[15] Although inspiring, imaginary feminism is locked into a rivalry with an other, a rivalry that is both erotic and aggressive. As I see it, the transitivism of this dual relation belies not only claims to having identified the woman's story or female meaning but perhaps more importantly, assurances that identification is liberating. Just as we cannot be sure who engenders the shadow-woman of "The Yellow Wallpaper," neither can we be sure that the story we're reading is the woman's story; indeed, it may be the case that in reading "The Yellow Wallpaper" we are reading the story of John's demands and desires rather than something distinctively female. If so, then the assurance that identification is liberating becomes highly problematic, for it too appears to be an assurance generated and sanctioned by the very ancestral structure that feminists have found so confining.[16]

In "The Yellow Wallpaper," the narrator does not move out into open country; instead, she turns an ancestral hall into a haunted house and then encrypts herself therein as a fantasy figure.[17] If we wish to consider the result of this turn to be a feminist monument, then perhaps it would be better to read such a monument as a *mememto mori* that signifies the death of (a) woman rather than as a memorial that encloses the body essential to a viable feminist literary criticism. Unlike a memorial, a *memento mori* would provoke sympathy rather than identification and in so doing, would encourage us to apprehend the turn to the imaginary not as a model of liberation but as a sign of what may happen when a possible operation of the feminine in *language* is repressed.

If such an apprehension seems an uninspiring alternative for those of us committed to feminism, then I suggest that we look to Gilman rather than to the narrator of "The Yellow Wallpaper" for the inspiration we seek. By representing the narrator as in some sense mad, Gilman can be said to have preferred sympathy to identification, a preference which becomes all the more significant once we recall that much of "The Yellow Wallpaper" is based on Gilman's personal experience. However, Gilman did more than sympathize, for as Dolores Hayden has documented, she also involved herself in efforts to change the material conditions of social existence through the construction of kitchenless houses and feminist apartment hotels—new architectural spaces in which alternative social and discursive relations might emerge.[18] Although those of us interested in literature may find Gilman's concern for the material conditions of social life a troubling defection,[19] it is also quite possible to consider that concern a thoughtful deferral based on a recognition that the prevailing social structure made it idealistic, if not dangerously presumptuous to lay claim to having identified either the woman's story or female meaning. Indeed, it may just be that what Gilman learned in writing and reading "The Yellow Wallpaper" was that as yet, a woman could only *imagine* that she had found herself, for until the material conditions of social life were radically changed, there would be no 'real' way out of mankind's ancestral mansion of many apartments.

Notes

1. When Howells requested permission to include "The Yellow Wallpaper" in his collection, Gilman responded that the story "was no more 'literature' than [her] other stuff, being definitely written with a purpose." See *The Living of Charlotte Perkins Gilman: An Autobiography* (New York: D. Appleton-Century Company, 1935), p. 121. For evidence of Howell's familiarity with Gilman's interest in the 'woman question,' see p. 113.

2. William Dean Howells, ed., *The Great Modern American Stories* (New York: Boni & Liveright, 1920), p. vii.

3. For the letters by M. D. and Horace Scudder, see *The Living of Charlotte Perkins Gilman,* cited above, pp. 119–20. For Gilman's account of Walter Stetson's response, see Mary A. Hill, *Charlotte Perkins Gilman: The Making of a Radical Feminist 1860–1896* (Philadelphia: Temple University Press, 1980), p. 186.

4. John Milton, *Paradise Lost,* ed. Merrit Y. Hughes (Indianapolis: Odyssesy Press, 1962), p. 226. To my knowledge, no critic has yet noted in print the connection between *Paradise Lost* and the ending of "The Yellow Wallpaper." That connection rests only on John's response to his "mad" wife but also on the narrator's statement to John that the "key" to the room is to be found in the garden under a "plantain leaf." In *Paradise Lost,* Eve tells Adam

that she first "espi'd" him, "fair indeed and tall/Under a Plantan" (Book IV, 11.447–8). Although a plantain leaf is not exactly the same as a Plantan or plane tree, there is a sound resemblance between the two words as well as an etymological connection by way of *plátano, plátano*, the Spanish words for plane tree. Since I am interested in other matters, I do not deal at length with the connection between "The Yellow Wallpaper" and *Paradise Lost;* nevertheless, I trust that the reader will keep the connection in mind, for it does have a bearing on both my interpretation of the story and my response to critics who read the story as a feminist monument.

5. Elaine R. Hedges, "Afterword" to Charlotte Perkins Gilman's *The Yellow Wallpaper* (Old Westbury, N.Y.: The Feminist Press, 1973), p. 39.

6. Although much of this monumentalizing occurs within classes devoted to women's studies or women's literature, at least three influential publications treat the story as both a memorial and a boundary marker: Sandra Gilbert and Susan Gubar, *The Madwoman in the Attic: The Woman Writer and the Nineteenth-Century Literary Imagination* (New Haven: Yale University Press, 1979), pp. 89–92; Annette Kolodny, "A Map for Rereading: Or, Gender and the Interpretation of Literary Texts," *NLH* 11 (1980). 451–67; and Jean Kennard, "Convention Coverage or How to Read Your Own Life," *NLH* 13 (1981), 69–88. Hereafter, Gilbert and Gubar's book will be cited as *Madwoman.*

7. Charlotte Perkins Gilman, *The Yellow Wallpaper* (Old Westbury, N.Y.: The Feminist Press, 1973), p. 9. Subsequent references to "The Yellow Wallpaper" will be to this edition.

8. For a more theoretical explanation of why and how a discourse based on binary oppositions is bound to destroy itself in unheard of contradictions, see the work of Jacques Derrida, especially *Of Grammatology*, trans. Gayatri Spivak (Baltimore: Johns Hopkins University Press, 1976).

9. The term *écriture féminine* names the desired or hypothetical specificity of woman's writing; as a concept, it underwrites the work of certain French feminists, most importantly Helene Cixous's "The Laugh of the Medusa," trans. Keith and Paula Cohen, *Signs,* 1 (1976), 875–93, and Luce Irigaray's *Ce sexe qui n'en est pas un* (Paris: Minuit, 1977). Irigaray's text has been translated by Catherine Porter as *This Sex Which Is Not One* (Ithaca: Cornell University Press, 1985). In both France and America, the concept of *écriture féminine* has occasioned much debate; for a French questioning of the appeal to *écriture féminine*, see "Variations sur des themes communs" in *Questions feministes* 1 (1977), translated by Yvonne Rochette-Ozzello as "Variations on Common Themes" in *New French Feminisms*, pp. 212–30; for Anglo-American responses to the postulate of *écriture féminine*, see the following: Ann Rosalind Jones, "Writing the Body: Toward an Understanding of L'Ecriture Feminine," *Feminist Studies* 7 (1981), pp. 247–63; Helene Vivienne Wenzel, "The Text as Body/Politics: An Appreciation of Monique Wittig's Writings in Context," *Feminist Studies* 7 (1981), pp. 264–87; Carolyn Burke, "Irigaray Through the Looking Glass," *Feminist Studies* 7 (1981), pp. 288–306; Elaine Showalter, "Feminist Criticism in the Wilderness," in *Writing and Sexual Difference*, ed. Elizabeth Abel (Chicago: University of Chicago Press, 1982), pp. 9–35; Mary Jacobus, "The Question of Language: Men of Maxims and *The Mill on the Floss*," in *Writing and Sexual Difference*, pp. 37–52; and Hester Eisenstein and Alice Jardine, eds., *The Future of Difference* (Boston: G. K. Hall & Co., 1980). As this essay indicates, I am both sympathetic to the utopian political impulse that underwrites appeals to *écriture féminine* and wary of various and sundry claims to having produced or identified a demonstrably feminine writing. Like Mary Jacobus, I think such claims too often "founder on the rock of essentialism

(the text as body) [or] gesture towards an avant-garde practice which turns out not to be specific to women." See Jacobus's essay cited above, p. 37.

10. Luce Irigaray, "The Power of Discourse and the Subordination of the Feminine" in *This Sex Which Is Not One,* trans. Catherine Porter, p. 81 and p. 76, respectively.

11. Although the significance of the Symbolic order is best apprehended in terms of its relationship to what Lacan calls the Imaginary and the Real, it is possible to describe the Symbolic as if it were a determinate space in which the relations between subject and sign as well as subject and other are mediated by the law of the signifier or the structure of Language. This triadic relation in which the subject is alienated in and by the symbolic mediations of language rests on a necessary separation of the paternal role from the biological father, a separation effected by the subject's awakening not only to the "Name-of-the-Father" but also to the general naming function of language. It is this separation which allows me to claim that discourse is a structure in which nobody is or can be at-home; by (dis)placing the subject in a chain of signifiers, the symbolic institutes a double disruption between on the one hand, biological need and articulate demand and on the other, articulate demand and unconscious desire. For a more detailed exposition of the Symbolic order, see the following texts: Jacques Lacan, *The Language of the Self,* trans. Anthony Wilden (New York: Dell Publishing Co., 1968); Jacques Lacan *Ecrits* (Paris: Editions du Seuil, 1966); Jacques Lacan, *Ecrits: A Selection,* trans. Alan Sheridan (New York: W. W. Norton, 1982); Jacques Lacan, *The Four Fundamental Concepts of Psycho-analysis,* ed. Jacques-Alain Miller, trans. Alan Sheridan (New York: W. W. Norton, 1978); Anika Lemaire, *Jacques Lacan,* trans. David Macey (London: Routledge & Kegan Paul, 1977); Samuel Ysseling, "Structuralism and Psychoanalysis in the Work of Jacques Lacan," *International Philosophical Quarterly* 10 (1970), pp. 102–17; Martin Thom, "The Unconscious Structured Like a Language" in *Economy and Society* 5 (1976), pp. 435–69; Frederic Jameson, "Imaginary and Symbolic in Lacan: Marxism, Psychoanalytic Criticism, and the Problem of the Subject," *YFS* 55–56 (1977), pp. 338–95; Richard Wolheim, "The Cabinet of Dr. Lacan," *NYRB* 25 (January, 1979), pp. 36–45; Juliet Mitchell, *Psychoanalysis and Feminism* (New York: Random House, 1975), pp. 382–98; Jane Gallop, *The Daughter's Seduction: Feminism and Psychoanalysis* (Ithaca: Cornell University Press, 1982), pp. 1–55; and Juliet Mitchell and Jacqueline Rose, eds., *Feminine Sexuality: Jacques Lacan and the Ecole Freudienne,* trans. Jacqueline Rose (New York: W. W. Norton, 1982).

12. Joseph Riddel, "The Crypt of Edgar Poe" *Boundary 2,* 7 (1979), pp. 117–44; the reference to 'de-constructed architecture' appears on p. 125.

13. Although the significance of the Imaginary is best apprehended in terms of its relationship to what Lacan calls the Symbolic and the Real, it is possible to describe the Imaginary as if it were a specific kind of psychic space wherein bodies or forms are related to one another by means of such basic oppositions as inside-outside and container/contained. Developmentally speaking, the Imaginary originates in what Lacan calls the "mirror stage," that period between six and eighteen months during which the infant becomes aware of its image in the mirror, thereby fixing the self in a line of fiction, a line of imaginary doubles. Although this doubling is the precondition of primary narcissism, it is also the source of human aggression, for in both cases there is a transitivistic substitution of images, an indifferentiation of subject and object which leads the child who hits to image that s/he is being hit. For more on the Imaginary, see the works cited in note 11.

14. For the appeal to "the woman's story," see Gilbert and Gubar, *Madwoman;* for the appeal to "female meaning," see not only Annette Kolodny's "A Map for Rereading: Or, Gender and

the Interpretation of Literary Texts" but also her more controversial essay, "Dancing Through the Minefield: Some Observations on the Theory, Practice and Politics of a Feminist Literary Criticism," *Feminist Studies* 6 (1980), pp. 1–25; for the appeal to *écriture féminine* as a body, see Helene Cixous's "The Laugh of the Medusa;" for the appeal to a maternal subtext, see Judith Kegan Gardiner's "On Female Identity and Writing by Women," in *Writing and Sexual Difference*, ed. Elizabeth Abel (Chicago: University of Chicago Press, 1982), pp. 177–91. In "Feminist Criticism in the Wilderness," Elaine Showalter distinguishes between feminist critics who appeal to the difference of the woman's body and feminist critics who appeal to the difference of a woman's language, psychology, or culture; in practice, however, much feminist criticism belies the theoretical distinction Showalter makes, for the identification of a woman's language, psychology, or culture is often presented as though it were the discovery of a distinctly feminine body, even though that body may now be defined structurally rather than biologically.

15.　Since the imaginary is associated with pre-oedipal relations with the mother, the thrust of Lacanian psychoanalysis is to value the symbolic over the imaginary. Like many other feminists, I do not accept wholeheartedly this value judgment; however, I also do not believe that a simple reversal wherein the imaginary is valued over the symbolic suffices. Thus, I ask for skepticism rather than either denigration or celebration of the imaginary. For a more detailed exploration of the claims of the imaginary and the symbolic as well as an account of Julia Kristeva's attempt to effect a semiotic displacement of the Lacanian Imaginary, see Jane Gallop's *The Daughter's Seduction: Feminism and Psychoanalysis*.

16.　Although "identity" is often considered to be one of the key benefits of the women's liberation movement, it seems to me that the relationship between identity and liberation is much more problematic than we sometimes care to admit. To the extent that identity means being at-one with oneself, then it necessitates the repression of a difference within, a repression which Jacques Derrida sees as characteristic of the phallologocentric discourse of the West. However, even though I am not willing to equate identity with liberation, neither am I willing to claim that it is either possible or desirable to forgo identity; again, I ask only for a more skeptical approach to the issue of identity, an approach that refuses to accept wholeheartedly the notion that identity is liberating.

17.　For a meditation on crypts and encrypting, especially as they relate to the psychoanalytic processes of introjection and incorporation, see Jacques Derrida's "Fors," trans. Barbara Johnson in *The Georgia Review* 31 (1977), pp. 64–116.

18.　Dolores Hayden, *The Grand Domestic Revolution: A History of Feminist Designs for American Homes, Neighborhoods, and Cities* (Cambridge: MIT Press, 1981), pp. 182–277.

19.　Some such discomfort may account for Gilbert and Gubar's defensive insistence that "we can be sure that Gilman . . . knew that the cure for female despair must be spiritual as well as physical, aesthetic as well as social" (*Madwoman*, p. 92).

7

Teaching "Women in America": Some Notes on Pedagogy and Charlotte Perkins Gilman

Maria Bruno

I had the opportunity to teach a course entitled "Women in America" at Michigan State University in the spring of 1988. Primarily developed and monitored by the Women's Studies Department, the course combines composition with the content area of twentieth-century women's history and literature. For the most part, the course is enrolled with female students (95% of my students were female)—I'm not sure why. Perhaps the title alone scares male students away. Maybe they think it is a trivial endeavor, or maybe they think if they're "caught" taking it, they'll be marked for life: labeled a wimp, scorned and left dateless by discerning women who prefer "real" men, blacklisted from fraternities or any future membership with Club Med. Whatever the reason, I found myself developing a composition course primarily for women students and I took up the challenge enthusiastically. I wanted to support their efforts to use language to free themselves from restrictions imposed by cultural and educational traditions. I wanted to provide them with a female literary tradition and a knowledge of the history of women who have struggled, worked and created in private and public life.

I knew I would give my usual opening lecture on Hypatia, the Alexandria Neo-Platonist philosopher-teacher, who, while driving to the academy where she taught, was attacked by a gang of jealous monks. They dragged her from her chariot, carried her into a church, stripped her, and scraped the flesh from her body with oyster shells. Then I'd follow this with the tale of "The Witch of Newbury" who, while surfing skillfully on a makeshift board in a moat, was attacked by a gang of jealous knights while she was hanging ten. They ambushed her, dragged her from the water, slashed her head, beat her and shot her. They displayed what was left. (By this time, the students should hear a major CLICK coming from their collective unconscious. Then I would cover various imprisonments, hangings, and burnings, before I'd end with Nathaniel Hawthorne berating that "damn mob of scribbling women." He wrote in a letter to editor James T. Fields "all women as author's (*sic*) are feeble and tiresome . . ." and "should be forbidden to write, on pain of having their faces scarified with an oyster shell."[1] (CLICK) I would then ask my students: "What's more horrible, Hawthorne knowing about Hypatia and still making that statement? Or his not knowing of her at all?"

What better way to dispel Hawthorne's nineteenth-century paranoia than to begin my "Women in America" with a study of Charlotte Perkins Gilman's "The Yellow Wallpaper." Is it not the perfect addition to the theme of silencing women and silencing voices? Although Gilman professed didacticism, claiming in her autobiography, "I have never made any pretense of being literary,"[2] "The Yellow Wallpaper" remains a classic tale of Gothic horror which W.D. Howells included in his *Great Modern American Stories* of 1920. Her original intent, though, was "to reach Dr. S. Weir Mitchell, and convince him of the error of his ways."[3] Mitchell, it seems, was effective in silencing hundreds of depressed women—including, for a while, Gilman—by advocating "a rest cure" which kept women immobile, confined to a room and a bed (with nary a chariot or a surfboard, not to mention books or pens or paper). An initial decoding of "The Yellow Wallpaper" using feminist criticism takes it way beyond a Gothic descent into madness. Feminist critics have already made the necessary connections between the sex role of the protagonist and how it relates to themes of enclosure, silencing, and women's role in the act of creation.

"The Yellow Wallpaper" is an excellent beginning, but it is by no means a place to end when considering the body of Gilman's works. It seems to me, as I listen to some of my colleagues speak about "revising the canon of literature," they tend to create their own rigid canon of women's literature too. Some figure they can add "The Yellow Wallpaper" to their already male-dominated syllabi, or maybe *The Awakening* or *The Color Purple* then they have their bases covered and the Women's Studies people will leave them alone. But much of Gilman's work is an excellent example of an emerging woman's voice. Not only did she excel in her literary pursuits but in her sociopolitical tracts as well.

Before I discuss Gilman further, I want to provide a rationale for the course, "Women in America," and how I developed my objectives and the proposed curriculum.

I wanted to create a course that would provide the particular legacy germane for the female writing student. She has probably had a lifetime of cultural and educational messages that label her experience marginal, unheroic, "outside" of what is considered "real" human experience, because by virtue of her gender, those experiences are not male. She has, probably, not traveled the Mississippi River on a raft or struggled to build a fire in the Alaskan wilderness or gone trout fishing in the Big Two-Hearted River. She has suffered from the invisibility of the women writing before her, believing there are no serious women writers at all, because she has been denied a knowledge of a female literary tradition. She probably saw only two or three works by women in her school texts and anthologies, and those were most likely poems: one conceit about a spinning wheel by Anne Bradstreet and two very short poems by Emily Dickinson. (She may have memorized their first lines as I did, secretly reciting them for years, at the time not knowing why. "There is no frigate like a book," I whispered. "I heard a fly buzz when I died.")

Besides a lack of knowledge, the woman student may bring to class a culturally imposed timidity based on years of being rewarded for good behavior (i.e., passivity) in the classroom. Her timidity is also based on her real fear of male antagonism, coupled with the unspoken or unrecognized need for a female audience to validate her perceptions and experiences. Perhaps the female student lacks confidence and believes it is improper, even "unfeminine," to be creative at all. She has seen too few women painters, sculptors, novelists, poets, and film directors—to name a few—and believes, as I did long ago, that there are simply no serious women artists. She has seen too few female heroes, except perhaps a socially acceptable smattering: Florence Nightingale (nursing), Betsy Ross (sewing) and Emily Dickinson, again, of whom, I might add, my tenth-grade teacher said almost sorrowfully: *"But,* she never married."

I remember my first graduate-level poetry writing course. I was lectured by a fellow male student who did not like my use of the word "cervix" in a poem. "Why did I have to hear that word anyway?" he demanded, waving his arms in the air. (His poem that week, I remember, was about the industrial military complex and M-16s.) I thought, well, maybe it was offensive to him—the poem was about a male doctor cauterizing my cervix, and maybe the thought of the procedure for this student was "unpleasant." I was sufficiently silenced for the class period, pretending to take notes in the large margins of the paper. In actuality, I was doodling the word "ovary" running the words together like an angry stream: ovaryovaryovary.... The next week he brought in a poem about abortion, in which he used the word *cervix* four times, slamming it together with adjectives like "eroded," "swollen," "cauterized," and "perforated." I felt as if I had been slapped in the face. In all fairness, the male instructor made the student analyze the reasons he wrote the poem in the first place; but the student talked around his motivations, neglecting what I think was the real reason: he wanted to show me that a man could write about female experience and female body parts better than any woman could.

In an environment of mutual respect, women will no longer have to write for men. They will not have to sacrifice their own voice to convention; they will be able to create a language that grows from their own lives. They will transcend the cultural assumptions of conformity and passivity and begin to write. The primary goal of this woman-centered course is connecting the process of learning to write well with the student's own reality and not, as Adrienne Rich says in her description of goals for a minority developmental writing course, ". . . to simply teach him/her how to write acceptable lies in standard English."[4]

According to Elaine Showalter, the concept of creativity, literary history, or literary interpretation is based entirely on male experience and put forward as universal.[5] If we make the assumption that writers learn to write by discovering the validity and variety of their own experience, and, in the instance of women, if the cultural message is that male experience is the only valid experience ("A writer must have balls," quips Norman Mailer), how can women, as writers, take themselves seriously? And if the literary role models are male, how can a woman writer take her predecessors seriously? And if the cultural messages to women have been that they live passive and compliant lives, and with female intelligence devalued, then we find women writers in every century, including our own, inhibited "both by economic dependence and by the knowledge that true writer signifies assertation while true woman signifies submission."[6] And if the language is patriarchal ("The oppressor's language," Adrienne Rich calls it), how does a woman writer find the basic linguistic tools to write and validate her own experience?

In *The Madwoman in the Attic,* Sandra Gilbert and Susan Gubar describe the ways the woman writer experiences her own gender as "a painful obstacle or even debilitating inadequacy."[7] They describe the loneliness of the female artist, who lives alienated from the standard male literary canon and yearning for validation from a female audience, and her very real anxiety about the impropriety of female invention.[8] The woman writer, suggests Gilbert and Gubar, faces greater obstacles than her male peers: ". . . all these phenomena of inferiorization mark the woman writer's struggle for artistic self-definition and differentiate her efforts at self creation from those of her male counterpart."[9]

It seems clear—judging from these critics and from the life experience of most women—that women experience definite problems of language and gender and silence. If all writers need to value and to speak the truth of their own experience, how can we get women writers to value their own "selves" and to handle what Joanna Russ calls "the unlabeled, disallowed, disavowed, and even consciously perceived experience which cannot be spoken about because it has no embodiment in existing art"?[10] Women writers are the outsiders, the "Other," people living outside the patriarchy, outside current fictional myths reinforced on the existing canon of literature; they do not even own the language. According to Nina Baym, little is expected of them in their role in the drama of creation: ". . . [E]ither she is to be silent, like nature, or she is the creator of conventional works, the spokesperson of society, what she might do as an innovator in her own right is not perceived."[11]

Charlotte Perkins Gilman was an innovator in her own right, and for pe-
dogogical purposes, serves students as a model of a feminist visionary and a
writer. Throughout history, when women have chosen to write, they have been
haunted by what Gilbert and Gubar call an "anxiety of authorship." In order to
write at all they had to defy societal assumptions of what was feminine and
proper, let alone what was a writer (which translates to writer = male; women
do not write). A female writer who was presumptuous enough to defy cultural
stereotypes and write became an anomaly, a freak, or at the very least, "unfeminine." And if she demonstrated the least bit of fervor, political or otherwise,
she could be branded "a hyena in petticoats" (Mary Wollstonecraft), or a "tran-
scendental heifer" (Margaret Fuller), or in Gilman's own case, after relinquish-
ing custody of her daughter Katharine to Charles Stetson in order to write, an
"unnatural mother." So women apologized for their writing and hid behind male
pseudonyms. Or to survive as writers, they imitated male texts. Or they be-
haved, in style and thematic approach, like conventional modest ladies. But
Gilman did none of this, except, perhaps, write her fiction in the "commonly
shared forms and structures of her day—farces, domestic novels, mysteries,
adventure stories," but she "infused them with her own brand of feminism and
socialism."[12] She defied patriarchal assumptions and took risks as a woman, a
humanist, and as a writer. The themes that she introduced in her fiction and
political tracts are still relevant to contemporary women.

Perhaps this is why Carl Degler calls *Women and Economics* the treatise
that propelled her into being "the leading intellectual in the woman's movement
in the United States during the first two decades of the twentieth century."[13] In
Women and Economics, Gilman studies the origins of patriarchy, the sexuoeconomic relationship of marriage, the women's movement as a catalyst for
"economic equality and freedom," the equitable division of labor in the home
and marketplace. In the second half of the treatise, Gilman becomes increasingly
radical. She deconstructs motherhood, removing it from the realm of a holy,
duty-bound mission, and introduces the prototype of the "kitchenless home"
which would ultimately eliminate sex-segregated household tasks by utilizing
professional housekeepers and food preparers. She foresaw the future of increased numbers of women in the workforce by advocating professionally
staffed childcare centers. Similar heretical themes can be found in *Concerning
Children, The Man-Made World, The Home,* and *Human Work.*

The topics of her fiction sound as if they could be listed on the production
rosters of Oprah, Donahue, or Sally Jessy Raphael: women as careerists, artists,
adventurers; women who are into sisterhood, living alone, having their own
money. Women who love men, but love their independence more. Women who
want men, turn into men, turn away from men. Gilman's men are not always
monsters, but often redeemable and capable of changing. Her women are intelli-

gent, resourceful, and willing to defy convention, and often (despite the ending of "The Yellow Wallpaper") break away from limiting circumstances to emerge whole and fully integrated.

The introduction of women writers as models becomes critical to a woman-centered writing course and it can spur students onto their own creative efforts. We have to convince them that published writings by women, and their own writings, are not merely trivial extensions of a male-defined code. We have to encourage our women students to examine the literary world of women, and the world of women in general, to break the culturally imposed stereotypes that damage confidence and suggest that women are enemies, especially enemies of literary creation.

So I began "Women in America" with Charlotte Perkins Gilman. Since most of her work is not anthologized in editions readily available to students, I developed a course pack that I felt encompassed the majority of her themes and concerns. I included "The Yellow Wallpaper," several of her other short stories, excerpts from her autobiography and political essays. She became a springboard for my students who, throughout the term, struggled to find their own voices in first-person narratives, oral and written family histories, journals, and research papers which included topics that Gilman would have approved of: childcare, comparable worth, sexual harassment in academia and the workplace, androgyny, women's health, and so on. She became also for my students a model of a woman who defied the societal restrictions of the domestic sphere, and who transcended patriarchal definition (all the monks and knights and Hawthornes of her era) to emerge as the leading intellectual of the feminist movement in the twentieth century.

Notes

1. Quoted in Joyce Warren's *The American Narcissus: Individualism and Women in Nineteenth-Century American Fiction* (New Brunswick, NJ: Rutgers University Press, 1984), p. 191.

2. Charlotte Perkins Gilman, *The Living of Charlotte Perkins Gilman* (New York: Arno Press, 1972), p. 284.

3. Gilman, p. 121.

4. Adrienne Rich, "Taking Women Students Seriously," in *On Lies, Secrets, and Silence* (New York: W. W. Norton & Co., 1979), p. 239.

5. Elaine Showalter, "Feminist Criticism in the Wilderness," in *Feminist Criticism* (New York: Pantheon Books, 1985), p. 247.

6. Alicia Ostriker, "The Thieves of Language: Women Poets and Revisionist Mythmaking," in *Feminist Criticism*, ed. Elaine Showalter (New York: Pantheon Books, 1985), p. 315.

7. Sandra M. Gilbert and Susan Gubar, *The Madwoman in the Attic* (New Haven: Yale University Press, 1979), p. 257.

8. Gilbert and Gubar, p. 50.

9. Gilbert and Gubar, p. 50.

10. Joanna Russ, *How to Suppress Women's Writing* (Austin: University of Texas Press, 1983), p. 160.

11. Nina Baym, "Melodramas of Beset Manhood: How Theories of American Fiction Exclude Women Authors," in *Feminist Criticism,* ed. Elaine Showalter (New York: Pantheon Books, 1985), p. 77.

12. Ann J. Lane, "The Fictional World of Charlotte Perkins Gilman," in *The Charlotte Perkins Gilman Reader* (New York: Pantheon Books, 1980), p. xviii.

13. Carl Degler, "Introduction" to *Women and Economics* (New York: Harper & Row, 1966), p. xiii.

8

The Gothic Prism: Charlotte Perkins Gilman's Gothic Stories and Her Autobiography

Juliann Evans Fleenor

Fictional forms can sometimes pervade the manner in which women shape their autobiographies. A case in point is the Gothic, a literary genre popular with female readers and authors for nearly two centuries. Identified as women's fiction and analyzed by feminist critics for evidence of women's experiences, it has been suggested that the Gothic has been used to voice rebellion and anger over the status of women; its themes of madness and disintegration have been analyzed for proof of women's victimization. The female experience, it has been suggested, is that of victim in an androcentric society, and the Gothic form with its ambivalent female symbolism and its psychological effect has been congenial for expressing that ambivalent experience for both readers and writers. In particular, the Gothic has been a form which has expressed women's need for and fear of maternity. Women writers have used the Gothic to convey fear of maternity and its consequent dependent mother/infant relationship as well as a fear of the mother and a quest for maternal approval.

I would like to propose in the following discussion that the Gothic form is one framework through which Charlotte Perkins Gilman shaped her autobiography as well as generalized about the female experience. Its use is both limiting and yet revealing—limiting in that it reduces Gilman's life to that of a victim; revealing in that its use suggests that the major conflict in Gilman's life was with her female self, with her mother, and with the very act of creation. Nancy K. Miller has suggested that women's fiction has been about the plots of fiction and not about life.[1] Might it also be possible that women's autobiography, at least in this instance, is about the plots of fiction *and* about life? In an attempt

This article originally appeared in *The Female Gothic*, ed. Juliann Fleenor (Montreal: Eden Press, 1983), pp. 227–41.

to answer that question, let me first discuss the nature of autobiography and the nature of women's autobiographies.

Whatever division existed between fiction and autobiography has been disappearing for some time, if it ever existed at all.[2] Once, autobiography was commonly assumed to be real and fiction unreal. Increasingly, critics of autobiography have been seeking form, shape, and unity, all common to literary forms. But that literary basis has been difficult to discover or define. Some critics have suggested that autobiographical form is determined by the writer's desire to discover one identity based on one facet of the personality.[3] Reality is simplified, and a pattern is imposed on the writer's life with a coherent story. On the other hand, Francis Hart has maintained that writers have complicated and shifting intentions which account for autobiography as a changing and varied form within the same work.[4] William Spengemann has attempted to synthesize these two poles by asserting that: "We must view autobiography historically, not as one thing that writers have done again, and again, but as the pattern described by the various things they have done in response to changing ideas about the nature of the self, the ways in which the self may be apprehended, and the proper methods of reporting these apprehensions."[5]

In his study, *The Forms of Autobiography,* Spengemann examines fiction and autobiography by men, claiming that autobiography has been found "to assume fictive forms in the modern era."[6] The questions Spengemann asks about autobiography are, how does the self know the self, and how is the self to be reconciled with the absolute. He concludes: "What makes *Sartor Resartus* and *David Copperfield* autobiographies . . . is not the inclusion of autobiographical materials but their efforts to discover, through a fictive action, some ground upon which conflicting aspects of the writer's own nature might be reconciled in complete being."[7]

Spengemann's conclusions have only limited application to women's autobiographies. Estelle Jelinek suggests that women's autobiographies differ generally from those written by men. She points out these three characteristics: an emphasis in male autobiographies on the public life, while women write about their personal lives; understatement in women's autobiographies as women camouflage their feelings and distance themselves from their lives; and irregular narratives in women's autobiographies rather than an orderly linear chronology.[8] The first two appear contradictory; the emphasis upon the personal leads a reader to expect that women would reveal their feelings; yet distancing occurs. Gilman's autobiography only partially fits these general characteristics. She writes consistently about her public life, stressing her commitment to the social welfare rather than the private. She writes of her personal experience; but it is always generalized to the plight of other women. Finally, her narrative is linear, beginning with her early life and proceeding chronologically to her death.

Spengemann has suggested that fiction and autobiography seek a reconciliation of the writer's nature into what might be construed as an absolute, a quest for completeness. Women's autobiographies have for the most part ignored that quest by keeping to the private sphere, not the public one. Thus, the female identity has been defined through its relationships with others, not by its own dimensions. Gilman's autobiography fits this definition.

Spengemann's approach to fiction through autobiography, however, is intriguing.[9] I would suggest that if fiction can be analyzed through autobiography, then autobiography might in turn be analyzed through a literary form, the Gothic. The Gothic paradigm has been and continues to be an important vehicle for women writers. If he is correct, and if autobiography is the thing that writers "have done in response to changing ideas about the nature of self," then the form might not be so fluid and changing in relation to women's autobiographies. The Gothic form can be used to suggest that the nature of the female self has not been fluid and changing, but limited within a patriarchal culture. Women's autobiography could be described as the Gothic has been, as ambivalent and concerned with women's lives in the private sphere. In this instance *The Living of Charlotte Perkins Gilman* offers a unique opportunity to relate Gilman's puzzling autobiography to her Gothic stories. This analysis also reveals that she wrote in response to the ideas of the nature of woman and woman as mother. Such a study gives an opportunity to move between fiction and autobiography and perhaps further define the nature of women writers and the nature of the mother-author conflict women face.

Moving between Gilman's short story, "The Yellow Wallpaper," and her autobiography is not a novel suggestion. Readers have consistently connected Gilman's story and her life. Perhaps the popularity of the Gothic itself has also prepared women readers for this connection, for the story graphically describes the nervous breakdown of a woman after she is confined to her country home by her physician-husband and told not to work but to rest. Since Gilman herself experienced a similar breakdown, readers have generally accepted her assertion that the story was a literal transcription of her life. She writes in her autobiography that:

> [T]he real purpose of the story was to reach Dr. S. Weir Mitchell, and to convince him of the error of his ways. I sent him a copy as soon as it came out, but got no response. However, many years later, I met someone who knew close friends of Dr. Mitchell's who said he had told them that he had changed his treatment of nervous prostration since reading "The Yellow Wallpaper." If that is a fact, I have not lived in vain.[10]

Ann Douglas, Gail Parker, Patricia Meyer Spacks, and Elaine Hedges have all accepted Gilman's statements and have interpreted the story accordingly as "the form of her life," as the story of Gilman's "blighted, damaged" yet "transcendent" life, and as the story of "a woman who is denied the right to be an adult."[11] These feminist critics move, as Gilman intended, from the story to the autobiography and back again. Her journals and letters support this interpretation as well. Sandra Gilbert and Susan Gubar have recently suggested that Gilman's story is a tale of all literary women trapped in a house which rapidly becomes the narrator's own body.[12]

Although it is not generally known, Gilman wrote at least two other Gothic stories around the same time as "The Yellow Wallpaper." All three were published in *The New England Magazine*. At the time that "The Rocking Chair" and "The Giant Wistaria" were written, Gilman and her young daughter, Katharine, were living in the warmth of Pasadena, separated from her husband, Charles Walter Stetson. Gilman later noted in her papers: "'The Yellow Wallpaper' was written in two days, with the thermometer at one hundred and three in Pasadena, Ca."[13] Her husband was living on the east coast, and, perhaps coincidentally, all three stories appear to be set in a nameless eastern setting, one urban and two rural. All three display similar themes, and all three are evidence that the conflict, central to Gilman's Gothic fiction and later to her autobiography, was a conflict with the mother, with motherhood, and with creation.

In all three stories women are confined within the home; it is their prison, their insane asylum, even their tomb. A sense of the female isolation which Gilman felt, of exclusion from the public world of work and of men, is contained in the anecdote related by Zona Gale in her introduction to Gilman's autobiography. After watching the approach of several locomotives to a train platform in a small town in Wisconsin, Gilman said, "'All that, . . . and women have no part in it. Everything done by men, working together, while women worked on alone within their four walls!'"[14] Female exclusion, women denied the opportunity to work, or their imprisonment behind four walls, led to madness. Her image, interestingly, does not suggest a female subculture of women working together; Gilman was working against her own culture's definition of women, and her primary antagonists were women like her own mother.

"The Rocking Chair" perhaps suggests conflict with an androcentric society. A beautiful, golden-haired girl sits in a clumsy, brass rocking chair, "something from the old country."[15] She is visible to two young men, but only from a distance. They describe her in terms of a feminine enigma: "Hers was a strange beauty, infinitely attractive, yet infinitely perplexing." They can never see her while they too are in the house, only while they are outside. The chair and its origins represent the effect that an androcentric tradition has upon women and men. The fact that she cannot be seen except from a distance indicates how the man relates to the woman. In this case she is in a rocking chair rather than on a pedestal. Originally the story was called "Inanimate," with the adjective modifying perhaps the girl, perhaps the chair. Her existence is created by the two men. They are doubles of each other, together since childhood, at school, as college roommates, and now as hack journalists. They "are organisms so mutually adapted that they never seem to weary each other." But that is not true of their relation to the unnamed girl.

The chair the girl occupies is described by Maurice, the narrator: "I never saw a chair so made to hurt as that one. It was large and heavy and ill-balanced, and every joint and corner so shod with brass." When asked about its origin, the landlady, whom they call Mrs. Sphynx, replies, "It is Spanish . . . Spanish oak, Spanish leather, Spanish brass, Spanish —." Maurice describes it in detail:

> It was a strange ill-balanced thing that chair, though so easy and comfortable to sit in. The rockers were long and sharp behind, always lying in wait for the unwary, but cut short off in front; and the back was so high and so heavy on top that what with its weight and the shortness of the front rockers, it tipped over forward with an ease and a violence equally astounding.
>
> This I knew from experience, as it had plunged over upon me during some of our frequent encounters with it. Hal also was a sufferer, but in spite of our manifold bruises, neither of us would have had the chair moved, for did not she sit in it, evening after evening, and rock there in the light of the setting sun?

Each man sees the other in the chair with the girl in his arms, and each claims to be sitting in the chair alone. Consequently, each grows suspicious of the other; they quarrel and end their friendship. Gilman appears to be satirizing the male proclivity to worship of a nonexistent woman.

In the manuscript the landlady is identified as the girl's mother. There is also the assertion that the mother/landlady keeps the girl away from the two men and the neighbors. The neighbors pity the daughter because the mother refuses to be sociable and keeps the daughter from being so. Neither leaves the house; the narrator notes: "Of course we made covert inquiries in the neighborhood, but nothing new could be elicited. That there was a pretty daughter, often seen in the window, that the mother was reserved and disagreeable neither calling nor returning calls, and that everybody pitied the daughter—that was all." The implication is that the mother imprisoned the girl. However, this description is eliminated from the published story, leaving it much tighter in focus. The omission of the neighbors' account makes the existence of the girl and the mother less possible.

Gilman could not or would not draw the mother/daughter relationship with any sense of reality. There are no conversations between them in either the manuscript or the published version. The narration is restricted to the male point of view. In fact, although the landlady is identified as the mother, at one point she denies it. All this takes place in an empty house in an unnamed city, where the light is usually shut out. The narrator describes the scene: "A waving spot of sunshine, a bright signal light, that caught the eye at once on a waste of commonplace houses and all the dreariness of a narrow city street. Across some low roof that made a gap in the wall of masonry, shot a level brilliant beam of the just setting sun, and struck directly on the golden head of a girl in an upper window." Nature is kept out of this place, except when it enters through one "brief signal light" which ends on the nonexistent girl.

There are similarities between "The Rocking Chair" and "The Yellow Wallpaper" other than those mentioned above. The men beg at the door for the young woman to open it, as does the husband in "The Yellow Wallpaper." They search for her: "Door after door I knocked at, tried and opened; room after room I entered and searched thoroughly—in all that house, from cellar to garret, was no furnished room but ours, no sign of human occupancy. Dust, dust and cobwebs everywhere—nothing else." The house is empty, actually having never been occupied, and they discover they are the only occupants. The girl here becomes one of the figures behind the wallpaper in the later story, and the landlady/mother becomes the woman outside of the wallpaper.

The friends are separated by this vision, one dies, killed with the same kind of slashes left by the rocking chair. The narrator returns to his room:

> The room was empty, both rooms utterly devoid of all life. Yes all, for with the love of a whole lifetime surging up in my heart I sprang to where Hal lay beneath the window and found him cold and dead.
> Dead, and most horribly dead—those heavy merciless blows—those deep three-cornered gashes—I started to my feet—even the chair had gone.
> And again that whispered laugh!

With that nearly comic image of the rocking chair inflicting mortal wounds Gilman ends her Gothic tale, one which combines satire with horror, as she satirizes the male need to create charming young women to pursue even when that pursuit leads to the death of a best friend, or perhaps a part of themselves.

The setting in "The Rocking Chair" is the city; in "The Giant Wistaria," it is the country. "The Giant Wistaria," however, is similar to "The Yellow Wallpaper" in that both have as a theme the punishment of women, by both women and men, for being women. In fact, women are punished for having babies because doing so imprisons them in the social structure symbolized by the house. The house is again employed as a major symbol; it is haunted, as is the manor house in "The Yellow Wallpaper," by female vulnerability and the sin of maternity.

The young woman in "The Giant Wistaria" has had an illegitimate child, given to a servant by her parents. The woman wears a carnelian cross, one of agate, which could be either flesh colored or deep red. Like Hester Prynne, she wears a symbol of her adultery. Unlike "The Rocking Chair," however, the maternal conflict is explicit here: the mother tells the daughter "Meddle not with my new vine child! See! Thou hast already broken the tender shoot! Never needle or distaff for thee, and yet thou wilt not be quiet!" The parents even lock her in her room, binding her to keep her there.

A hundred years later, after the death of all those involved, four young people—two women and two men—visit the house and find a huge wistaria vine covering the house. Nature now runs wild:

> The old lilacs and laburnums, the pires and syringa, nodded against the second-story windows. What garden plants survived were great ragged bushes or great shapeless beds. A huge wistaria covered the whole front of the house. The trunk, it was too large to call a stem, rose at the corner of the porch by the high steps, and had once climbed its pillars; but now the pillars were wrenched from their places and held rigid and helpless by the lightly wound and knotted arms.
> It fenced in all the upper story of the porch with a knitted wall of stem and leaf; it ran along the eaves, holding up the gutter that once supported it; it shaded every window with a heavy green; and the drooping, fragrant blossoms made a waving sheet of purple from roof to ground.

Like the house in Shirley Jackson's novel, *We Have Always Lived in the Castle,* nature has reclaimed the house. Like "The Yellow Wallpaper," the four visitors begin to see female figures throughout the grounds, even though the house is unoccupied. A group of trees look like "a crouching, haunted figure" of a woman picking huckleberries. For one of the visitors the vine itself takes on human form and appears as "'a writhing body—cringing—beseeching!'" One of the men begins to dream of the young mother, and soon they discover that she has been buried under the porch in the roots of the giant wistaria. The woman, through the vine has held the house in her arms, and her baby—dead at the age of a month—lay in the old well in the basement. Thus, pregnancy leads first to ostracism and then to death for both mother and child.

This fate might be construed as apt punishment for illegitimacy, but no such confusion exists in "The Yellow Wallpaper." Diseased maternity is explicit in Gilman's third Gothic story. The yellow wallpaper symbolizes more than confinement, victimization, and the inability to write. It suggests a disease within the female self. When the narrator peels the wallpaper off, "It sticks horribly and the pattern just enjoys it! All those strangled heads and bulbous eyes and the waddling fungus growths just shriek with derision."[16] This passage describes more than the peeling of wallpaper: the "strangled heads and bulbous eyes and waddling fungus" imply something strange and terrible about birth and death conjoined, about female procreation, and about female physiology. Nature is perverted here, too. The narrator thinks of "old foul, bad yellow things." The smell "creeps all over the house." She finds it "hovering in the dining-room, skulking in the parlor, hiding in the hall, lying in wait for me on the stairs." Finally, "it gets into my hair."

The paper stains the house in a way that suggests the effect of afterbirth.[17] The house, specifically in this room, becomes more than a symbol of a repressive society; it represents the physical self of the narrator as well. She is disgusted, perhaps awed, perhaps frightened of her own bodily processes. The story establishes a sense of fear and disgust, the skin crawls and grows clammy with the sense of physiological fear that Ellen Moers refers to as the Female Gothic.[18]

My contention that one of the major themes in the story, punishment for becoming a mother (as well as punishment for being female), is supported by the absence of the child. The child is taken away from the mother, almost in punishment, as was the child in "The Giant Wistaria." This differs from Gilman's experience; she had been told to keep her child with her at all times. In both the story and in Gilman's life, a breakdown occurs directly after the birth of a child. The narrator is confined as if she had committed a crime. Maternity— the creation of a child—is combined with writing—the creation of writing—in a way that suggests they are interrelated and perhaps symbiotic, as are the strange toadstools behind the wallpaper.

The pathological nature of both experiences is not surprising, given the treatment Gilman received, and given the fact that maternity reduced women to mothers and not writers. Childbirth has long been a rite of passage for women. But the question is, where does that passage lead? Becoming a mother leads to a childlike state. The narrator becomes the absent child.

All three of these stories have similar themes related to the Gothic as it is used by women. All depict women trapped and driven insane in a patriarchal society. They illustrate a conflict with the mother or with maternity itself, for all are about the act of creating a narrative; they are all processes of discovery. In "The Rocking Chair" the young man pieces together the story for the reader; in "The Giant Wistaria" the two couples discover through intuition, dreams, and finally the removal of the old porch, the secret of the house; and in "The Yellow Wallpaper" the narrator—this time nameless—reads the wallpaper, creating figures and a diseased nature from its faded surfaces.

Imagination is diseased in these stories, like the overgrown gardens in "The Giant Wistaria," like the abandoned garden in "The Yellow Wallpaper," and like the darkened city street where one beam of sunlight reaches the head of the young woman. In two of these stories the creation of an infant is related to the creation of the narrative. In both the infants are conspicuous by their absence, further evidence of a diseased female imagination. In the hands of a female writer, diseased imagination and madness become diseased maternity; for literary creation is directly related to the creation of a child. How these themes relate to Gilman's autobiography, written some twenty-five years later, is the subject of the remainder of this essay.

When Gilman begins her autobiography she makes her mental breakdown the most significant event in her life. Her daughter, Katharine, or perhaps Zona Gale, or both, chose to end the biography with her suicide note, thus, making the breakdown and the suicide important. Readers have since been making a similar emphasis. For example, Ann J. Lane, in her recent edition of Gilman's fiction, chooses to begin her introduction with Gilman's suicide. Lane presents it as an indication of "the struggle and the triumph of her life."[19] Seeing it as a "choice," "an act of will, of rationality, of affirmation," Lane sets it within the shape of Gilman's life, as described by Gilman. Perhaps Lane is correct in asserting that Gilman's death was a rational act, and it certainly agrees with the persona described by Gilman in her autobiography—the woman who reasoned everything out and then acted solely on reason. The problem is not one of truth but of choice and emphasis. The problem is also one of reading an autobiography as a factual transcription of a life rather than as a literary form.

While Gilman's suicide might seem both heroic and rational, it is also a familiar ending in fiction by women. Madness, death, and suicide have predominated in women's fiction, and the Gothic form, with its themes of madness and disintegration, pervades the fiction of such writers as Shirley Jackson, Doris Lessing, Charlotte and Emily Brontë, and Sylvia Plath, not to mention the ending of such works as *The Awakening, Wuthering Heights,* and *The Mill on the Floss.* Here is an instance of autobiography being conceptualized as literary form and perhaps with the aid of literary form. I am not suggesting that Gilman's life was conflict-free and that art and fiction shaped her life. No, Gilman's autobiography was written within the context of the conflict with her society. She was repeatedly labeled an outcast. We need not rely upon her autobiography for testimony to that fact. The California newspapers reported unfairly upon her divorce from Walter Stetson, for example, making her a notorious woman. Surely this conflict shaped her autobiography. Even if conflict had not been so open and so frequent throughout her life, such conflict frequently molds the writing of women's autobiographies. As Norine Voss observes: "The act of writing autobiography reawakens and exacerbates the autobiographer's life-long conflict between rigid definitions of femininity and her need for self-esteem and a vocation. The conflicts between egoism and unselfishness, self-love and self-effacement can affect the narrative mode and the form of autobiography."[20] While Voss is writing about women autobiographers in general, her observation has particular revelance to Gilman. Certainly she had a lifelong conflict between what she termed "service" and her role as a woman and mother, and between her egotism and her desire to be unselfish.

Yet that conflict was not as great as one might expect, for Gilman's feminism is, of course, not the feminism of 1982. Like her contemporaries, she apparently believed that women were morally superior to men and the role of social reformer adapted itself well to this belief. Building on Lester Ward's theory, that woman is the basis of society and man only the appendage, and upon Social Darwinism, Gilman wrote the following passages in *Women and Economics* (1898):

The naturally destructive tendencies of the male have been gradually subverted to the conservative tendencies of the female, and this so palpably that the process is plainly to be observed throughout history. Into the male have been bred, by natural selection and unbroken training, the instincts and habits of the female, to his immense improvement.

With a full knowledge of the initial superiority of her sex and the sociological necessity for its temporary subversion, woman should feel only a deep and tender pride in the long patient ages during which she has waited and suffered, that man might slowly rise to full racial equality with her. She could afford to wait. She could afford to suffer.

In her subordinate position, under every disadvantage, through the very walls of her prison, the constructive force of woman has made man its instrument, and worked for the upbuilding of the world.

Women can well afford their period of subjection for the sake of a conquered world, a civilized man.

The woman's movement rests not alone on her larger personality, with its tingling sense of revolt against injustice, but on the wide, deep sympathy of women for one another.

A society whose economic unity is a sex-union can no more develop beyond a certain point industrially than a society like the patriarchal, whose political unit was a sex-union, could develop beyond a certain point politically.[21]

In these excerpts Gilman expounds the theory of the innate superiority of the female based on the nineteenth-century doctrine of the spheres. This position made the work of Jane Addams and her contemporaries possible; it did not limit them. So the conflict that Gilman felt was not over the definition of femininity but the definition of motherhood.[22]

It is this conflict, over her abandonment of her daughter to her father, viewed by her contemporaries as "unnatural" that most concerns her. It is this conflict which causes her to suggest that she is a mortally wounded woman, scarred for life, and that continues to shape her life and autobiography. Also, it is not surprising to find that it surfaces most in her Gothic stories and in her autobiography. As Lynn Z. Bloom has noted, women autobiographers assume the maternal role in the act of writing their life stories; they become their own mothers. The woman autobiographer "becomes the recreator of her maternal parent and the controlling adult in their literary relationship."[23] Such a role must surely result not in control but in excess and pathos when an autobiographer such as Gilman is trying to atone for what she considers her guilt. In addition, since she so completely rejected the role her mother had played—that of the submissive, long-suffering wife—the autobiography is also a self-justification for this rejection. But, as I pointed out above, others were doing similar service to their society and fitting it within the prescribed role; however, Gilman was unique; she was a mother, and she had rejected that role soundly and publicly.

Thus it is not surprising to find that as in her Gothic stories where women were punished for being women and for having children, in Gilman's autobiography she, too, is punished for having a child. Gilman suggests in the autobiography that Mitchell, the male physician, is punishing her as woman. She writes; "He had a prejudice against the Beechers. 'I've had two women of your blood here already,' he told me scornfully."[24] After his treatment of her for hysteria fails, she descends into madness. Furthermore, her description of that madness consists of a rejection of her child: "I made a rag baby, hung it on a doorknob and played with it. I would crawl into remote closets and under beds—to hide from the grinding pressure of that profound distress. . . ." (95). By hanging the baby on the doorknob, she figuratively destroys it; or she retreats into closets or under beds—to escape even that representative. Gilman needs to build a very strong case for the loss of her daughter, and she does so by claiming that the mental breakdown scarred her permanently, breaking her mind at the age of twenty-four:

> The result has been a lasting loss of power, total in some direction, partial in others; the necessity for a laboriously acquired laziness foreign to both temperament and conviction, a crippled life. . . . After the debacle I could read nothing—instant exhaustion preventing. As years passed there was some gain in this line; if a story was short and interesting and I was feeling pretty well I could read a little while. (98–99)

Yet letters to her second husband, Houghton Gilman, indicate that she read voraciously and even that he planned readings for her (much as her father had sent her reading lists years before).[25]

Further proof of my contention that Gilman's central conflict was with the role of mother and not woman is found in her description of her mother, Mary Fitch Perkins. Gilman complains about her mother's long-suffering passivity and describes herself positively as recreating herself—Athena-like—out of her own intellect and will. Her dissatisfaction with her mother's performance as a mother is clear in the autobiography. She argues that motherhood requires rationalism, discipline, and independence not "devotion to duty, sublime self-sacrifice" (11). Gilman attacks the traditional belief that maternal instinct exists and that every woman can be a mother simply because she has a womb. This attack arises from her argument that knowledge is to be acquired; it is not innate; nor is moral judgment innate. This position is in direct conflict with the one she took in *Women and Economics*. There, as pointed out above, she maintained that women were innately superior. Here she maintains that women must be taught motherhood. Yet, in her biography of Gilman, Mary Hill has pointed out that Gilman, who had no education to be a mother, regarded herself as a superior parent.[26] This contradiction appears to be necessary in order for her to argue that she had to give up her child on a logical basis, not because she could not stand the responsibility and self-sacrifice required of a mother.

Rejecting her mother and her actions in the autobiography, Gilman searches for mother figures, women she hoped would give her the approval and love she needed but could not herself give. She creates a sense of a female community which needs and supports the rational and independent self of the autobiography. The support and admiration of women nurtures the Gilman of the autobiography to the point that Gilman de-emphasizes her dependence upon men, particularly her long (and apparently happy) relationship with Houghton. This is consonant with her comment in *Women and Economics* that the woman's movement "rests . . . on the wide, deep sympathy of women for one another" (139).[27] Yet these relationships are misrepresented. Gilman is frequently the preacher, not the teacher, and her relationships with women, particularly her two love-relationships, are not warm and sustaining but at times sharp and bitter. In her autobiography she is particularly bitter about her relationship with the anonymous "Dora," a woman she lived with while still separated from Stetson and living on the west coast.[28] She also does not admit to the rifts between herself and Grace Channing, the woman who later married Stetson and raised Katharine for some years.

Since the purpose of this paper is to draw a relationship between the Female Gothic and Gilman's conflict with motherhood and creation, I will not dwell on the contradictions, omissions, and misrepresentations concerning her relationships with women that appear throughout Gilman's biography. That Gilman tied the two together is clear, both in her autobiography and in her Gothic stories. Once approval was denied to Gilman, rage, depression, and guilt followed. Her letters to Houghton give a graphic account of the psychological wounds she suffered. yet she was able to write numerous books, begin her own publishing company (Charlton) with Houghton, and write her own journal, *The Forerunner*. All of this was accomplished even though she claims in the autobiography that:

> When I am forced to refuse invitations, to back out of work that seems easy, to own that I cannot read a heavy book, apologetically alleging this weakness of mind, friends gibber amiably, "I wish I had your mind!" I wish they had, for a while, as a punishment for doubting my word. What confuses them is the visible work I have been able to accomplish. They see activity, achievement, they do not see blank months of idleness; nor can they see what the work would have been if the powerful mind I had to begin with had not been broken at twenty-four. (98–99)

Gilman, the unsuccessful mother, becomes the unsuccessful or suffering mother. Maternity and creation become thus intertwined in a most destructive and painful way. Contrary to her many claims, woman as author is depicted in the autobiography not as the forceful, decisive woman she intended, but as a wounded woman in constant torment.

Because of this conviction the autobiography does not end on the positive note one would expect from a woman stressing her long and successful life. Suicide in the context of this life is not an affirmation. The result is that the heroine of this work is damaged, controlled by others—male and female, permanently scarred, and not the logical, self-supporting, and successful woman she appeared to others.

She was undoubtedly both Gilmans—the highly emotional self and the logical self. She does try to draw for her readers the successful, creative Gilman, even to the point of omitting or misrepresenting some events. Yet the heroine of the autobiography is an injured woman, wounded in part by being female and most certainly by maternity. Her search for a mother to save and to guide her is a fruitless one. Precisely because of this search, this conflict, and these ambiguities, I would maintain that her autobiography resembles a literary form—one she was familiar with, and one congenial to expressing such ambivalences and such conflict—the Gothic.

The autobiography bears a startlingly close relationship to Gilman's Gothic stories. On the surface these stories, like her autobiography, convey her continued rebellion and anger over the treatment women received in a patriarchal society. On closer examination, however, they also reveal an ambivalent relationship with the mother, one that is duplicated in the autobiography. And, finally, they reveal an ambivalence about the capacity of female imagination and female creativity. Gilman's autobiography was shaped, like the stories, through a Gothic prism.[29] We see a woman at odds with her society, at odds with those of her own sex, and primarily at odds with herself. In her lifelong attempt to redefine American motherhood—not American womanhood—Gilman was singularly out of step with her contemporaries. Constantly under attack—both provoked and unprovoked—she lived her life as a Gothic heroine might: impetuously, righteously, and reasonably. Yet she insisted that she lived it virtually alone. The Gothic prism had become the Gothic prison.

Notes

1. Nancy K. Miller, "Emphasis Added: Plots and Plausibilities in Women's Fiction," *PMLA* 96 (January 1981), p. 46. Miller notes: "The point is . . . that the plots of women's literature are not about 'life' and solutions in any therapeutic sense, nor should they be. They are about the plots of literature itself, about the constraints of rendering a female life in fiction."

2. Earlier biography had been used to interpret fiction, a practice discarded in the practice of modern literary criticism. The attempt to link fiction and autobiography is a different endeavor and recognizes that autobiography, like fiction, has literary form and tradition.

3. For a full discussion of the many problems in defining autobiography, see William C. Spengemann, *Forms of Autobiography: Episodes in the History of a Literary Genre* (New Haven and London: Yale University Press, 1980), pp. 183–89.

4. Frances R. Hart, "Notes for an Anatomy of Modern Autobiography," *New Literary History* 1 (1970), pp. 485–511.

5. Spengemann, p. xiii.

6. Ibid.

7. Ibid., p. 132.

8. Estelle C. Jelinek, "Introduction: Women's Autobiography and the Male Tradition," in *Women's Autobiography: Essays in Criticism,* ed. Estelle C. Jelinek (Bloomington: Indiana University Press, 1980), pp. 1–20.

9. For Spengemann autobiography is a changing form, "an idea that changes with every new statement about it . . ." (p. 84). This essay does not attempt to generalize about women's autobiographies and the Gothic form, only to speculate on the connection of the two in the case of Charlotte Perkins Gilman.

10. Charlotte Perkins Gilman, *The Living of Charlotte Perkins Gilman,* Foreword by Zona Gale (1935; rpt., New York: Harper & Row, 1975), p. 121.

11. Gail Parker, "Introduction," in *The Oven Birds: American Women on Womanhood, 1820–1920,* ed. Gail Parker (Garden City, N.Y.: Doubleday, 1972), pp. 52–53; Patricia Meyer Spacks, *The Female Imagination* (1972; rpt.,New York: Avon Books, 1976), pp. 268–69; and Elaine Hedges, "Afterword," to "The Yellow Wallpaper" (Old Westbury, N.Y.: The Feminist Press, 1973), pp. 37–63.

12. Sandra M. Gilbert and Susan Gubar, *The Madwoman in the Attic: The Woman Writer and the Nineteenth-Century Literary Imagination* (New Haven and London: Yale University Press, 1979), pp. 88–89.

13. Folder 222, The Charlotte Perkins Gilman Collection, Schlesinger Library, Radcliffe College.

14. Gilman, *Living,* p. xxiv.

15. All quotations from "The Rocking Chair" and "The Giant Wistaria" have been taken from the published and manuscript copies of these stories on file at Schlesinger Library, Radcliffe College, Folder 222.

16. *The Yellow Wallpaper* (Old Westbury, N.Y.: The Feminist Press, 1973).

17. See Ellen Moers's discussion of *Frankenstein in Literary Women* (Garden City, N.Y.: Anchor Books, 1977), pp. 140, 142.

18. Ibid., p. 138.

19. Ann J. Lane, *The Charlotte Perkins Gilman Reader* (New York: Pantheon Books, 1980), p. [ix].

20. Norine Voss, "'Saying the Unsayable': An Introduction to Women's Autobiography," in *First Labor: An Interdisciplinary Women's Studies Journal,* ed. by Graduate Women in English (Bloomington, IN: Hysteria Press, 1980), p. 106.

21. *Women and Economics: The Economic Factor Between Men and Women as a Factor in Social Evolution* (1898; rpt., New York: Harper & Row, 1966), pp. 128, 129, 133, 134, 139, 144.

22. Jill Conway points out that "Once Addams had met Lester Ward at Hull House in the decade in the 1890s, she accepted Ward's assumption that the female was the prototype of the human being and the most highly evolved of the two sexes" ("Women Reformers and American Culture, 1870–1930," originally printed in the *Journal of Social History* 5 [Winter 1971–72], pp. 164–77; rpt in *Our American Sisters: Women in American Life and Thought*, eds. Jean E. Friedman and William G. Shade, 2nd ed. [Boston: Allyn & Bacon, 1976], pp. 307–308.) This acceptance by Addams, Lillian Wald, and Charlotte Perkins Gilman left these female reformers unable to cope with the later popularized Freudian stereotypes of women. In fact, as Conway points out, they may have contributed to the Twenties' frenzy over the flapper by never challenging the sexual stereotypes in their culture.

23. Lynn Z. Bloom, "Heritages: Dimensions of Mother-Daughter Relationships in Women's Autobiographies," in *The Lost Tradition: Mothers and Daughters in Literature*, ed. Cathy N. Davidson and E. M. Broner (New York: Frederick Ungar Publishing Co., 1980), p. 292.

24. *The Living of Charlotte Perkins Gilman*, p. 95. Subsequent references to this work will be placed in the text.

25. Letters to Houghton Gilman on file in the Charlotte Perkins Gilman Collection, Schlesinger Library, Radcliffe College.

26. Mary A. Hill, *Charlotte Perkins Gilman: The Making of a Radical Feminist* (Philadelphia: Temple University Press, 1980), pp. 230–31.

27. Gilman's autobiography demonstrates her lifelong search for mother figures and for women who would love and approve of her unconventional life.

28. The woman is identified in Gilman's papers as Adeline E. Knapp. For a discussion of this relationship see Mary A. Hill, pp. 189–94.

29. The title of this essay was suggested by the collection of essays, *The Prism of Sex: Essays in the Sociology of Knowledge*, eds. Julia A. Sherman and Evelyn Torton Beck (Madison, Wis.: The University of Wisconsin Press, 1979).

9

Brittle Jars and Bitter Jangles: Light Verse by Charlotte Perkins Gilman

Carol Farley Kessler

We do not usually think of the feminist Charlotte Perkins Gilman (1860–1935) as a funny woman. But even in her easily available autobiography, *The Living of Charlotte Perkins Gilman* (1935), Gilman shows us glints of sharp rejoinder and quick humor. For example, she explains

> Audiences are always better pleased with a smart retort, some joke or epigram, than with any amount of reasoning. In the discussion after a Forum lecture in Boston, an address on some aspect of the Woman Question, a man in the gallery, who evidently took exception to a dull rose fillet I wore in my hair, demanded to know how women could expect to equal men "so long as they took so much time fixing up their hair and putting ribbons in it?" There was some commotion, and cries of "Put him out!" but I grinned up at him cheerfully and replied, "I do not think it has been yet established whether it takes a woman longer to do her hair than it does a man to shave." This was not an answer at all, but it seemed to please every one but the inquirer.[1]

Do not believe Gilman's alleging that reason was absent from her repartee. On the contrary, how better to silence male objections to female ways than to point out a comparable "weakness"! Fanny Fern (Sara Payson Willis Parton, 1811–72) used the same technique when in her column "The Woman Question" (in *Caper-Sauce*, 1872), she suggested that men seek themselves to attain the degree of moderation-in-all-things that they would require of women as qualification for the ballot.[2]

Much of Gilman's light verse is less funny than the passage just quoted. In fact the light verse of *In This Our World* (1895) is often not funny at all, but rather satiric, sarcastic, even sardonic.[3] Because this volume is relatively scarce,

---

This article originally appeared in *Regionalism and the Female Imagination* 4 (1979): 35–43.

I shall quote liberally. I have, however, deliberately omitted those few verses now easily available.[4] We will see that Gilman's verse is to be valued not so much for its belletristic merit as for its social critique. Her verses question the basic assumptions that underlie our social structure and thus have unquestionably radical intent. Even in its first and briefer 1893 edition, Gilman noted, "That little book of verse brought small returns in cash but much in reputation" (*Living*, p. 169).

Gilman divided *In This Our World* into three parts: "The World," "The Woman," and "The March." The third section being uniformly humorless and the first, though often humorous, largely informed by now-discredited social Darwinist thinking, I have selected only from "The Woman"—in volume one quarter of the book. A quick survey of Gilman's themes in "The Woman" indicates that even before 1893, her thought focused upon the concerns that would inform her later books. We find verses which in their treatment of women's status point to *Women and Economics* (1898), others on motherhood and housekeeping that suggest *Concerning Children* (1900) and *The Home: Its Work and Influence* (1903). (Gilman's sociology as developed in *Human Work*, 1904, is suggested by the sections "The World" and "The March.")

A good verse to look at first is called "Woman of To-Day." Gilman heaps sarcasm and scorn upon the limited roles available to women, limitations starting to recede only in the decade of the 1970s. Gilman begins,

> You women of to-day who fear so much
> The women of the future, showing how
> The dangers of her course are such and such—
>   What are you now?

She continues with mock-heroic inflation,

> Mothers and Wives and Housekeepers, forsooth!
> Great names! you cry, full scope to rule and please!
> Room for wise age and energetic youth!—
>   But are you these?

And then she proceeds to negate women's effectiveness in each sacred female role:

> Housekeepers? Do you then, like those of yore,
> Keep house with power and pride, and grace and ease?
> No, you keep servants only! What is more,
>   You don't keep these!
> Wives, say you? Wives! Blessed indeed are they
> Who hold of love the everlasting keys,
> Keeping their husbands' hearts! Alas the day!

> You don't keep these!
> And mothers? Pitying Heaven! Mark the cry
> From cradle death-beds! Mothers on their knees!
> Why, half the children born—as children die!
>   You don't keep these!
> And still the wailing babies come and go,
> And homes are waste, and husbands' hearts fly far,
> There is no hope until you dare to know
>   The thing you are! (128–29)

In spite of her scorn, Gilman still hopes women will "dare to know" the ineffective and failing beings such limited roles have permitted.

Other verses further explicate the roles of wife, mother, and housekeeper. One selection, "The Modest Maid," details traditional—and deplorable—qualifications for the marriage market. Dated San Francisco, 1895, the verses follow:

> I am a modest San Francisco maid,
>   Fresh, fair, and young,
> Such as the painters gladly have displayed,
>   The poets sung.
>
> Modest?—Oh, modest as a bud unblown,
>   A thought unspoken;
> Hidden and cherished, unbeheld, unknown,
>   In peace unbroken.

(Four stanzas in which the Modest Maid excoriates the New Woman intervene. We will survive without those!)

> As veined flower-petals teach the passing bee
>   The way to honey,
> So printer's ink displayed instructeth thee
>   Where lies my money.
>
> Go see! In type and cut across the page,
>   Before the nation,
> There you may read about my eyes, my age,
>   My education,
>
> My fluffy golden hair, my tiny feet,
>   My pet ambition,
> My well-developed figure, and my sweet,
>   Retiring disposition.
>
> All, all is there, and now I coyly wait.
>   Pray don't delay.

My address does the Blue Book plainly state,
And mamma's "day." (166–67)

Not in the last "modest," this maid is striking for her vanity and ignorance.[5] Such heights of female desirability are rather depths and could hardly provide grounds for satisfactory companionship.

"Wedded Bliss," in the manner of a fable, suggests the nature of the "bliss" in store for married woman and man, according to Gilman's view of the differential socialization of the sexes:

"O come and be my mate!" said the Eagle to the Hen;
   "I love to soar; but then
   I want my mate to rest
   Forever in the nest!"
   Said the Hen, "I cannot fly,
   I have no wish to try,
But I joy to see my mate careering through the sky!"
They wed, and cried, "Ah, this is Love, my own!"
And the Hen sat, the Eagle soared, alone.

"O come and be my mate!" said the Lion to the Sheep;
   "My love for you is deep!
   I slay, a Lion should,
   But you are mild and good!"
   Said the Sheep, "I do no ill—
   Could not, had I the will—
But I joy to see my mate pursue, devour, and kill."
They wed, and cried, "Ah, this is Love, my own"
And the Sheep browsed, the Lion prowled, alone.

"O come and by my mate!" said the Salmon to the Clam;
   "You are not wise, but I am.
   I know sea and stream as well;
   You know nothing but your shell."
   Said the Clam. "I'm slow of motion,
   But my love is all devotion,
And I joy to have my mate traverse lake and stream
   and ocean!"
They wed, and cried, "Ah, this is Love, my own!"
And the Clam sucked, the Salmon swam, alone. (157–58)

The moral is clear: by rearing and interest the human sexes differ as much as species, yet are expected to live together in "wedded bliss." Gilman unveils the reality—such "love" is loneliness.

Examining in particular now the woman's role in marriage, in "To the Young Wife," Gilman asks hard questions: Are you as wife "content" to be wife, housekeeper, mother? Are you "convinced" that these only are women's duties? "Have you no dream of life in fuller store?" Then with sarcasm Gilman concludes,

> What holds you? Ah, my dear, it is your throne,
>   Your paltry queenship in that narrow place,
>   Your antique labors, your restricted space,
>   Your working all alone!
>
> Be not deceived! 'T is not your wifely bond
>   That holds you, nor the mother's royal power,
>   But selfish, slavish service hour by hour—
>   A life with no beyond! (131)

Her description suggests what the psychoanalyst Robert Seidenberg has aptly labelled the "trauma of eventlessness."[6] Gilman offers heavy content, though rendered in singsong patter—a disguise for her serious intent.

Further developing the role of mother, Gilman in "The Mother's Charge" shows the "two-edged humor-and-pathos" that Emily Toth finds in the work of Dorothy Parker, with the difference that Gilman was outspokenly profemale whereas Parker was not.[7] In this selection one female generation charges the next to be equally limited:

> She raised her head. With hot and glittering eye,
> "I know," she said, "that I am going to die.
> Come here, my daughter, while my mind is clear.
> Let me make plain to you your duty here;
> My duty once—I never failed to try—
> But for some reason I am going to die."
> She raised her head, and, while her eyes rolled wild,
> Poured these instructions on the gasping child:
>
> "Begin at once—don't iron sitting down—
> Wash your potatoes when the fat is brown—
> Monday, unless it rains—it always pays
> To get fall sewing done on the right days—
> A carpet-sweeper and a little broom—
> Save dishes—wash the summer dining-room
> With soda—keep the children out of doors—
> The starch is out—beeswax on all the floors—
> If girls are treated like your friends they stay—
> They stay, and treat you like their friends—the way
> To make home happy is to keep a jar—
> And save the prettiest pieces for the star
> In the middle—blue's too dark—all silk is best—
> And don't forget the corners—when they're dressed
> Put them on ice—and always wash the chest
> Three times a day, the windows every week—

We need more flour—the bedroom ceilings leak—
It's better than onion—keep the boys at home—
Gardening is good—a load, three loads of loam—
They bloom in spring—and smile, smile always, dear—
Be brave, keep on—I hope I've made it clear."

She died, as all her mothers died before.
Her daughter died in turn, and made one more. (160–61)

Showing a grim humor, also suggestive of E. M. Broner's recent work, *Her Mothers* (1975),[8] the mother reveals an *un*clear mind, totally muddled—we surmise, from her having lived a woman's life. The mélange of immediate directives—"the starch is out," "we need more flour"—with general housekeeping tips regarding washing, ironing, cleaning, and gardening as well as admonitions to "smile always" and "be brave" suggest a person unable to sort out her thoughts because overwhelmed by the minutiae of daily chores. More horrifying is the fact that this is a mother charging her daughter. Gilman's flip final couplet belies a sobering reality.

Two verses placed earlier in the collection particularize this reality also mentioned in "To the Young Wife." "Six Hours a Day" (136–37) details a mother's daily toil to serve her family's meals: "to refuse to cook is held the same/ As to refuse her wife and motherhood. Six mortal hours a day to handle food. . . ." Thus "each living man,/ Strive as he may" must acknowledge that "'His mother was a cook!'" Truly funny as well as pointed is "The Holy Stove," extolled in grand mock-heroic measure. It requires no comment beyond quotation:

O The soap-vat is a common thing!
    The pickle-tub is low!
The loom and wheel have lost their grace
In falling from the dwelling-place
    To mills where all may go!
The bread-tray needeth not your love;
    The wash-tub wide doth roam;
Even the oven free may rove;
But bow ye down to the Holy Stove,
    The Altar of the Home!

Before it bend the worshippers,
    And wreaths of parsley twine;
Above it still the incense curls,
And a passing train of hired girls
    Do service at the shrine.
We toil to keep the altar crowned
    With dishes new and nice,

And Art and Love, and Time and Truth,
We offer up, with Health and Youth,
        In daily sacrifice.

Speak not to use of a fairer faith,
        Of a lifetime free from pain.
Our fathers always worshipped here,
Our mothers served this altar drear,
        And still we serve amain.
Our earliest dreams around it cling,
        Bright hopes that childhood sees,
And memory leaves a vista wide
Where Mother's Doughnuts rank beside
        The thought of Mother's Knees.

The wood-box hath no sanctity;
        No glamour gilds the coal;
But the Cook-Stove is a sacred thing
To which a reverent faith we bring
        And serve with heart and soul.
The Home's a temple all divine,
        By the Poker and the Hod!
The Holy Stove is the altar fine,
The wife the priestess at the shrine—
        Now who can be the god?

Similarly lighthearted is "Feminine Vanity," whose final lines recall Gilman's fondness for animal fables as a way to puncture humanity's (often men's) assurance of being superior. Typically as in "The Modest Maid," she proceeds to show that her subject is the opposite of what she has labelled it to be.

FEMININE Vanity! O ye Gods! Hear to this man!
        As if silk and velvet and feathers and fur
        And jewels and gold had been just for her,
            Since the world began!

Where is his memory? Let him look back—all
        of the way!
        Let him study the history of his race
        From the first he-savage that painted his face
            To the dude of to-day!

Look at the soldier, the noble, the king!
        Egypt or Greece or Rome discloses
        The purples and perfumes and gems and roses
            On a masculine thing!

Look at the men of our own dark ages!
        Heroes too, in their cloth of gold,

> With jewels as thick as the cloth could hold,
>> On the knights and pages!
>
> We wear false hair? Our man looks big!
>> But it's not so long, let me beg to state,
>> Since every gentleman shaved his pate
>>> And wore a wig.
>
> Feminine Vanity! O ye Gods! Hear to these men!
>> Vanity's wide as the world is wide!
>> Look at the peacock in his pride—
>>> Is it a hen? (164–66)

Jarring brittle minds, jangling sometimes bitterly at numbed sensibilities, Gilman prods her audience to reconsider, to question the roots of traditional ways of being. The light tone of her verse I take to be a strategic calculation to disarm. In keeping with the contemporary authors Judy Little has examined, Gilman too attacks through satire, sarcasm, or scorn the traditions that are considered basic to social functioning: she "satirizes the norm."[9]

Because my aim has been to let Gilman speak for herself and thus call attention to this lesser known facet of her work—namely, her light verse, I have quoted much and analyzed little. In keeping with this practice, Gilman will have the last word. The final verses I include, although originally directed against woman suffrage opponents, seem today equally topical with reference to ERA opponents. Gilman calls these "The Women Do Not Want It."

> When the woman suffrage argument first stood
>> upon its legs,
> They answered it with cabbages, they answered it
>> with eggs,
> They answered it with ridicule, they answered it
>> with scorn,
> They thought it a monstrosity that should not have
>> been born.
>
> When the woman suffrage argument grew vigorous
>> and wise,
> And was not to be silenced by these apposite
>> replies,
> They turned their opposition into reasoning severe
> Upon the limitations of our God-appointed sphere.
>
> We were told of disabilities,—a long array of these,
> Till one would think that womanhood was merely
>> a disease;
> And "the maternal sacrifice" was added to the plan

Of the various sacrifices we have always made—
    to man.

Religionists and scientist, in amity and bliss,
However else they disagreed, could all agree to this,
And the gist of all their discourse, when you got
    down to it,
Was—we could not have the ballot because we
    were not fit!

They would not hear to reason, they would not
    fairly yield,
They would not own their arguments were beaten
    in the field;
But time passed on, and someway, we need not ask
    them how,
Whatever ails those arguments—we do not hear
    them now!

You may talk of woman suffrage now with
    an educated man,
And he agrees with all you say, as sweetly as he
    can;
'T would be better for us all, of course, if woman-
    hood was free;
But "the women do not want it"—and so it must
    not be!

'T is such a tender thoughtfulness! So exquisite
    a care!
Not to pile on our fair shoulders what we do not
    wish to bear!
But, oh, most generous brother! Let us look a little
    more—
Have we women always wanted what you gave to
    us before?

Did we ask for veils and harems in the Oriental
    races?
Did we beseech to be "unclean," shut out of sacred
    places?
Did we beg for scolding bridles and ducking stools
    to come?
And clamor for the beating stick no thicker than
    your thumb?

Did we seek to be forbidden from all the trades
    that pay?
Did we claim the lower wages for a man's full work
    to-day?

Have we petitioned for the laws wherein our shame
    is shown:
That not a woman's child—nor her own body—
    is her own?

What women want has never been a strongly act-
    ing cause
When woman has been wronged by man in churches,
    customs, laws;
Why should he find this preference so largely in
    his way
When he himself admits the right of what we ask
    to-day? (154–57)

Notes

1. Charlotte Perkins Gilman, *The Living of Charlotte Perkins Gilman* (New York: Harper Colophon, 1975), p. 328. All references are to this edition.

2. See quotation in Carol F. Kessler, "The Feminist Mock-Heroics of Elizabeth Stuart Phelps (1844–1911)," *Regionalism and the Female Imagination (RATFI)*, III (2 & 3), (Fall-Winter 1977–78), pp. 20–21.

3. Charlotte Perkins Stetson Gilman, *In This Our World* (Boston: Small, Maynard & Company, 1899). All quotations are from this edition. A somewhat smaller edition first appeared in Oakland, Cal.: McComb & Vaughan, 1893. A second edition was published in San Francisco: J. H. Barry and J. H. Marble, 1895. The same year T. G. Unwin, London, published an edition. Small, Maynard brought out their first edition in 1898, with others following in 1899, 1908, and 1913. In 1911 the New York firm of Charlton Company brought out a 24-page *Suffrage Songs and Verses*. The anthology, *A Book of American Humorous Verse* (Chicago: Herbert S. Stone & Co., 1904), included "Similar Cases" from the section "The World." The foregoing information comes from *The National Catalog: Pre-1956 Imprints*, Vol. 200 (London: Mansell, 1972).

4. Four selections are available in current anthologies: "Two Callings" in Gail Parker, ed., *The Oven Birds: American Women on Womanhood 1820–1920* (New York: Doubleday/Anchor, 1972), pp. 335–38; "She Walketh Veiled and Sleeping," "The Anti-Suffragists," "The Prophets" in Louise Bernikow, ed., *The World Split Open: Four Centuries of Women Poets in England and America, 1552–1950* (New York: Random/Vintage, 1974), pp. 223–26.

5. Another work by Gilman concerning premarital female ignorance is *The Crux: A Novel* (New York: Charlton, 1911), where the issue is the effect of venereal disease upon the unsuspecting bride and her unborn children.

6. Robert Seidenberg, "The Trauma of Eventlessness," *Psychoanalytic Review* 59 (1972): pp. 95–109; also available abridged in Jean Baker Miller, ed., *Psychoanalysis and Women* (Baltimore: Penguin, 1973), pp. 350–62.

7. Emily Toth, "Dorothy Parker, Erica Jong, and New Feminist Humor," *RATFI*, III (2 & 3) (Fall-Winter 1977–78), pp. 70–76, especially p. 72.

8. E. M. Broner, *Her Mothers* (1975; rpt. Bloomington: Indiana University Press, 1985).

9. Judy Little, "Satirizing the Norm: Comedy in Women's Fiction," *RATFI*, III (2 & 3), (Fall-Winter 1977–78), pp. 39–49.

10

Charlotte Perkins Gilman
and the Whitman Connection

Joann P. Krieg

Since the rediscovery in the past decade of Charlotte Perkins Gilman's short story "The Yellow Wallpaper," Gilman's name has once again come to the fore. Certainly the best piece of fiction she ever produced, the story has earned for its author a reputation almost as great as that which she enjoyed in her own lifetime. That reputation, though far-reaching, was mixed; for Gilman, whose literary output ranged far beyond "The Yellow Wallpaper," was well known early in this century as an ardent feminist socialist. Her treatise on *Women and Economics* (1898) is a textbook of the effects on nineteenth-century womanhood of industrial capitalism, and her attack on *The Home* (1903) offered a plan for women's economic independence that would take them into fields of labor outside the home, leaving their children in the care of others.

This is the same Charlotte Perkins Gilman who was one of the principal speakers at the final meeting of the Walt Whitman Fellowship in 1919, choosing as her subject Whitman's views on women. One wonders what Whitman's reaction would have been to a feminist ideal that took mothers from their homes and children, he who in *Democratic Vistas* had called for "a new founded literature [that] as perhaps the most precious of its results" would insure to the nation "a strong and sweet Female Race, a race of perfect Mothers. . . ."[1] Why was this arch feminist among the speakers at the Fellowship, and what connection could there have been between her philosophy and Whitman's? With no precise knowledge of what Gilman said on that occasion (the text of the address has not been found), all that can be done in an attempt to answer is to trace the connecting tissue of events, people, and ideas that led to the occasion.

This article originally appeared in *Walt Whitman Quarterly Review* 1 (March 1984): 21–25.

The first tenuous connections between Gilman and Whitman were remote ones, involving others more directly than they themselves. Nellis Tarr O'Connor, wife of Whitman's great champion, was aunt to Grace Ellery Channing, the woman to whom Gilman refers in the foreword of her autobiography as "my more than sister." So close were these two women that when Gilman and her first husband Walter Stetson divorced in 1893 and Walter promptly married Grace, the friendship was not affected. Grace Channing's parents had offered the comfort of their California home to William Douglas O'Connor in 1887 when he was suffering with a variety of illnesses. Just a year later they did all in their power to help establish Charlotte Gilman (then Stetson) who, with her daughter Katharine, had moved to Pasadena from Rhode Island for a trial separation from her husband.

That separation came after the events so terrifyingly fictionalized in "The Yellow Wallpaper," Charlotte's mental collapse following the birth of the child and her (mis?)treatment by Dr. S. Weir Mitchell. The story was first published in 1892 in *The New England Magazine,* and in 1899 Small, Maynard & Co., who had already published *Women and Economics,* brought it out as a small volume. The publishers then are the next connecting link between Gilman and Whitman, for it was to Small & Maynard that Whitman's literary executors committed his works. Small & Maynard were also the source for Grace Channing's volume of poems, *Sea-Drift* (names for Whitman's collection of sea poems) that was published at the same time as "The Yellow Wallpaper." Included among the poems was one written in Italy where Grace Channing was at the time of Whitman's death. Titled "The Voiceless Syllables of Grass," the poem gracefully contrasts the laurel, symbol of Italy's golden past, with Whitman's symbol, "The common herb One taught to sing." Horace Traubel noticed both volumes in *The Conservator* of March 1899 with a very positive review of Charlotte Perkins Stetson's "The Yellow Wallpaper" on one page, faced by Grace Channing Stetson's poem on Whitman on the other. (Charlotte did not acquire the name Gilman until her marriage to George Houghton Gilman in 1900.)[2] The year before, *The Conservator* had highlighted two of Gilman's poems from her published collection called *In This Our World,* which Traubel urged his readers to get either at a bookstore or library.[3]

Traubel was far more aware of Charlotte, however, than he was of Grace. The reason was simple: Charlotte had moved from being a convert in 1890 to the Nationalists's cause, to being in 1896 a confirmed Socialist and delegate to the International Socialist and Labor Congress in London. To facilitate her increased activities in the Socialist movement, she had, in 1894, sent their daughter to her ex-husband just before his marriage. Her ex-husband married Grace, who then assumed in practice the duties of motherhood that Charlotte espoused in theory.

Again and again in the years following this abdication of responsibility,

Gilman, who earned much of her reputation and her livelihood from the speaker's lectern, unhesitatingly spoke her thoughts on "The New Motherhood." An abstract of her lecture on the subject that appeared in the first volume of *The Forerunner,* the periodical Gilman wrote and published from 1910 to 1916, encapsulates the standards of The New Motherhood:

> First: The fullest development of the woman, in all her powers, that she may be the better qualified for her duties of transmission by inheritance; Second: The fullest education of the woman . . . concerning her great office and in her absolute duty of right selection—measuring the man who would marry her by his fitness for fatherhood. . . . Third: Intelligent recognition that child culture is the greatest of arts. . . .[4]

This, then, is the ground on which finally Gilman and Whitman meet, the glorification of the female as mother. Like Whitman, Gilman had little interest in women's suffrage; indeed, her interest in economics and what is now called sociology was all predicated on her belief that once freed from the confines of the home and made economically independent through their own labor, women would no longer feel obliged to choose husbands for economic reasons and could engage in selective mating. Such selective mating, she believed, would produce a higher civilization which women would acculturate. Though not so cosmic as Whitman's, it was a vision of perfect motherhood deeply akin to his. With what joy Gilman must have read Whitman's words in *Democratic Vistas,* " . . . I promulge new races of Teachers, and of perfect Women, indispensable to endow the birth-stock of a New World."[5] As another feminist admirer of Whitman, Mabel MacCoy Irwin, urged women to heed the poet's call and awaken to the need for what she termed a "Justified Motherhood," so Gilman developed the idea of The New Motherhood which demanded the full development of a woman's mental and physical powers, these to be brought to bear on the all-important selection of a father for her children.

Later, in the pages of *The Forerunner,* Gilman gave fictional form to this idealization in her Utopian myth, *Herland,* a picture of an all-female welfare state in which the highest welfare is that of its future citizens. It was during the years she published *The Forerunner* that Gilman came into contact with Whitmanites, though in 1919 she claimed, "When for some years my personal possessions were limited to one truck [this would have been in the first years after her divorce] I carried two books always: Olive Schreiner's 'Dreams' . . . and Whitman the Great."[6] Oddly enough, it was the Canadian disciples of Whitman to whom she became attached, that second generation of Whitmanites who after the death of Dr. Richard M. Bucke found their leadership in the feminist Flora MacDonald Dennison.

Dennison, a Gilman counterpart in the Canadian feminist movement, had a deep and sustained appreciation for Whitman. The last years of her life, from

1910 to her death in 1921, were devoted to fostering the Whitmanite movement in Canada. In 1910 she purchased "Bon Echo," a large tract of land, now a public park, in Peterborough, Ontario, where the Whitman followers had summer houses, and where Whitman was extolled at meetings devoted to his life and work. A huge hanging cliff that juts out over a lake there was dubbed "Old Walt," and here might be found of a summer Traubel, Henry S. Saunders—and Charlotte Perkins Gilman, who visited in 1918 and perhaps sooner. In the June 1916 *Forerunner* Gilman speaks glowingly of the summer community, claiming to have been there, and urges on her readers the periodical Flora MacDonald edited for the Whitman Club, *The Sunset of Bon Echo*. In the same year MacDonald refers, in the pages of *Sunset*, to "The Gilman Cottage" at Bon Echo, adding that Charlotte is "always welcome."[7]

The Whitman Club at Bon Echo was probably the final link in the chain of events, people, and ideas that led to Charlotte Perkins Gilman's participation in the last meeting of the Walt Whitman Fellowship in 1919. She was Mrs. Houghton Gilman by then, living with her husband in New York City while still working steadily for feminist and Socialist causes. Horace Traubel admired her greatly and no doubt it was he who invited her to speak at the Whitman Centenary. Judging by David Karsner's description of that night, Gilman must have been right at home. The after-dinner speeches had "a distinctly revolutionary flavor,' Karsner says, with applause for the mention of such names as Eugene V. Debs and Emma Goldman.[8] Traubel, sick as he was, relished every moment.

That summer Traubel insisted on traveling to Bon Echo for the Whitman Club's centenary celebration in August for which he had written a poem, "Walt, at Bon Echo, August 1919."[9] Charlotte Gilman had also written a small piece, called simply "Walt Whitman," that appeared in the summer issue of *The Sunset of Bon Echo*. In it she makes the point that Whitman's is the poetry that meets one's maturity when "besides music and emotion, we want thought, vision, strength in poetry."[10] Though Traubel died at Bon Echo in September of 1919 and Gilman lived on until 1935, they had shared in their lifetimes that maturity of poetic sensibility described by Gilman. Still, when one thinks of Traubel telling of the special appeal mothers always had for Whitman, how he spoke of the beauty and inspiration to be found in the sight of "a hale old woman, full of cheer as of years, who has raised a brood of hearty children," one wonders what he would have made of Gilman's "New Motherhood."[11]

Notes

1. Walt Whitman, *Prose Works 1892*, ed. Floyd Stovall (New York: New York University Press, 1964), 2:372.

2. Gilman's ancestry included the illustrious New England Beechers and Edward Everett Hale, whose review of *Leaves of Grass* in the *North American Review* for January 1856 was one of the few friendly early reviews Whitman received.

3. Horace Traubel, "Reviews," *The Conservator* 9 (August 1898), p. 109.

4. C.P. Gilman, "The New Motherhood," *The Forerunner* 1 (December 1910), p. 17.

5. *Prose Works*, 2:364.

6. C. P. Gilman, "Walt Whitman," *The Sunset of Bon Echo* 3 (Summer 1919), p. 28.

7. Flora MacDonald Dennison, "Short Stories," *The Sunset of Bon Echo* 1 (March 1916), p. 17.

8. David Karsner, *Horace Traubel, His Life and Work* (New York: Egmont Arens, 1919), pp. 25–26.

9. Karsner, p. 28.

10. C. P. Gilman, "Walt Whitman," p. 28.

11. Horace Traubel, *With Walt Whitman in Camden* (Boston: Small, Maynard & Co., 1906), 1:332.

11

What Diantha Did: The Authority of Experience

Sharon M. Rambo

The goal of this article is primarily to provoke further discussion of the serial novels of Charlotte Perkins Gilman by suggesting the richness of her text, and secondly, to encourage republication of them. On a more personal level, I embrace this opportunity to assess a twenty-year fascination with Gilman as woman and writer.

Much of Gilman's short fiction has become available in the last ten years, and *Herland* has a considerable following as an early feminist utopia. Further, even though Gilman's fiction rarely receives the amount of attention drawn by her feminist tracts, especially *Women and Economics,* the autobiographical "The Yellow Wallpaper" (1892) retains its preeminence. Although that story abounds with the themes of contemporary women's literature, especially the ever-popular heroine/victim, in order to assess her contribution more clearly, we must savor the long narrative, the serial novel.

What Diantha Did (1909) is the first of seven serial novels that Gilman published in *The Forerunner,* Volume 1, in fourteen issues.[1] Each issue contains one titled chapter and a short introductory verse that focuses the chapter. The 1910 Charlton edition is "affectionately dedicated to 'The Housewife':[2] With earnest love and a warm wish to help; with the highest respect for her great work and the desire to see it done more easily, pleasantly, scientifically, economically, hygienically and beautifully; hoping for her a happier life, a large income, better health, and full success in living . . ." (2).

The novel's heroine, Diantha Bell, struggles for nine years against the prejudices of family, love, and society to demonstrate through a successful business that everyday housework could be done more easily, pleasantly, scientifically, economically, hygienically, and beautifully while liberating the wife and providing a secure, respectable living for young, single women. Diantha grows from a twenty-one-year-old woman betrothed to Ross Warden into a successful business woman and recognized international authority on house-keeping.

Diantha's story begins after she resigns a teaching position,—"I don't like it, I don't do it well, and it exhausts me horribly" (28)—leaves her parents (a "virtuous" mother who closely resembles Gilman's own self-sacrificing New England one, and a tyrannical, patriarchal father who is incompetent at business) and separates from her fiancé, Ross Warden, and his "burdens" (8). Warden is the sole support of four 'true womanhood' sisters and a healthy, Southern belle mother. He longs to fulfill his dream of a life with Diantha on a farm and of selective breeding experiments with guinea pigs. Instead, he runs the family store, hating both his job and his "duty." When Diantha declares herself free to "develop the work, to earn money, to help my family, and to—well, not hinder [him]" (55), he demeans her with the familiar misogynist responses: "I cannot believe that the woman I love would—could take such a position. . . . Dear, brave foolish child!" (56). "I don't for one moment doubt your noble purposes. But you don't get the man's point of view—naturally. What's more you don't seem to get the woman's," and finally, "I can't stop you—I see that. If you think this thing is your 'duty' you'll do it if it kills us all. . . . What ever happens, darling—no matter how you fail—don't ever be afraid to come back to me" (58).

Upon relocating in "Orchardina," California, Diantha begins her career as housekeeper to the young Porne family: Isabelle, an established architect, who intended to become a homemaker after marriage and children only to discover that she hated the endless and unavoidable tasks of housekeeping; Mr. Porne, her husband, and their infant child. "Miss Bell's" domestic skills save the Porne household from ruin, and Diantha uses the situation to research domestic specialization as a business opportunity. Soon she organizes the servant girls of the community by providing domestic education, a safe place to live, and employment services. Her philosophy promotes community, privacy, and autonomy in place of the exploitation that characterizes most of their lives: "You are not servants—you are employees. . . . Each of us must do our best to make this new kind of work valued and respected" (179).

In addition to her effort to reform housework through a housecleaning business, Diantha begins a food preparation business, which offers home-delivered meals, and undertakes the management of a hotel complex, complete with housekeeping cottages, childcare facilities, and food service. Diantha's many business endeavors are made possible in large part through the spiritual and financial assistance of Mrs. Viva Weatherstone, a widow and former schoolmate of Isabelle Porne, who becomes Diantha's close friend. Diantha's mother also contributes to her success by relocating in order to become the accountant of the business.

Four years after leaving home, Diantha marries Ross when the sale of his store enables him to buy a ranch with two houses—one for himself and one for his mother and sisters—and he overcomes his aversion to the idea of a successful, working wife enough to "accept" Diantha for what she is. Several years and several children later, Ross finally comes to recognize the importance of Diantha's accomplishments. In a letter written while on a travel lecture tour, Ross confesses that he has "at last begun to grasp the nature and importance of your work . . . what brave, strong, valuable work you have been doing for the world. Doing it scientifically, too . . ." (249). Diantha gives thanks.

When, if at all, scholars have discussed *What Diantha Did*, their condescending responses are of two general types: ridicule of Gilman's social feminism ("a romantic advocate of benevolent capitalism"),[3] and denigration of the narrative ("concerned less with literary style and inventiveness than with propaganda for the emancipation of women"[4] . . . "Gilman subordinated story to theme").[5] One important and different voice is that of Ann J. Lane, who appreciates *What Diantha Did* as a companion to other of Gilman's works that show women, "through struggle and hardship, ultimately achieving autonomy, usually through work. With that autonomy, they are then complete enough to love and be loved."[6] Her sensitive reading is thematic and omits formulaic or structural analysis.

Rachel Blau DuPlessis's general discussion of the development of *Künstlerromane* ("to bear my mother's name") by women, specifically Charlotte Perkins Gilman, is a particularly good starting point for rediscovering Gilman's fiction.[7] DuPlessis limits her discussion to narratives of the female artist ("woman of genius") as the everywoman struggling against the misogyny of bourgeois ideology. These artist-heroes represent a "particular exaggeration of bourgeois individualism" and their struggles interweave the conventional romantic notions of womanhood and genius into the lives of women with strong middle-class values and gender caste (Chopin's Edna Pontellier, and Barrett Browning's Aurora Leigh, to name two).

In accommodating the contradictions of heterosexual love and vocation, twentieth-century female political narratives break with their predecessors by "writing beyond the ending" (*WBE* 91). Accordingly "The Yellow Wallpaper" is "transitional" in the resolution of the nineteenth-century contradictions between the love plot and the *Bildungs* plot. Gilman's main character is a potential artist whose husband's/doctor's emotional control and repressive tolerance cause rebellion from, not resignation to or complicity with, his heterosexual love. Because the "text" is autobiographical in source, "The Yellow Wallpaper" grows as a critique of the narrative of heterosexual love and marriage. The contradiction of the dominant and muted meanings embedded in the work (a characteristic of the *Künstlerromane*) results in two contradictory and simultaneous opinions about the main character: The muted subtext says that the narrator's tearing the wallpaper in order to release her double is not madness but [to use Emily Dickinson's term], 'divinest sense,' whereas the dominant "perspective of normalcy" makes the muted appear irrational and delusive (*WBE* 92–93). These interpretive paradigms signify a politics of narrative which reflect Gilman's early 1890s analysis of the tragedy of women's oppression. Transitional "The Yellow Wallpaper" may be, but its importance is in its intimate, first-person narration, experimental and experiential.

The third-person narrative *What Diantha Did* includes many women's stories—most, but not all, of them white women—and describes the struggle of a collective hero, not of the individual/artist (a construct that is often elitist/patriarchal). The women in *Diantha* struggle to expose and reform the tyranny of housewifery as well as to challenge the myths of marriage and motherhood. Embedded in the narrative is a critique of heterosexual love—the myth that woman's emotional, spiritual needs must be fulfilled through men, not other women. Gilman's women empower themselves and each other, different though their lives may be, and their common struggle against oppression enables them to develop lifelong bonds. The muted text also portrays marriage as a means to ensure species survival through impregnation and rejects the myth of romantic thralldom.

In twentieth-century women's *Künstlerromane* the conflict between women's patriarchal roles (marriage, motherhood, housewifery) and vocational roles evolves so that 'role' becomes "the filial completion of a thwarted parent's task" (*WBE* 94). This narrative pattern features mother and daughter as "collaborators, coauthors, separated by a generation," the mother as passive muse to a daughter-creator who completes the fragmentary and potential work of her mother (*WBE* 94). Significantly, the maternal "muse and reparenting motifs are strategies that erode, transpose, and reject narratives of heterosexual love and romantic thralldom" (*WBE* 94). These patterns are particularly helpful in decoding *Diantha*, especially as the collective hero, in contrast to the solitary artist model, enables a fuller, less intimate exploration of the oppression of housewifery: "The quiet everyday tragedy of that distasteful life—the slow withering away of youth and hope and ambition into a gray waste of ineffectual submissive labor—not only of her life, but of thousands upon thousands like her . . ." (58). This description accompanies that of Diantha's separation from family and financé, and represents a rededication of the novel to her thwarted muse, the housewife. Diantha rejects a life of "interminable dull tragedy . . . literally a lifetime, in the conscientious performance of duties she did not love . . . the chafe and fret of seeing her husband constantly attempting against her judgment, and failing for lack of the help he scorned" (23). Diantha rejects not only her mother's world of exhaustion from housework and childcare, but also the genteel world of Widow Warden, her future mother-in-law, a world which forbids women to 'work' because of that world's insistence on the husband's ability to provide servants (who, in turn, are oppressed by their employer). She also rejects the emptiness of Ross's sisters' passive lives. Diantha records the silent suffering of her mother, whose "needle trembled irregularly under and over, a tear or two slid down her cheeks" (32); "the faint creak of her light rocking chair. She could not sleep—she was sitting with her trouble, bearing it quietly as she had so many others" (58). This awareness of women's suffering enables Diantha to undertake the ethical role of trying to change the life in which she and other women are immersed.

As her search for happiness leads to questioning the very foundation of patriarchy—woman's role in the family—Diantha's emergence as a "woman of genius" rests on her appreciation of her mother's experience as wife and mother. In refusing to accept marital restraints on women, Diantha refuses to accept the either/or choice demanded of women, a situation that requires a woman who chooses marriage to lose her self to gender. Like Diantha herself, her collaborators are New Women.[8]

In place of single maternal muse, Diantha collaborates and coauthors with a series of muses. Her inspiration comes from two general sources: recurring and stereotypic characters, predominantly female.

The women of Orchardina are an interesting mixture of New and Old. Isabelle (Belle) Porne, Diantha's first employer, resumes her work as architect because of Diantha's efficient and economic housewifery. Both she and her husband become enthusiastic supports of Diantha as an enabler and embodiment of the New Woman. The New Woman network expands to include Viva Weatherstone, the young, wealthy widow with whom Diantha enjoys a financial, emotional, and intellectual relationship. Significantly, and suggestive of nineteenth-century female friendships as discussed by Carroll Smith-Rosenberg,[9] Isabelle and Viva were schoolmates. As collaborator, Viva's status as widow further widens the description of woman to include an adult female who, because her mother-in-law lives with her, must live by a code not of her own making. Viva's eventual liberation from both her stepson and Madame Weatherstone results from the insight into woman's role she receives from Diantha.

In a scene reminiscent of public meetings in Elizabeth Robins' semibiographical *The Convert*,[10] Diantha, the New Woman, addresses the Orchardina Women's Club at Mrs. Weatherstone's request. Representing the Old Woman, one who identifies by social class and its privileges, not by sex, President Mrs. Dankshire points out that the Club was formed "to serve The Home . . . interests which stand first . . . in every human heart" (108), and that the aim is Culture, "not only in the curriculum of institutions of learning, not only in those spreading branches of study and research which tempt on from height to height. . . . Most of us, however widely interested in higher education, are still—and find in this our highest honor—wives and mothers" (109). She bemoans that the young woman who must toil for a living prefers the "din and tumult of the factory" or "the dangerous exposure of the public counter" to the "true advantages of domestic service" (110). Diantha's speech, "The True Nature of Domestic Service," then openly challenges Mrs. Dankshire's assumptions. Reflecting that "whoso had met and managed a roomful of merciless children can easily face a woman's club," Diantha's attack on bourgeois housewifery reflects Gilman's theoretical work on housework: Although some "domestic work" has been socialized (confectioners replace baking; rug cleaners replace vacuuming), the housemaid is the last remnant of woman's ancient status as slave. Diantha catalogues the exploitative working conditions of housemaids and shows the system to be economically wasteful. Her vision of the kitchenless house is not "cooperative housekeeping . . . the feared perdition of capitalism" or the "dubious import . . . the commune," but individual domiciles in which each family is a distinct unit with separate living quarters and a garden (114). Diantha posits that delivered, cooked food and skilled wage labor will free wives from the oppression of housework and will product respectable well-paid professionals who have their own homes and families. As expected, Diantha's "heresy" creates a "schism" as Belle, Viva, the aptly named Miss Eagerson (a self-described "journalist"), and others contest Mrs. Dankshire's "generalship," which is "content with marking time." These rebel-women break away to form the New Woman's Club of Orchardina (120). Thus, as Diantha effects changes, she is joined by like-minded women.

The collaboration of Viva Weatherstone and Diantha changes both their lives. Together they shatter the illusion that the chief end of a bourgeois wife is "to serve an endless series of dignified delicious meals, notably dinners" (127). They also expose the fact that sexual harassment is a reality among domestic servants. When Viva and Diantha rescue Ilda, "a helpless child, a foreigner, away from home, untaught, unprotected" (155), from the lechery of Matt, Viva's stepson, their commitment to changing the nature of housework intensifies. Diantha's reorganization of the Weatherstone household permits Viva greater freedom, and with her encouragement, Diantha establishes the Girls' Club, an educational enterprise, which provides lessons in arithmetic, simple dressmaking, easy and thorough methods of housework, and use of the public library.

Diantha's vision continues to become reality as she succeeds in an enterprise beneficial to, not exploitative of, working women oppressed by disability and race. With the financial backing of female friends and her own savings, Diantha opens the Union House, a boarding house for female day-laborers, and soon expands it to include a "caffeteria" (*sic*) serving a businessmen's lunch menu of three items, five cents each: coffee, "dropcakes," and a selection of five sandwiches. Similar to other *Diantha* stereotypes are two female domestic workers who join Union House: Mrs. Thorvald, a Danish laundress whose disabled husband is the porter, and Julianna, the cook, who is a single mother and "'person of color'" (160).

Inevitably, the success of Union House draws the attention of the town gossips who speak threateningly of the "social atmosphere" of the establishment, and sparks the "active malignity of Mrs. Thaddler," social dictator (161). Unwanted publicity from local and San Francisco newspapers convinces Diantha to emphasize her own respectability and that of her establishment by asking her mother, Mrs. Henderson Bell, to act as matron of Union House. Not only does Union House gain respectability, but Diantha at last has a bookkeeper to organize accounts. Appropriately, the maternal muse thrives in her work: "Small dragging tasks were forgotten and a large growing business substituted. . . . Eyes grew bright again, she held her head as she did in her keen girlhood" (187). Enabled in part by her mother's active collaboration, Diantha establishes cooked food delivery ("c.f.d."). While in Europe, Viva Weatherstone discovers a technologically advanced aluminium food container and has it adapted to serve Diantha's c.f.d. needs. This "new heresy" adds to the "stealthy inroads of lunches and evening refreshments . . . [and] this new kind of servant who wasn't a servant at all" (194), becomes reality, once again, through the cooperative effort of many, including the Pornes, who eagerly list the economic and aesthetic benefits they enjoy as patrons. Further, in a final assault on Orchardina male privilege, Mr. Porne praises c.f.d. for liberating him from the symbol of bourgeois masculinity, carving at his own table; he claims inability, no pleasure and a desire to eat, "not saw wood" (197). The initial success of the home-delivered food moves Diantha to complete her resolve "to get 'housework' on a business basis . . . and prove, *prove*, PROVE what a good business it is" (226).

Orchardina men, particularly the religious and business community, support Diantha's efforts by patronizing her business, extending to her the same preferential conditions accorded her male competitors, and generally supporting her ventures. Several clergy offer her support and sometimes, unsought advice. The Reverend Mr. Eltwood offers marriage; Mr. Thaddler, spouse of a quintessential Old Woman, so respects Diantha's ability that his quiet financial help enables Ross to buy his dream farm near Orchardina.

Muted in the Orchardina men's acceptance of the changes which Diantha effects is the obstructive behavior of Old Women of Orchardina, particularized in Mrs. Thaddler, Mrs. Dankshire, Madame Weatherstone, and Mrs. Warden as representatives of the traditions of Boston, New York, Philadelphia, and the South.

Ross Warden's eventual accommodation to the woman's world comes quickly and with little embellishment. Throughout Diantha and Ross's separation, verbal declarations of devoted love, in letters mostly, constitute the romance formula. Throughout Diantha's struggles, Ross continually reflects the values of true womanhood which his mother embodies. He blames Diantha for "cruel obstinancy" and "cold blood" (221) because she rejects his demand that she compromise herself by abandoning her life's work to live on the Orchardina ranch in a situation which meets his requirements for scientific experimentation and family life. Having met the patriarchal requirements for marriage, Ross resumes his campaign to make Diantha conform to his bourgeois fantasy of woman as dependent and passive. His freedom to pursue his dream of scientific experiments is overwhelmed by his need to enslave Diantha to bourgeois tradition. Their disputes become so prevalent that there was "grave danger of an absolute break between them" (222).

While Mrs. Warden takes her son's side, painting Diantha as "an unnatural monster of hardheartedness," Diantha receives solace and advice from her mother and Belle Porne. In a declaration which echoes Edna Pontellier's, Diantha resolves that she would marry him tomorrow, "but I will not give up my work" (225). Ross's willingness to compromise comes only after Mr. Thaddler confronts him with accusations of "pigheadedness" (223) and the truth that out of respect for Diantha's accomplishments and a wish for her happiness, Thaddler family largesse has enabled Ross to relocate. His advice: "And now you've got what you want—thanks to her, mind you, thanks to her!—and you ain't willing to let her have what she wants. . . . You're breaking the heart of the finest woman I ever saw. You can't bend that girl—she'll never give up. A woman like that has got more things to do than just marry!" (234). Ross's capitulation brings reconcilation and marriage: "Dear, I have been a proud fool—I am yet—but I have come to see a little clearer. I do not approve of your work—I cannot approve of it—but will you forgive me for that and marry me? I cannot live any longer without you" (235).

Even in marriage, Ross continues to want his wife "there, in the home—his home—his wife—even when he was not in it himself" (239). And even the levelheaded Diantha "is beset with an unexpected uprising of sentiments and desires she had never dreamed of feeling," jealousy, treason and neglected duty all assail the bride. She upbraids herself for allowing such a traditional view of woman to dilute her happiness; soon she discovers a blank wall between herself and Ross, his sense of protest against her public life. His acceptance of her success comes only after hearing international praise of her work. As a self-designated "man of science," Ross parallels the husband/physician of "The Yellow Wallpaper." Yet his eventual endorsement of Diantha discloses his complete acceptance of the value of her work and his desire to share in the happiness of her accomplishments, an ending that acknowledges and legitimizes heterosexual love in women's lives.

What Diantha Did is Gilman's novel of visionary housewifery, and its ethical realm is based on human ties and seeks human change. In offering alternative vicarious experiences, not blueprints for implementation, and by analyzing the past and projecting a future, the novel conforms to the utopian works of United States women between 1836–1920.[11] Reflecting the nineteenth-century feminist critique of marriage as the enemy of women's rights, the utopia of *Diantha* envisions changes to produce the "good" society, not the "superior" one common to the utopias of male writers. True to formula, the characters are not classically well-rounded because they are more embodiments of ideals, and commonly a collective protagonist points to the unity of social purpose.

This Gilman novel interweaves several major narrative structures character-istic of Gilman's generation of women writers. The important key to unifying these elements is the maternal muse figure so crucial to the gendering process of the *Künstlerromane* by women. Significantly, a collective and active muse signals the values of the woman-centered world, the "wild zone," which draws upon utopian traditions. Essential to the dreams of woman's culture is the concept of experience, not dogma, as the primary source of knowledge. Women of varied social groups, hence experiences, join together to construct a more integrated, even holistic, Orchardina. Diantha is not the solitary, outcast (ma-cho) model that informs much myth, and the experiences upon which this novel rests are not Gilman's alone.

Throughout the novel are reflections of Gilman's own childhood in a pater-nal yet woman-centered family, especially the New England Beecher Stowe clan. In addition, the novel echoes reminiscences of Gilman's life with her great aunt, Harriet, and of her experience as a resident in Hull House in the 1890s. Rooting her utopian scheming in the reality of woman's experience enables Gilman to signify ways of lessening woman's oppression through wage labor for domestic women workers, appropriate education, and cooperation.

Notes

1. A narrative structure listing the fourteen chapters of *What Diantha Did* titles, pages, and time passage suggests a pattern. The exact passing of time is indeterminable.

   THE ALIENATING WORLD: Patriarchal
   1. Handicapped (3–15) *3–123 = 6 months
   2. An Unnatural Daughter (16–42)
   3. Breakers (43–59)

   THE FERTILE/GREEN WORLD: Woman-centered; Orchardina
   4. A Crying Need (60–72)
   5. A Friend in Need (73–90)
   6. The Cynosure (91–104)
   7. Heresy and Schism (105–20)
   8. "Locked Inside" (121–35)
   9. "Sleeping In" (136–55)
   10. Union House (156–69)
   11. The Power of the Screw (170–98)

ACCOMMODATING THE WORLD: Utopian Integration
   12. Like a Banyan Tree (199–219)
   13. All This (220–35)
   14. And Heaven Beside (236–50) *Four years in 12 years.

2. Charlotte Perkins Gilman, *What Diantha Did* (New York: Charlton, 1910). Subsequent page references to this edition will be included in the text.

3. Dolores Hayden, "Charlotte Perkins Gilman and the Kitchenless House," *Radical History Review* 21 (Fall 1979), p. 230.

4. Madeleine B. Stern, "Introductions," *Forerunner* 1 (1909–10), p. v.

5. Gary Scharnhorst, *Charlotte Perkins Gilman* (Boston: Twayne, 1985), p. 75.

6. Ann J. Lane, "The Fictional World of Charlotte Perkins Gilman," in *The Charlotte Perkins Gilman Reader* (New York: Pantheon, 1980), p. xxxix.

7. Rachel Blau DuPlessis, *Writing Beyond the Ending* (Bloomington: Indiana University Press, 1985) pp. 84–104. Subsequent page references to this edition will be included in the text with the abbreviation *WBE*.

8. The term "New Woman" signifies one who exercises choice and was a frequent motif of Gilman's contemporaries. For example, Anne Warner (1869–1913), whose story, "The New Woman and the Old" tells of a mother-daughter struggle to individuate in patriarchy.

9. See Carroll Smith-Rosenberg's "The Female World of Love and Ritual; Relations between Women in Nineteenth-Century America," *Signs* 1 (1975) pp. 1–30.

10. Elizabeth Robins, *The Convert* (Old Westbury, NY: The Feminist Press, 1980). Originally published in 1907.

11. Carol Farley Kessler, Introduction to her *Daring to Dream—Utopian Stories by United States Women: 1836–1919* (Boston: Pandora, 1984), pp. 1–25.

12

Mothers and Children: "Rising with the Resistless Tide" in *Herland*

K. Graehme Hall

Now if I were to live as we dream—alone with you—with a circle of souls like ourselves, and the quiet atmosphere of mutual love and perfect accord. . . .
      CPG in a letter to Martha Luther, September 4, 1881

I could make a world to suit me. All that inner thirst for glorious loveliness could be gratified now, at will, unboundedly.
      CPG in her autobiography, remembering nights in childhood

As a child, Charlotte Perkins was put to bed early by her mother and would lie, in that space before sleep, imagining "pleasant things . . . lovelier, stranger things . . . wonders . . . and once a year . . . anything I wanted to!"[1] She made a commitment early to "improve the world," and learned the importance of giving form to her ideals. Her concretization of a socialistic community of women in *Herland* has brought us all a step closer to transforming through into reality, achieving a society where women are autonomous and self-actualizing. Its similarities to other recent utopian novels by women, such as Sally Miller Gearheart's *Wanderground*, demonstrate the strength of Gilman's intellect and vision. While feminist readers today may choose to refine Gilman's dream, its message of humanism and woman-empowerment is as pertinent now as it was in 1915, when *Herland* was first published serially in *The Forerunner*.

A radical feminist, Gilman saw that change was necessary from the "root" of society.[2] Her many contrasts between life in Herland and in the United States during the early twentieth century show the failure of the American system to allow women full humanity. The fact that two thousand years were necessary for the evolvement of society in Herland is not particularly encouraging, and is evidence of Gilman's frustration with the extreme invasiveness of sexism and with the role women sometimes play in maintaining their own subservience. Gilman's vision is both future and past: a reflection of her dreams for the future, shaped by her own life experience. Of particular concern to Gilman throughout much of her life were the concepts of motherhood and child-rearing. She saw children as, truly, the hope of the world; if change were to be created, it needed to begin with them. Why work to erase the erroneous beliefs of an older generation when a new generation was, at that very moment, quite literally being born? Improve the quality of child-raising and the education provided to children, and improvements in society would quickly follow. Similarly, a changed world would necessitate new views on children, as traditional views link(ed) children with women in a situation of powerlessness.

Increasing the value society places on motherhood—still a feminist struggle today—was particularly timely during this period of compulsory and involuntary motherhood. In *Herland,* motherhood entered as a miracle. After the men living there had been killed, and the two boy children had died, residents feared their people would become extinct. When a young woman first produced a child, "they decided it must be a direct gift from the gods."[3] Gilman reminds us that the original purpose of mothering was procreation for the survival of the human species. As in the biblical version, it is a power bestowed on women from God(s). This "longed-for motherhood was not only a personal joy, but a nation's hope" (57).

Motherhood became the "religion" of Herland, as narrator Vandyck Jennings describes it. Gilman proceeds to make several contrasts between the Maternal Pantheism of Herland and the Christianity of Western civilization, as practiced. Gilman finds the Christian religion "requires a fuller 'change of heart' and change of life than any preceding it; which may account at once for its wide appeal to enlighten peoples, and to its scarcity of application."[4] The women of Herland have a Temple of Maaia—their "Goddess of Motherhood."[5] This goddess, while comparable with the idol of Mary used in the Catholic Church for the past several hundred years, is seen as representative of the values of motherhood, beliefs which form the foundation of their very lives; she does not exist because of her part in the birthing of a male child, or because of her suffering in his sacrifice. Because Gilman suggests the Goddess of Maaia existed before the women of Herland first experienced parthenogenesis, there is no association of virginity or virgin birth. There is, similarly, no association with subservience to a god or dominant power, and there is no indication that Maaia ever represented the passive "feminine virtues" attributed to Mary, often held up as a role model to women in the Catholic Church. What the women of Herland consider as their version of "God" is an "Indwelling Spirit," a power which resides within them all, as opposed to a power over them. The two thousand years in which they have been developing the values of Maaia are equivalent to the age of Christianity; the different levels of attainment of the respective ideals in these religions is obvious.

The Herlanders' commitment to perpetuate ideals of "Beauty, Health, Strength, Intellect, Goodness" permeates every aspect of their lives, including work and prayer (59). While beauty and goodness were generally associated with mothers in the early twentieth century, health, strength, and intellect were considered masculine virtues. By attributing these characteristics to mothers, Gilman eliminates, as she does frequently in *Herland,* any false, artificial division of femininity and masculinity, embracing instead a common set of human qualities. These values are the foundation of the Herlanders' belief system. They are demonstrated through their commitment of "Human Motherhood—in full working use," "the literal sisterhood of our origin," and the "far higher and deeper union of our social growth" (66). Again, Gilman provides the biblical parallel of humans sharing (brotherhood and) sisterhood as descendants from a single (set of) ancestors(s).

As the country began to encounter problems of overcrowding, with each woman producing five female offspring, it became necessary to create a form of birth control. With mind literally overtaking matter, women of child-bearing age voluntarily limited themselves to only one child, focusing their energies of mothering on other children of the land during their other four potentially fertile times, an interesting biological reduction in frequency of female fertility. The only "class" system in the land is determined by mothering capabilities: women who are considered unfit to be mothers are denied the right of even one child; a few other women, Over Mothers, are paid the highest of tributes by being allowed to bear more than one child. The entire system depends on the willing cooperation of all of Herland's inhabitants; since the practice has been designed for the common good, it seems unlikely to the Herlanders any woman would disregard it.[6]

Obviously, these "Conscious Makers of People" have only begun their task at the time of childbirth. The transformation of girl into woman is a massive task, particularly according to the standards Gilman holds, and demonstrates, through the attention paid to children in Herland: "The children in this country are the one center and focus of all our thoughts. Every step of our advance is always considered in its effect on them—on the race" (66). Gilman first encountered this affection for children in her own mother, Mary Perkins: "My mother was a baby-worshiper, even in her own childhood, always devoted to them, and in her starved life her two little ones were literally all; all of duty, hope, ambition, love and joy" (*L* 10).

Despite the importance Gilman's mother placed on motherhood, Gilman developed values about child-raising which were different from Mary Perkins's. Perkins was a strict disciplinarian who kept her daughter close at hand. Believing that if Gilman never experienced affection, she would never long for it or hurt from its loss if denied her, Perkins withheld signs of love. As she told her daughter in later years, "I used to put away your little hand from my cheek when you were a nursing baby. . . . I did not want you to suffer as I had suffered" (*L* 10). When Gilman discovered, finally, that her mother would sometimes cuddle her after she was asleep, she would take great pains, even using pins, to stay awake. Feigning sleep, she would "rapturously" enjoy her mother finally taking her into her arms, holding her and kissing her (*L* 11).

While Gilman inherited "something of [her] mother's passion for children," she more accurately felt a "deep sympathy" for them, "a tenderness for these ever-coming strangers, misunderstood, misjudged, mistreated, even when warmly 'loved'" (*L* 153). She developed her own methods of child-raising to use with her daughter, ideas which were radical in their time and brought disdain from friends and neighbors. Instead of discipline, Gilman depended on suggestion, cooperation, logic, and honesty in bringing up Katharine; she strove to gain her daughter's confidence rather than obedience. She taught Kate to associate reason with action—to shut the door, for instance, because the air was cold. "Children are naturally reasonable, and, most of them, well meaning." She believed in the importance of building a base of information which could readily be called upon by either parent or child in answering necessary questions. Gilman recalls that she talked to her daughter casually, as she would to a friend, instead of using the authoritarian distance she had experienced as a child. And, as an alternative to punishment, Gilman taught consequence. It would be consequences which would follow the adult Katharine's actions; there was no reason not to learn that lesson as a child. "Childhood is a transient condition; what we are trying to 'raise' is a competent adult" (*L* 157).

Kate was thirty years old at the time *Herland* was published; Gilman was fifty-five. She had had time to reflect on the appropriateness of her "people making" methods. The values Gilman demonstrates in *Herland* are similar to the ones she recalls in her autobiography as the basis of her own parenting techniques.[7] The theory in Herland is that the mind, like the body, is natural, alive and growing, and in need of nourishment. Both body and mind must be fed and exercised.

In Herland, babies are provided with an environment designed to stimulate the mind. As early as possible, they are given "choices, simple choices, with very obvious causes and consequences" (106). The babies are taught interrelationships, one step at a time. Their physical safety is ensured by the removal of any possible dangers from the houses and gardens they inhabit. The babies are raised in the warmer climates of the country, and experience no disease. "Shortcomings and misdeeds" are presented "merely as errors and misplays—as in a game." Most importantly, children are seen as people: "the most precious part of the nation" (100).

While women value their ability to bear children, their education is trusted to those best able to provide it. Childcare is shared by a variety of people, including the child's mother and educators. The teaching of children is seen as a specialized craft; only the most competent in Herland may engage in it. Mothers are glad to have the finest education available to their children, and are then free to concentrate their energies on other kinds of work.

The education, or making, of people extends into adulthood: "their ethics, based on the full perception of evolution, showed the principle of growth and the beauty of wise culture" (102). As the country provides a natural learning environment for children, drawing purely from the child's own natural curiosities, so the land equally encourages the growth of adults. Women undertake areas of specialization, in addition to the common knowledge necessary to everyone. Most engage in several fields, keeping the mind active and preventing "disused portions of the brain" from atrophying (105). The three male adventurers are amazed on their journey of Herland to discover how well their audiences are acquainted with the information they have shared about the United States and the world, and that these women possess a "highly developed mentality quite comparable to that of Ancient Greece" (85).

The country's inhabitants have undertaken a world view that recognizes a single cycle of life, all-encompassing. The women extend their mothering capabilities into their work with Mother Earth, and her growth and birth capacity. The two forces work as one in the creation of food for human and animal nourishment: "All that they ate was fruit of motherhood, from seed or egg or their product. By motherhood they were born and by motherhood they lived" (59). The women treat the Earth with the same respect they do every mother. Life in Herland, as in the United States, is very human-species oriented, however. What is not potentially useful to the women and their children, and infringes on their lives, has been eliminated, such as cows and tree-eating moths. Cats, once their bird-killing instincts have been overcome, are allowed to remain to destroy small animals threatening the food supply. Once cats are accepted as contributing to the life cycle, respect is extended to them as well.

Because there is no need for "possession" in Herland, there are also no private residences or homes. The entire country is home to the Herlanders. Their work takes them to different places; to have a single "abode" is impractical. Indeed, they have no word for the American concept of "home," just as they have no word for "family" (94). If a woman is not a mother or daughter, she is sister and compatriot. Aware of their common ancestry, they are free to interact as "family" in a different sense: in a sense of sisterhood.

The traditional family unit, more common in the United States in 1915 than today, was inconceivable in Herland. Surely, Gilman did not experience it as successful in her own life, nor could she imagine it being truly beneficial to its members. Her own father left her and her mother when Gilman was a child.

Similarly, Gilman divorced her first husband, raising her daughter until Katharine went to live with her father and his second wife.

Gilman's own experiences as child and mother also taught her that compulsory child-rearing is not necessarily in the best interests of either mother or child. Gilman's own mother "lost" her son and daughter as they rebelled against her stringent controls and her lack of knowledge about the proper way to raise children. After Gilman marries—a decision made with ambivalence—and gives birth to a daughter, she suffers a breakdown; she had assumed temporary conformity to a lifestyle she did not want but felt pressured, as a woman, to undertake. Gilman very much wanted to have children, but she also wanted—and needed—to continue writing. An arrangement such as she later created in Herland would have allowed her to enjoy both aspects of life more fully. The joy of motherhood was lost for her when it became a burden.

Gilman's views of woman's sexuality are also very revealing, as demonstrated in *Herland*. Contemporary readers might at least expect to find frustration, if not allusions to sexual relationships between women or to masturbation. Gilman makes no attempt to deviate from accepted conservative norms of the time; those norms were very much in line with her own views regarding sexuality. Many children who protest that their mother "only did it once" when they first learn about sexual intercourse might enjoy its absence in the novel, for these mothers remain sexually "pure." Gilman appears to have believed that sex was only necessary for procreation; if parthenogenesis was ensuring survival of the species, then no sexual activity was needed. She felt its frequency in American society was due to psychological—not physiological—need. When Vandyck explains to Ellador that couples have sex "without regard to motherhood," as Ellador puts it, she is quite confounded: "But—but—it seems so against nature! None of the creatures we know do that." Gilman makes a substantial differentiation, however, between affection and sex.

At the age of seventeen, Charlotte Perkins began a romantic friendship with a young woman, Martha Jessie Luther; for four years they enjoyed an intense relationship Gilman considered the most passionate of her life. In "Audacious Fancies," Juliet Langley provides excerpts of some of the letters Perkins wrote Luther; Gilman suggests she destroyed the letters Luther sent her so they would not be discovered. "Little Pet," Perkins writes at age twenty-one, "It has got to where I don't need the slightest excuse to write to you pussy, not the least incident, not a grain of news. Simply that I love you."[8] And nine days later, "It is no longer friendship between us, it is love."[9] Perkins trustingly poured out her feelings to Luther: "It seems improbable to me that two souls could be so perfectly matched as ours seem now. There must be places in each that we don't either of us know about yet—undiscovered countries where we may go together, and may not."[10]

When Martha Luther began to consider marrying Charles Lane, the young

Perkins, at first openly supported her: "You are to be your own sweet self, marry all you please. . . . But be your home as charming as it may, I am to have a night key, as it were, and shall enjoy in you and yours all that I don't have myself."[11] Perkins had already decided not to marry, telling Luther: "You will make up to me for husband and children and all that I shall miss."[12] "So no gentlemen for me just now," she writes, "I have friends enough, and one love. I have more work that I dare think of. . . ."[13] Perkins became as fearful as Luther seemed more intent on the engagement, and began to discourage it, trying to persuade her friend that her gentleman's feelings were probably not honorable. In the fall of 1881, there is a sudden break in the friendship. As Gilman writes later in her autobiography: "Four years of satisfying happiness with Martha, then she married and moved away . . . and I had no one else" (*L* 80). Gilman tentatively reached out to her in 1889, as Mary Hill tells us, at the time she was writing "The Yellow Wallpaper": "No one has ever taken your place, heart's dearest. No one has ever given me the happiness you did, the peace, the rest, the everpresent joy. I do not forget."[14]

It is this happiness Gilman attempts to convey in *Herland*. The women do not lack anything emotionally with the absence of men; they imagine that, if they can know such joy with only one sex, surely life will be more splendid with two. As Susan Gubar notes, "While tenderness and affection characterize the relationships between women in *Herland*, as they did in Gilman's life, sexuality is fairly closely identified with heterosexuality, as it is in "The Yellow Wallpaper."[15] Sexuality and love are distinct to Gilman.

Physical demonstrations of love Gilman enjoys; they are part of emotional caring, and not indicative of a sexual relationship. She writes Luther in 1881, "I could spend hours in cuddling if I had you here."[16] As Ann Lane notes, Gilman complains twice in her diary, just days after her marriage to Walter Stetson in 1882, that he is displeased with her for being "too affectionately expressive."[17] Gilman also makes clear that her relationship with Luther was never sexual; she closes one of her letters, "Yours is a calm ordinary, wellbehaved friendly (not intimate) masculine! way."[18] She states in her autobiography that with Luther, "there was not Freudian taint, but peace of mind, understanding, comfort, deep affection" (*L* 80). To add a sexual element to the relationship would have corrupted it, in Gilman's eyes, and was probably inconceivable.[19]

At a time of rapidly changing sexual values, Gilman's remained steadfast: "It is essential to the best growth of humanity that we practice the virtue of chastity; it is a human virtue, not a feminine one."[20] Gilman believed sexual activity should be reserved for marriage, with one's own spouse; the assumption is that the relationship will be heterosexual. In her autobiography, she criticizes the "lowering of standards in sex relations, approaching some of the worst periods in ancient history." Gilman is appalled that "now the very word 'chastity' seems to have become ridiculous." She feels that a large part of the problem is "the psycho-philosophy, the sexuo-pathic philosophy, which solemnly advocates as 'natural' a degree of indulgence utterly without parallel in nature. A larger knowledge of biology, of zoology, is what is wanted to offset this foolishness." "Monogamy," Gilman declares, "is a 'natural' form of sex relationship practised widely among both birds and beasts" (*L* 323).

The women of Herland are without "sex-feeling," or have very "remote stirrings." As Susan Gubar has pointed out, "What Gilman calls into question is the idea that there is or can be or should be a single definition of what constitutes the female. . . . Historically such a core definition has fixated on the sex-function, and therefore Gilman gives us women with no sexual desire at all."[21] In *Herland,* Gilman presents three different responses from the men to these "sexless" creatures. Jeff "worships" Celis and, in Van's words, has become "so deeply convinced of the almost supernatural advantages of this country and people that he took his medicine," although Celis is pregnant by the novel's end (123). Terry is the other extreme, attempting to show his "mastery" of Alima in attempted marital rape. Ellador is open to a demonstration of what Van is making such a fuss about, and he finds in her eyes "a remote clear look as if she had gone far away even though I held her beautiful body so close." Ellador tells him afterward that she is not convinced such interaction will help develop their love, as Vandyck has told her; she "cannot do as you wish" until she is convinced that it is right.

Appearing feminine in American culture has been part of the economic process in which women have had, by necessity, to participate to survive. As Gilman writes in *Women and Economics,* "She gets her living by getting a husband. . . . The sex-functions to her have become economic functions."[22] Because appearance and dress are the first measures of a woman's "femininity," the strong, healthy physical appearance of women in Herland and their comfortable, practical non-"feminine" clothing and hairstyles provoke the first surprised comments from the male adventurers. They know these creatures must be women because of "that sparkling beauty, and yet none of us was certain at first."

Coupling is, further, an economic arrangement, rather than an arrangement in the best interests of rearing children. With a woman being taught to depend financially on her husband for survival, the husband "gets his wife by getting a living . . . it is to his individual sex-advantage to secure economic gain."[23] Similarly, society expects that unit of husband and wife to support its children financially, implying private responsibility, even possession, of children. In *Herland,* Moadine and Somel are questioned by the male explorers as to why their children do not carry their mother's name. Terry asks, for instance, "why not sign 'em," as Americans do; the women do sign works of art, architecture, and furniture, for example, but because they want to know "to whom to be grateful." Moadine answers his query: "Because the finished product is not a private one" (76). Surnames imply ownership. The children "belong" to themselves, first, and are the pride of all of Herland—not just their birth mothers. As in some animal species, Gilman may have expected that the father would serve his necessary role in parenting the child with the mother, but that the unit would dissolve when it was no longer needed. In Herland, with only one parent required for the birth of a child, and a whole community engaged in meeting her needs, coupling is unnecessary.

"There are three governing laws of life," Gilman writes in *The Forerunner." "To Be; To Re-Be; To Be Better."*[24] We are, as people and especially as women, struggling to be ourselves; we "re-be" through our children, as we give them life; we become better, as individuals and a collective society, through work and education. Gilman presents life—being—as the foundation of existence, and the extension of that life—growth—as a natural force. The movement toward achieving a state where oppression is overcome because it is antilife and antinature, forces beyond man/womankind, is a "resistless tide." Motherhood epitomizes the ideals Gilman sees society necessarily assuming in the future, a time when women and children alike will be empowered:

> With Motherhood at last awake—
> > With Power to Do and Light to See—
> Women may now begin to Make
> The People we are Meant to Be![25]

Notes

1. Charlotte Perkins Gilman, *The Living of Charlotte Perkins Gilman.* (New York: Harper & Row, 1935), p. 20. Subsequent page references will be made in the text to (*L*).

2. As Sonia Johnson points out in *Going Out Of Our Minds: The Metaphysics of Liberation* (Freedom, Calif.: The Crossing Press, 1987, p. 351), the word "radical" comes from the Latin *radicalis,* or *radix,* and means "at the root." Gilman saw the oppression of women as one of the roots of our society and its structures, and knew that those structures would have to change if oppression were to be eliminated.

3. Charlotte Perkins Gilman, *Herland* (New York: Pantheon Books, 1979), p. 56. Subsequent references will be made in the text.

4. Charlotte Perkins Gilman, *The Man-Made World, or Our Androcentric Culture* (New York: Charlton Co., 1911) p. 129.

5. Maia means "mother" or "nurse." In Greek mythology, Maia was a nymph of Mount Cyllene in Arcadia, the eldest daughter of Atlas and Pleione. She bore Zeus a son, Hermes, who was very precocious, stealing Apollo's cattle on the first day of his life. Maia also raised Callisto's baby, Arcas. Maia was known for her quiet manner, her beautiful hair, and was very much loved by Zeus. There was also a goddess called Maia in early Roman times, a supporter of Vulcan, the fire god; the month of May was named in her honor. Maaia also resembles the name of Mary, the name of Gilman's mother and the Virgin Mary, although the names of

Mary and May have different origins. Primary source: Pierre Grimal, *The Dictionary of Classical Mythology*, trans. A. R. Maxwell-Hyslop (New York: Basil Blackwell, 1986), p. 270.

6. It is stated in *Herland* (p. 82) that as part of their plan of evolution, if a woman with undesirable qualities chose to bear a child, it would be raised by other women.

7. It must be kept in mind that Perkins may have been prone to exaggerate in her autobiography at times, adjusting her life to more accurately depict her values than what was necessarily lived.

8. Juliet A. Langley, "'Audacious Fancies': A Collection of Letters from Charlotte Perkins Gilman to Martha Luther," *Trivia: A Journal of Ideas* 6 (Winter 1985), p. 57, letter dated August 6th, 1881.

9. Langley, p. 59, letter dated August 15th, 1881.

10. Langley, p. 58, letter dated August 10th, 1881.

11. Langley, p. 55, letter dated July 29th, 1881.

12. Langley, pp. 54–55, letter dated July 24th, 1881.

13. Langley, p. 58, letter dated August 15th, 1881.

14. Mary Hill, *The Making of a Radical Feminist* (Philadelphia: Temple University Press, 1980), p. 159, quoting from letter dated August 1889.

15. Susan Gubar, "*She* in *Herland:* Feminism as Fantasy," in *Coordinates* (Carbondale: Southern Illinois University Press, 1983), p. 146.

16. Langley, p. 54, letter dated July 24th, 1881.

17. Ann Lane, "The Fictional World of Charlotte Perkins Gilman," *The Charlotte Perkins Gilman Reader* (New York: Pantheon Books, 1980), p. xi.

18. Langley, p. 58, letter dated August 10th, 1881.

19. To choose a single label for Gilman's relationship with Luther, as either a romantic friendship or lesbian relationship, seems unnecessary. While today, the relationship would be considered lesbian based on the definition of "affectional preference," it is doubtful Gilman would ever have considered herself a lesbian, particularly with the connotations present at that time. Gilman does seem fearful that their relationship will be misinterpreted, judging from her request that Luther destroy her letters, and from Gilman's apparent destruction of Luther's letters. What is most important is the deep affection these two women shared. Gilman's intellectual views about women being sexual with one another are demonstrated in *Herland:* "Those who had at times manifested it ["sex-feeling"] as atavistic exceptions were often, by that very fact, denied motherhood" (92). To Gilman, sex would have been unnecessary between women, regardless of the feeling involved, because no child would be produced by the act. For further discussion of romantic friendship in this period, see Lillian Faderman, *Surpassing The Love of Men* (New York: William Morrow and Co., 1981).

20. Gilman, *Man-Made World*, p. 133.

21. Gubar, p. 142.

22. Charlotte Perkins Gilman, *Women and Economics* (New York: Harper & Row, 1966), p. 110.

23. Ibid., p. 110.

24. Charlotte Perkins Gilman, "A Small and a Large Goddess," *The Forerunner* 1:1 (November 1909), p. 2.

25. Gilman, untitled poem, *The Forerunner* 1:3 (January 1910), p. 11.

13

Charlotte Perkins Gilman's
Steady Burghers: The Terrain of *Herland*

Christopher P. Wilson

In the Utopian romance *Herland* (1915), during a chapter entitled "Rash Advances," author Charlotte Perkins Gilman crafts a scene which, in several respects, foreshadows the byplay of the book as a whole. Here, we are introduced to a decidedly masculine adventurer named Terry Nicholson (nicknamed "Old Nick," the narrator tells us, "with good reason"), one of three men who have just entered the pastoral territory of Herland. Old Nick encounters—and tries to capture—the first young woman he espies. While clinging precariously to the limb of a tree where three of the country's "seemingly aboreal" inhabitants are perched, he reaches into his inner pocket and produces a box of purple velvet— pulling out a necklace, Gilman writes, "of big varicolored stones that would have been worth a million if real ones." His apparent prey reaches timidly out with her right hand—and then seizes the bauble with her left; as he clutches for air, she and her companions are gone, "swift as light." Such a scene, rippling with satire on the Eden myth, encapsulates much of the book: female agility counterpoints and defeats the knowledge, temptations, and "advances" of masculine exploit. Yet, as they avoid possession, the women also stay enigmatic, just out of reach.[1]

The scene also testifies to Gilman's often-neglected literary skills. True, in recent years, Gilman's reputation as a writer of fiction has experienced a modest renaissance—due, in part, to a recent Pantheon collection of short works, and the publication in book form of *Herland* itself. Interest in Gilman is generally on the rise. But few of even her devoted critics have, as yet, gone so far as to credit Gilman with being a self-conscious literary craftsperson. In

This article originally appeared in *Women's Studies* 12 (1986): 271–92.

part, this is due to her own dismissiveness: "I have never made any pretense of being literary," she wrote in her autobiography. "As far as I had any method in mind, it was to express the idea with clearness and vivacity, so that it might be apprehended with ease and pleasure." Gilman's analysts have generally agreed with this self-description. For instance, while acknowledging the wit, adroit sense of popular formulas, and ear for dialogue in Gilman's short fiction, Ann Lane writes that "Gilman gave little attention to her writing as literature, and neither will the reader, I'm afraid. She wrote quickly, carelessly, to make a point." Despite the fact that Gilman's earliest childhood writings were fanciful, that she was fascinated by word-puzzles and puns, or that fiction actually dominates *The Forerunner,* her writings are usually seen, as Lane puts it, as "lessons." With the worthy exception of "The Yellow Wallpaper," the reputation of Gilman's nonfiction far outweighs that of her imaginative writing.[2]

This is probably as it should be. And yet, as such, Gilman's fiction presents a recurrent critical dilemma, explored intriguingly by Myra Jehlen in the Summer 1981 issue of *Signs:* the problem of a female or feminist author who, despite her laudable political intentions (or, as Jehlen suggests, perhaps *because* of them), offers "scant nourishment" for our inherited literary tastes. To put it rather gently, whatever its political ingenuity or prescience, the bulk of Gilman's fiction does not elicit the reader-responses we commonly associate with "high" literary stature. Whatever the politics of our own critical vision, we do not often think of ourselves as deeply "moved" or enthralled; her characters, however modern, do often seem strangely lifeless, her plots typically aimed in some didactic direction. Whenever I assign *Herland* to today's undergraduate English majors, they habitually complain (at first) that the book, despite its wit, is "bloodless" and even downright dull. But as Jehlen writes, this has the effect of putting the appreciative critic or teacher in a double bind. If we accept the common feminist argument that standards derived from the so-called "Great Tradition" are masculinist mystifications, we should not find ourselves using them to apologize for a female author's supposed failings. On the other hand, to write forced apologias for such work risks sending the critic (and the writer) into isolation and irrelevance.[3]

One of the ways out of this critical borderland may be to reorient ourselves by reference to the unfashionable weathervane of authorial intention—a useful guide especially for interpreting the goals of a writer like Gilman, who was both critic and practitioner. The fact is that, despite her modest protestations, Gilman did indeed think seriously about aesthetics, wrote about them in *The Forerunner,* and implemented her literary ideas in fiction—especially in *Herland* itself. Critics have uniformly overlooked a body of *Forerunner* criticism which clarifies that the seemingly didactic style of Gilman's writing was not simply the function of "ideology" per se, as our New Critical ancestors might have concluded, but rather a result of the *kind* of ideology she proposed. When we reconstruct Gilman's literary principles, we discover that at least some of her lack of "affect" was entirely intentional. That is, her fiction often consciously lobbied to overturn her reader's preconceptions about what was "natural" or desirable in a work of literature—principally, by frustrating the ideological expectations of the literature of "adventure" and "romance" from her era. Furthermore, Gilman aimed to conceive of a feminist and socialist idiom partly by remodifying literary and pictorial conventions which linked standards of taste to received gender roles and expectations.

One can imagine Gilman herself scoffing at any overzealous praise. She is no Virginia Woolf. Nonetheless, I think we can better appreciate the intellectual conduit between her feminism and her literary style. Therefore, instead of reviewing the "lessons" of *Herland*—which have already received able explication—I want to explore some of its literary devices and its implicit commentary about art, gender, and property. In concluding, I want to suggest that Gilman's effort to counter what she saw as a bourgeois and masculine aesthetic often had elusive and paradoxical consequences. Like those young women in the trees, Gilman's own perspective was not always so easily "apprehended."

In his recently printed adaptation of a B.B.C. broadcast, *Ways of Seeing* (1972), British art critic, film maker, and novelist John Berger explores how some of our most fundamental artistic conventions partake of a shared rhetoric of property and gender roles. Berger's discussion, an interpretive and visual foray into the nexus of class, sexuality, patronage, art, and advertising, focuses principally on the social and ideological function of the European oil portraiture tradition. The principal appeal of oil for European patrons, Berger argues, was its special ability to "render the tangibility," the substance, of what it depicted. Oils, he writes, had "special qualities [which] lent themselves to a special system of conventions for representing the visible." Defining the real in terms of "that which you can put your hands on" (not unlike what Ian Watt once termed the philosophical "realism" of the early novel), oils more fully captured the potential for enhancing material objects—through light and shadow, scale and perspective, and new textures. But that "system of conventions" surrounding the realm of art was social as well as mimetic. Shaped by the demands of patronage, the realistic capabilities of oil conventionally serviced the needs of power and wealth. The "average" painting often served simply to celebrate property, symbols of adventure, exploit, or leisure—and, of course, to celebrate the patrons themselves. Oil only reinforced the tangible desirability of what was owned, and hence, of ownership.[4]

Berger also argues that the social use of the final product—the framed portrait hung on a wall—often only further underscored this social homage. He demonstrates, in particular, that the stances, postures, and even the gazes of conventionally depicted patrons served to reinforce the supposed legitimacy of their social station. As in modern ads, direct gazes at the viewer signalled challenge and forcefulness; "overhead" stares conveyed aloof pride and dignified proprietary right. Because such postures or body language usually accompanied artifacts of conquest, culture, leisure, or learning, the paintings legitimized—or, to use a more current term, "naturalized"—the patrons' social rule. What Berger has in mind, of course, is conventional art's role in fashioning ideological hegemony, in reaffirming the legitimacy of the world it represents.[5] This validation function of taste performed especially well in paintings that combined landscape and portraiture. In Gainsborough's well-known "Mr. and Mrs. Andrews," for example, the aloof pride of possession reveals itself in the countenances of the married couple. In turn, one can imagine that their pride is affirmed by what Berger calls the oil's ability to "render their land in all its substantiality" (108). Moreover, to inject a bit of what Irving Goffman calls "Gender Advertisements," one might also comment upon the sexual ritual of the piece. Mister stands, casual yet potent, gun in hand and loyal hunting dog attending. Missus is placed in diminished perspective, seated, stiff. The distance between the couple seems pronounced, as if to reassure us (and them) that Mister's proprietary right—over land and wife alike—is altogether "proper."[6]

Not surprisingly, then, such conventions also reaffirmed gender roles. In fact, Berger goes on to demonstrate how an aesthetic comparable to that of the landscape/portrait is at work in the standard depiction of the female nude. In the nude's conventionally passive gaze and reclined posture, Berger finds a classic statement of the patriarchal contract: men, one might say, are viewers, women essentially "sights." Normally, in the most common postures, the woman's face is either shyly demure, or turned outward to the viewer, as if personally engaging the intimacy of the viewer or patron. In other instances, she gazes at her own reflection. In any of these cases, the convention asks her to comply, via her supposedly "feminine" response or mystique, or her internalized vanity, with her possession by the patron. The nude thus becomes a sight arranged for her owner's (and selected guests') periodic consumption. In oils, then, a man's presence exists to define the power he possesses; a woman's, however, usually defines "what can and cannot be done to her" (46). Thus the social orchestration of "property"—what Lewis Hyde tells us is commonly defined as a "right to action"—is easily transposed to the key of gender.[7] The male patron, Berger writes, becomes the "surveyor," while the nude internalizes the patron's expectations and her own awareness of being "surveyed" (46). In Berger's terms, thus, nudity becomes a form of dress (54); to use words which appear in *Herland*, "'feminine charms' . . . are not feminine at all, but mere reflected masculinity—developed to please" (59) the male of the species. One might better understand this dynamic by recalling the tortured compact dramatized in Robert Browning's "My Last Duchess." Here, a guilt-ridden Duke narrates:

That's my last duchess painted on the wall,
Looking as if she were alive. I call
That piece a wonder, now: Fra Pandolf's hands
Worked busily a day, and there she stands.
Will't please you sit and look at her?

What we discover, of course, is that in all probability the Duke has ordered his former wife killed. But what interests us here is his second reflex: like the statue of "Neptune . . . / Taming a sea-horse" cited in the final lines of the poem, the Duke has asserted his "nine-hundred years-old name" and imprisoned his wife's image within a framed portrait. He refers explicitly to the look of "depth and passion" and the "spot of joy" he now privately commands by drawing the curtain as he pleases. In final irony, we discover that the projected "listener" of the Duke's tale is probably an agent sent to arrange the dowry settlement of the next duchess. Browning implies that art—like the other "mediators" and murderers in the poem—complies in the hypocrisy of property and hierarchy.

What does all this have to do with Charlotte Perkins Gilman? Primarily, Berger's analysis is illuminating because it highlights a series of artistic conventions against which, especially when transposed to literary forms, Gilman rebelled—consciously and otherwise. A bit of her understanding may even have derived from her own training in the fine arts—although, unfortunately, the extant material on her apprenticeship is still quite thin. Perhaps because household duties (which at the time included caring for her ill brother Thomas) had prevented her from pursuing her youthful vocation to the fullest, and perhaps because her democratic spine bristled at the pretensions of "connoisseurship," Gilman's memoirs are notoriously silent on this side of her nature.[8] (As may become clear subsequently, this "silence," to use Tillie Olsen's term, may itself be instructive.) We do know, however, that Gilman was a skillful artist and teacher from childhood onward, that she spent about two years at the Rhode Island School of Design, and that her first marriage was to Charles Walter Stetson, a painter whose specialties were portraiture, landscape, and the nude. Nevertheless, what is most striking about Gilman's own extant drawings (at the Schlesinger Library) is the absence of these same subjects. Despite the fact that Gilman apparently had rigorous training in classical composition—a fact revealed what is probably by an extant R.I.S.D. "quiz" on perspective—her own work, while not without the conventional still-life studies, was more fanciful. Her work more often ranged from fantastic doodlings to flower cards, from ornamental designs to clever advertisements for domestic products; only a few, however, even hinted at Gilman's prefeminist musings. For whatever reasons, Gilman seems not to have been swayed by the traditions that moved Walter.[9]

Another fragment helps to piece together the puzzle—which, again, was one of Gilman's own pastimes. Early in her first engagement, Walter Stetson proposed, as a present to his fiancée, to paint Charlotte's portrait. He recorded the effort in a love-poem:

> These many days I've tried to fix the face
> Of her I love on canvas, that it might
> Remain to tell of her, and glad the sight
> Of those to come with intellectual grace.
> Most patiently did she sit, and I did trace
> And study the marvellous eye that's dark and bright;
> The curve from the wide clear brow's fair height
> Along the cheek to the eloquent lip's red place;
> And then down the delicate smooth chin
> To the supple throat, until it was so lost
> In the [illegible] and heaving breasts' creamy white high
> mounds. . . .

What is striking about this otherwise conventional poem-portrait is that, for some reason, the painting was never finished, as the second stanza explains. Although Walter blamed the failure on himself, was it possible that Charlotte actually proved hesitant to "sit patiently" while this Duke-to-be recorded her blush? We may never know. Another small record we do have of Gilman's views of Walter's work recalls an incident where she criticized a painting, in her words, "so harshly from a moral point of view that he smash[ed] and burn[ed] it." Even more suggestively, as the marriage of Charlotte and Walter finally ceased, his own work became positively Dionysian.[10]

Such speculations are perhaps best left to Gilman's present and future biographers. But whether or not Gilman consciously understood these conventions in the fine arts, she wrote explicitly about them in regard to literature. What has been overlooked, specifically, are articles in *The Forerunner* which demonstrate Gilman's intention to fuse her feminist perspective with her literary practice. To begin with, she not only referred repeatedly to the mimetic power of art—citing the classical phrase of holding "the mirror up to nature"—she also spoke of literature's social function as the means by which societies made sense of the world. She certainly needed no training to understand implicitly the "naturalizing" role of art, because her career-long contention, in a wide array of fields, was that masculine values had been mistaken for a "human" point of view. She resented this state of affairs in literature only because she held the power of letters in high esteem—not because she dismissed them. Employing the biological analogy typical of her thinking, she said that literature "is the brain of society; and all our brains are steadily modified by it." Through art, Gilman wrote, "we know the past, govern the present, and influence the future." A masculine distortion, and particularly a distortion of perspective, could not purport to document the state of Nature. In a serialized chapter of "Our Andro-

centric Culture" entitled "Masculine Literature," she ridiculed the fact that females were patronizingly provided with "women's pages" and "feminine" features, while men's literature was simply taken for Literature itself. Men, the
public was led to believe, were "people"; women were but a "side issue." (A
"side issue" quite "literally," Gilman wrote, "if we accept the Hebrew leg-
end!")[11]

Gilman avoided the narrow-mindedness of condemning all imaginative
writing by men; for example, she repeatedly praised Dickens and Shakespeare.
Instead, her particular object of attack was a masculinist distortion which had
overtaken contemporary fiction. Her contention, incidentally, was entirely accurate. Immediately following the Gilded Age vogue of Robert Louis Stevenson
and Rudyard Kipling (whom Gilman often lambasted), American popular tastes
in the Progressive era were dominated by "masculine" naturalists like Jack
London, Frank Norris, and David Graham Phillips. In their own rebellion from
the "feminized" ethos of mid-Victorianism, these writers moved to the national
spotlight by emphasizing a prose style that was "vigorous" and topics that
ostensibly appealed to "real men." Popular editors in this period spoke of seeking out the "roast beef" of literature, and of favoring "manly" exhortation that
was direct and to the point.[12] This context is crucial to understanding Gilman's
own counterpointing style. Although the era's "naturalism" posed as scientific
realism, to Gilman it was brutal and mysoginist. Not unlike male-dominated
History, she wrote, this literature was infested with the disease of exploit. The
two main branches, she said, were the "Story of Adventure" and the "Story of
Romance." The first worked, as in Kipling, by inciting "predatory excitement"
in the reader by depicting fighting, robbing, and plunder. Romance, in turn,
capitalized on the story of the "premarital struggle." In either case, Gilman said,
there was an unconscious appeal to the thirst for conquest—and thus, as with
Berger's painterly conventions, an implied kinship between the related idioms
of property and gender hierarchy. The romance, Gilman wrote, was simply
another version of the Hunt: "It is the Adventure of Him in Pursuit of Her—and
it stops when he gets her!" Consequently, much like Berger, Gilman also felt
that the traditionally coy byplay of manners, so basic to what critics often call
"complication" in the romantic plot, only intensified the reader's appetites.
Instead of presenting men and women on equal footing, "Woman's love for
man, as currently treated in fiction is largely a reflex." Gilman said contemporary writers showed only "the way he wants her to feel, expects her to feel; not
a fair representation of how she does feel."[13]

Like Berger's nudes, then, the fictional female of Gilman's description
only reflected an identity given to her—and a fate. Inevitably, Gilman wrote,
this character is eventually "tamed" or domesticated, enclosed in a fiction (as
often in life) by the conventional resolution of a marriage scene. Gilman ridiculed this traditional ending in a romance, because it implied that women, once

possessed, were no longer on the stage of human action. Their "estate" was settled.[14] Furthermore, Gilman argued that implicit assumptions about gender were embedded into conventions of narration and description. "Do not women notice," she wrote, "that in the perennial love story the heroine is still described, for the most part, in terms of physical beauty?" Men's physiques were geared to action; women's were a matter of "charms." "The man is required to do something, to show character, action," Gilman wrote. "The woman, in spite of all our rational progress, is still most emphasized as something to look at."[15]

Given these objections, it is not surprising that, in *Herland*, the idiom of surveillance and ownership is not just treated thematically. Rather, it infuses and surrounds the language of the narrative itself. Perhaps hinting at her own motives—and perhaps more literary self-consciousness than she would admit it—Gilman names her masculine narrator "Vandyck" Jennings, as if alluding to the prominent seventeenth-century Flemish painter, Sir Anthony Van Dyck, (in)famous for abandoning his early mythological themes in favor of portraits of the European aristocracy.

Gilman's own Van, of course, is hardly the rake the original was.[16] But as a narrator of *Herland* he is both an apt and an ingenious choice. First of all, he is a sociologist who espouses what are, in Gilman's eyes, faulty Social Darwinist economisms about the struggle for existence. Gilman may imply here that, like his namesake, Vandyke is an unwitting servant of power, an articulator of the dominant way of seeing. Secondly, as Lane points out, Gilman was unusually sensitive to popular literary devices, and here, as in the classic utopian formula, the narrator chosen is an outsider, a principal opponent of the system he is asked to describe. Many utopian tales employ a seemingly skeptical observer who voices the reader's anticipated objections. In Edward Bellamy's restful Nationalist Boston, we follow a nineteenth-century upper-class insomniac; in the Altrurian dialogues of Howells the realist (an admirer of Gilman, and probably a model for *Herland*'s style), we hear from Mr. Twelvemough, the romancer; in a society of and for women, we have the story told to us by a male. But Van's aptness has more do with *how* he sees. What is most striking in the preliminary chapters of *Herland* is this narrator's frustration—and near inability—to tell the tale. The book, in fact, opens with a lament about what is to follow:

> This is written from memory, unfortunately. If I could have brought with me the material I so carefully prepared, this would be a different story. Whole books full of notes, carefully copied records, firsthand descriptions, and the pictures—that's the worst loss. We had some bird's-eyes of the cities and parks; a lot of lovely views of streets, of buildings, outside and in, and some of those gorgeous gardens, and most important of all, of the women themselves.

Nobody will believe how they looked. Descriptions aren't any good when it comes to women, and I never was good at descriptions anyhow. But it's got to be done somehow; the rest of the world needs to know about that country. (1)

To some, this lament might seem a device of convenience—simplifying Gilman's writing of the book by enlisting the reader's imagination. This is certainly one possibility. And yet, perhaps the "they" of the opening line of paragraph two is not unintentionally ambiguous. It is striking how the narrator focuses particularly on the loss of "pictures" of the land, and how, initially, the women are described essentially as a feature of the landscape. It is even more intriguing how the narrator complains of being dispossessed of his tools of explanation. The women and land are unable to be seen, and moreover, to be surveyed and described. This is a narrator who has been expropriated, and it creates a problem that constantly undermines his narration in the early going.

The male trio's first exposure to *Herland* is as surveyors. They fly over the terrain in an airplane, measure the land's proportions and state of civilization, and then decide to find "women"—by which they mean young and beautiful ones. ("'Woman' in the abstract is young." Van asserts, "and, we assume, charming. As they get older they pass off the stage, somehow, into private ownership mostly, or out of it altogether" [20]). But at first they are offstage completely: the men are cut off from viewing the young women as sights. Deprived of this basic "right" that had whet their appetite for exploration, they become doubly immobilized. The older women-captors (Terry calls them "Colonels") who encircle the men make Van feel like a child again, as "when my short legs' utmost effort failed to overcome the fact that I was late to school" (19). Furthermore, the women are not, in the devious malapropism of the vernacular (which Terry employs) "lookers"—they neither look, nor allow themselves to be looked at, conventionally. "The—the—reaction of these women is different from any that I've ever met," one of the male trio stutters. Vandyke agrees, and his friend rejoins: "They don't seem to notice our being men" (29–30). The men's presence, in other words, does not inaugurate the nuances of manner and gesture basic to the sexual ritual the adventurers expect. Looking at his loved one, Van remarks: "There was something so powerful, so large and changeless, in those eyes that I could not sweep her off her feet by my own emotion as I had unconsciously assumed would be the case. . . . There was not a shade of that timid withdrawal or pretty resistance which are so— provocative" (126). In turn "[t]heir dress and ornaments," Van remarks soon after, "had not a touch of the 'come and find me' element" (128).

Reading *Herland* seems to follow these new conventions of sight. Throughout the first four chapters, Gilman sprinkles chapter titles and phrases which play upon the masculinist and capitalist expectations of adventure itself. The story, again satirizing popular formula, is cast in the familiar form of an expedition—not unlike three civilized Tarzans in search of a savage Jane. But Gilman's imaginative phrases—"A Not Unnatural Enterprise," "Rash Advances," "Our Venture"—also make puns upon the imperial and sexual designs underwriting conventional narrative development. These men "advance" into *Herland* but make failed advances at the women; the men's "enterprise" (capitalism) is, in Gilman's view, hardly natural; their "venture" for profits and spoils is, as the prelude to the ad-venture, frustrated. Consequently, Gilman even has fun in these chapters with a twist on a conventional plot cliché. The male trio devise an altogether familiar hairbreadth escape, knot their bedsheets together in true Robin Hood fashion, climb down from a treacherous mountainside fortress, and escape over a moonlit landscape to their airplane. This Great Escape, however, is only in vain; again, they are surrounded and herded back like errant children. We should note, as well, the primary source of their embarrassment: during their entire escape, they had been under surveillance. (As we discover later, secrecy or privacy—those basic elements of suspense—have little place in *Herland*.) Not long after, in the course of his study of *Herland*'s education, Terry finds the children's tales sadly wanting—"punk" (44), he says, because they lack men and thrills. Van, however, signals his incipient conversion at the start of chapter five. "It is no use for me to try to piece out this account with adventures," he says. "There were no adventures because there was nothing to fight. There were no wild beasts in the country and very few tame ones" (49). A man who tries to be assertive, we are told, is "all out of drawing" (74). Adventure is entirely unmanned.

Van's second confession itself signals a change in the book's tempo: to reflect Van's own term (and to whom it refers), the action henceforth is far more tame. In fact, immediately following his confession, we witness a dialogue about the breeding of canines and felines, obvious symbols for a witty discussion on heredity, domestication, and gender stereotypes. (Cats, we discover, no longer cry, and serve *Herland* as practical, useful pets.) This discussion, apparently, sets the stage for a rather familiar utopian element: the question-and-answer style upon which the dramatic tension of so many utopian romances founders—as, for instance, in the tedious disquisitions of Dr. Leete in *Looking Backward* and *Equality*. And now we do hear—indirectly—about *Herland*'s history, its parthenogenic biology, its religion, and so on. But even in this respect Gilman's accounting seems rather unusual. That is, confined as we are to the narrator's eye and voice, in fact we don't *see* or *hear* much about Herland at all: no lengthy diatribes about its politics or economy, no visits of any substance to its workplaces, not much detail at all about its recent past. Of course, this is partly because Gilman's goal is satiric and not programmatic: Herland is conceived as a mythological Archimedean standing place, not a "mapped out" or realistic terrain. Nevertheless, my point here is that what we listen to can only loosely be called "dialogue" at all. Rather, the men are usually led into bold assertions of "civilized" belief; but their female counterparts only ask Socratic questions, look quizzical, or blanche in shock—and take notes. Their talk echoes their demonstrated skill at foiling linear "plots" (e.g., escape plots) with encirclement. Their "lines of interrogation," Van say "would gradually surround us and drive us till we found ourselves up against some admissions we did not want to make" (50). As a result the description of *Herland* is left to Van, or to characters who don't talk very much.

This is not entirely because Gilman is condensing to maintain reader interest, nor because she is taking any literary shortcuts. Rather, as some of her *Forerunner* commentary reveals, this reticence seems to have derived from her belief that literal "self-expression," a term which she sometimes used interchangeably with sheer exuberance of speech, was a masculinist failing, a kind of boasting that the men in this tale exhibit. (Sure enough, the naturalists themselves valued "forceful" speech as a key to literary success.)[17] Her distaste, however, led her down an interesting if problematic literary avenue. On the one hand, she was compelled, I think, to confront the problem of consciousness inherent in the utopian tale—and yet, to try to tell that tale through a narrator who is deprived of his normal means of telling. Part of his conversion involves losing his initial mode of expression—his original literature. This problem is fundamental to many a utopian tale, but to Gilman's credit, she is exceptional in the way she confronts it directly. She understands that it is a problem not merely of intellection, but of narration. As for her women, their talking, such as it is, is like their looking: a form of undefinable presence. Like Gilman's famous woman in the wallpaper, they seem to occupy a kind of terra incognita which we never fully see.

This central paradox becomes more elaborate in the final four chapters dealing with marriage, an institution that Van terms "The Great Adventure" (121). In the final part, each of the men is paired with a Herlander counterpart; again, however, the relationship developing between the narrator and his mate, Ellador (whose name may allude to Gilman's beloved Greece), is the most important one. Much of this section is quite witty and discursive, but there is a developing tension in Van's growing realization that he will no longer be able to see gender conventionally—that is, as part of a familiar terrain. (Ellador, we discover, is a forester.) As the book proceeds, Van initially expresses in traditional terms his satisfaction at the new relationship:

> As for Ellador: Suppose you come to a strange land and
> find it pleasant enough—just a little more than ordinarily
> pleasant—and then you find rich farmland, and then gardens,
> gorgeous gardens, and then palaces full of rare and curious
> treasures—incalculable, inexhaustible, and then—
> mountains—like the Himalayas, and then the sea. (89)

Gilman consciously employs natural imagery here because she wants to alter our perspective, subvert our notion of a "natural" relationship. Van is initially pleased with his exploration. "Then, as I got on further, the palace and treasures and snowy mountain ranges opened up" (90). Such heights are giddy—but, interestingly enough, also a bit cold, and the air is thin. After a time, of course, Van discovers that these women have practically bred the sex-instinct to extinction; they view it as a curiosity but not much more. At first, Van speculates rather hopefully that the males' arrival might awaken the old drive. But when he pursues his venture, with "hot" hands (127), Ellador responds about sex "as if she were discussing life on Mars" (127). Later, as Van holds her in his arms, "kissing her hungrily," he sees in her eyes a "remote clear look as if she had gone far away ... and was now on some snowy mountain regarding me from a distance" (138).

This change in location Gilman sets forth is a challenging one. Accordingly, it undermines the rhetoric of romance as much as adventure has been. We discover that, for the most part, Herland has no ritual of privacy—hence, no chance meetings or private retreats that are the stuff of romance or intrigue. Since there are no differences of class—the slaves of earlier reigns conveniently disappear—and none of wealth, and no gender distinctions, there are few available devices of farce or even the comedy of manners: no occasions for mistaken identities, no disguise, no false or misconstrued impressions. Even more fundamentally, there is no struggle or conflict about courtship. Hence, we discover, Herland has no conventional drama as the men understand it. Again speaking in landscape terms, Van remarks: "The drama of the country was—to our taste—rather flat" (99). We learn that it would strain plausibility, for example, to have Othello suffocate a Herlander with a pillow (132). Most importantly of all, however, Herlanders exhibit a subordinated sense of the personal. Children's names are almost superfluous; women don't view motherhood as an individual matter; mothers don't coo over their own children. Like the antipropertarian citizens of Annares in Ursula LeGuin's *The Dispossessed,* these women have dispensed with "egoizing."[18] The visiting men complain about the ever-present "we" that undermines intimate dialogue; they say they have married a nation, not individual women. Their property is never private.

In the end, of course, Van imbues the spirit of Motherlove, and we are told that his relationship with Ellador is unlike any that he has known. But Gilman, again entirely intentionally, chooses not to employ that capstone moment of romance—chooses not, in other words, to end with the marriage scene. Rather, she turns her narrative focus back to the most venturesome and rash man, Terry, as if to signal a final shift in mood. Asserting what he thinks is his proprietary right on his new bride—by trying to rape her—Terry is repulsed, tied up, anaesthetized, and ultimately sentenced to banishment from Herland. Gilman's distaste for conventional endings seems to have led her to a more provisional final episode. Even here, however, she returns to the imagery of vision and terrain. Prior to their final moments, the men are shown that it is they who have been surveyed. The Herlanders, having pieced together facts from their questioning, "had a great globe, quite fairly mapped out from the small section maps in that compendium of ours" (145). Van realizes how the tables have been turned: "Little had we thought that our careful efforts at concealment had been so easily seen through, with never a word to show us that they saw. They had followed up words of ours on the science of optics, asked innocent questions about glasses and the like, and were aware of the defective eyesight so common among us." (144) Defective eyesight indeed. The men have been "seen through" by doing all the talking. For a moment, as if sensing this reversal of surveillance, the women now do lecture the men before claiming their proprietary right and sealing off Herland from outsiders.

Perhaps this is why Gilman chose the possessive pronoun: ultimately, it is not "she-land," but Herland. And yet, even here, there is a sign of Gilman's enigmatic narration. We should remember that "Herland" is a name that *Terry* coins at the very start of his adventure. We never actually hear the country's real name.

If we return to Terry in the tree, we can see that his bauble is not merely material enticement—not just a lure. Rather, what he is offering Herland in that varicolored necklace is, in Gilman's view as in Berger's, femininity. Understandably, then, the gift is not "real" but synthetic, a device which, once worn, confirms his possession. But for the woman it is never hers. In this gesture the dual nature of Gilman's vision comes together. Her feminism and socialism have a common intellectual basis: she believes that women cannot be enticed to subordination if they renounce pride of ownership; she feels that if they reject a false femininity, they in turn transcend the rhetoric of possessiveness. Given this assumption, Gilman's rejection of literary "affect" and adventure followed directly. And yet, this leaves open what Gilman proposed to put in their place—in Jehlen's term, what kind of "nourishment" we do find. In *A Literature of Their Own*, for instance, Elaine Showalter argues that feminist utopias of this era, crafted principally in opposition to the male world (and impelled by some repugnance of intercourse and childbirth), offered worlds that "were not visions of primary womanhood," and which lacked a "theory of female art."[19]

There is much to be said for Showalter's basic point. Indeed, my own contention has been that Gilman's distaste for popular, "masculine" literary conventions led her to undercut many common literary strategies. But we should not mistake reticence for absence: *Herland* does infer an aesthetic of its own, if not a gender-specific one. (It should not surprise us that *Herland* lacks a female aesthetic, since Gilman argued that her position was "humanist," not feminist.) The key, I think, lies in the description of the country's cultural psychology. We discover, of course, that the Herlanders, much as they suppress the sex instinct, neither smoke nor drink. We hear, in addition, that the children in their nurseries do not cry as our children commonly do. This might be partly a reflection of contentment and security, but it also exhibits their training in self-control. Along the same lines, the mothers of Herland limit population via a kind of contraceptive voluntarism—by repressing the ecstasy that foreshadows the onset of pregnancy. "We each go without a certain range of personal joy," one citizen explains (71). Clearly, what Gilman offers here, in response to the trinity of possession, gratification, and "expression" is self-restraint, holding back. Herland's psyche is based not in self-expression, but in renunciation; its version of loving "up" (141) is a religious ideal. This is why, I think, Van remarks that Herland seems more "Christian" (115) than any society he knows. Moreover, this seems why, so paradoxically, the women (like their land) seem to have made "cultivation" appear as if it is a "natural condition" (72). They have made selfhood itself into something positively pastoral.

Re-viewing the "look" of the Herlanders seems to encapsulate what Gilman has in mind here. Van remarks quite early on: "Their attitude was not the rigid discipline of soldiers; there was no sense of compulsion about them. Terry's terms of 'vigilance committee' was highly descriptive. They had just the aspect of steady burghers, gathered hastily to meet some common need or peril, all moved by precisely the same feelings, to the same end" (22). In that Van invokes the spirit of Terry here, perhaps some caution is in order—our own form of self-restraint. But it seems altogether fitting that Vandyke, the name which evokes the favored artist of Charles I—and, as well, the typical dress of the Cavaliers—should be confronted by an ethic which is so essentially Puritan. This descendent of the Beechers, in other words, has given us something like an inverted captivity narrative—inverted, because it is not a female whose virtue is tested in the wilds, but "Old Nick" who is trapped among barely visible saints.[20] Despite Herland's banishment of an angry male God and even the sense of sin itself, this is an eminently rational and restorative terrain fashioned to trip up, surround, and baffle the incursions of the outside (old) world. It is the ideological basis of Gilman's own artifice.

My point here is not the familiar one that Gilman's views on sexual freedom were by and large conservative, nor that *Herland* exhibits any conscious appropriation of her Puritan forbears' ideas. Authorial intention can no longer be our guide. Rather, it is simply that Gilman's rejection of conventional literary discourse, when combined with her distrust of "expressiveness" as a masculinized trait, led her to evolve a literary-political idiom which was essentially renunciatory—that is, her own version of a "plain" style. Rejecting both the comedy of manners and the adventure formula, she chose instead a style that was akin to self-effacement: elusive, satirical, almost limnerlike in its immateriality. Recent thinking about Puritan aesthetics therefore provides an instructive caution. Just as we no longer believe the Puritans lacked literary devices altogether, so too is Gilman not without an awareness of narration, dialogue, plot, and imagery. If her style was enigmatic or reticent, likewise it only reflected her primary goal of exposing the vanities of the material world in a way the reader could apprehend them without conventional distractions.[21] This adjustment may allow us to revise some of our readings of *Herland* itself. For instance, Gilman's witty reversal of a cat's proclivities, or her positing of a parthenogenic world, are possibly not to be taken as "peculiar fantasies," nor as extensions of her eugenicist paranoia.[22] Rather, they may be satiric and symbolic creations, representations of an ideal natural order—not lessons, exactly, but images which provoke her readers (like the trio of men) to trip up and then reexamine their own teachings. If my own reader will indulge yet one more return to Terry in the tree, we will see that the Herlanders only appear to reject ornamentation; actually, they seize it with a sleight-of-hand.

The conduit between Gilman's feminism and this literary ethos of renunciation is also expressed in the essentially communal inferences about Herland's art. It is interesting, for example, how Gilman herself answered the charge that her vision of the future was somehow "asexual." In one of her earliest poems, she wrote about a drone in a beehive who confessed a dream of equality to others, only to encounter ridicule:

> Then fiercely rose the worker's all,
> For sorely were they vexed;
> "Oh wretch!": they cried, "should this betide
> You would become *unsexed*!"
>
> And yet he had not sight for eggs,
> Nor yet for royal mien,
> He longed to be a worker bee,
> But not to be a queen.

Herland, one often feels, is a bit like that beehive—thus, again, the resonance of Gilman's Puritan echoes. Even in "Masculine Literature," she had written that "if the beehive produced literature, the bee's fiction would be rich and broad," celebrating the work of comb-building, treating the "vast fecundity of motherhood," the passion of loyalty and "social service which hold the hive together." Herland's plays are actually annual communal festivals of "joyous, triumphant life" (99). She offered these adventures in place, furthermore, of the cult of individual self-realization implicit in a character, for example, like Ibsen's Nora. Briefly reviewing "The Doll House," Gilman once sardonically wrote that "[b]ird, beast, reptile, fish and insect are very busy realizing themselves, yet every one of them waves the right of the present Self, in favor of the future Self—the next generation."[23]

Many of Gilman's other characters and stories show this same paradoxical sense of self-realization. In many respects her *Forerunner* tales, in which women enter spheres of work and though previously monopolized by males, represent individual "cells" busily realizing themselves. For the narrator of "The Yellow Wallpaper," it is a cell of a different kind. To be fair, however, Gilman's description of the Herland pageants, like her brief mention of its supposedly "exquisite, imaginative" nursery tales, are indeed too cryptically described. But this cryptic quality, and Gilman's evocation of the steady and silent burgher-bee, only again indicate *why* Gilman's style is the way it is. Seeking a society in which selfhood lost itself in a renunciatory and communal endeavor, and employing a literary style which dispensed with conventional "affect" to describe that society, Herlanding had given "expression" itself a curious presence—or nonpresence—in Gilman's world view. Somewhat like the murals of socialist realism, *Herland* itself may present too voluntary a vision, too pastoral a terrain—and a literary ideal too elusive. But this is not an uncommon quality in a utopia—nor unforgivable in such a lively one which nevertheless refuses to be a "romance" at all. It was an adventure Gilman willingly undertook as part of her own quest for self-possession.

Notes

1. Charlotte Perkins Gilman, *Herland* (1915; rpt. New York: Pantheon, 1979), pp. 1, 16–17. All further citations in text.

2. *The Living of Charlotte Perkins Gilman* (New York: Appleton, 1935), p. 284–85. Ann Lane in her excellent introduction to *The Charlotte Perkins Gilman Reader* (New York: Pantheon, 1980), p. xvi. Carl Degler also writes in his introduction to *Women and Economics* (1899; rpt. New York: Harpers, 1966) that "Gilman's poetry, like her prose, was straightforward, lucid, but without much imagery or deep sensibility" (xiii), and that "[d]espite her feeling for words and the easy flow of language on paper and tongue, she showed little talent for imaginative writing" (xviii).

3. Myra Jehlen, "Archimedes and the Paradox of Feminist Criticism," *Signs* 6 (Summer 1981), pp. 575–601. I am also indebted to Jehlen's argument that certain patterns of "victimization" may be embedded in the conventions of the sentimental novel. See also Stuart Cunningham, "Some Problems of Feminist Literary Criticism," *Journal of Women's Studies in Literature* 1 (Spring 1979), pp. 159–78.

4. *Ways of Seeing* (New York: Penguin Books, 1977) p. 84 ff. All further citations in text.

5. On "hegemony," see Raymond Williams, "Base and Superstructure in Marxist Cultural Theory," in *Problems in Materialism and Culture* (London: Verso, 1980), pp. 31–49; on "naturalizing," see Roland Barthes, *Mythologies,* trans. Annette Lavers (New York: Hill and Wang, 1979), p. 129 ff.

6. Irving Goffman, *Gender Advertisements* (New York: Harper & Row, 1979).

7. Lewis Hyde, *The Gift: Imagination and the Erotic Life of Property* (New York: Vintage, 1983), p. 94. See also his discussion on gender and property, pp. 93–108.

8. For Gilman's skeptical views on art criticism, see "Painting Via Literature," *Forerunner* 7 (July 1916), pp. 186–87, and the poem, "Connoisseurs," in *In This Our World and Other Poems* (San Francisco: James H. Barry and John H. Marble, 1895), p. 170.

9. On her R.I.S.D. years, see *Living,* p. 45 ff.; cf. Mary A. Hill, *Charlotte Perkins Gilman: The Making of a Radical Feminist* (Philadelphia: Temple University Press, 1980), p. 105. My comments on Gilman's drawings are based particularly on Oversize Folder Number 4, Gilman papers, Schlesinger Library. This folder also contains the R.I.S.D. quiz.

10. For insight into Walter Stetson's style, see Charles C. Eldridge, *Charles Walter Stetson: Color and Fantasy* (Lawrence: University of Kansas Press, 1982). For this episode, see Hill, p. 138.

11. "Masculine Literature," *Forerunner* 1 (March 1910), pp. 18–22; "Effects of Literature Upon the Mind," *Forerunner* 3 (May 1912), pp. 133–39. See also "The Only Hero," *Forerunner* 2 (August 1911), p. 209; "With a Difference (Not Literature)," *Forerunner* 5 (February 1914), pp. 29–32.

12. On this trend, see my "American Naturalism and the Problem of Sincerity," *American Literature,* 54 (December 1982), pp. 511–27; and for another woman author's reaction to this trend, see Gertrude Atherton, "Literary Merchandise," *New Republic,* 3 (July 1915), pp. 223–24. For Gilman's specific reaction to literature of this type, see her review of Phillips's "The Grain of Dust," in *Forerunner* 2 (June 1911), p. 170.

13. "Masculine Literature." See also "The Dress of Women," *Forerunner* 6 (April 1915), esp. pp. 102–108 on dress "conventions." See also the poem comparing prostitution and flirtation, "As a Business," *Forerunner,* 3 (December 1912), p. 325.

14. On what Raymond Williams calls "that typical interest which preoccupied the nineteenth century middle class imagination," see his *The Country and the City* (New York: Oxford University Press, 1973), p. 174 ff. One might also note that, in "The Yellow Wallpaper," Gilman locates the action on a decayed estate—broken up, we are told, by legal battles between the heirs and co-heirs. This use of concentric "states" was common in the socialist aesthetics of the era. See Sinclair Lewis's review of H. G. Wells, "The Relation of the Novel to the Present Situation: The Passing of Capitalism," in *The Man from Main Street,* eds. Harry E. Maule and Melville H. Cane (New York: Random, 1955), pp. 327–39. Note also that Gilman spoke with Shaw about literary matters; see *Living,* p. 203.

15. "Her 'Charms,'" *Forerunner* 6 (January 1915), p. 26.

16. For a book from Gilman's time, see *Sir Anthony Van Dyck* (London: George Newnes, Ltd., 1904).

17. Cf. "American Naturalism and the Problem of Sincerity."

18. Ursula K. LeGuin, *The Dispossessed* (New York: Avon, 1974). See also Lucy M. Freibert, "World Views in Utopian Novels by Women," *Journal of Popular Culture* 17 (Summer 1983), pp. 49–60.

19. *A Literature of Their Own* (Princeton: Princeton University Press, 1977), pp. 4–5, 191–92.

20. On these captivity narratives, see especially Richard Slotkin, *Regeneration Through Violence* (Middletown: Wesleyan University Press, 1973), pp. 94–145.

21. Compare the comments in Robert Daly, *God's Altar: The World and the Flesh in Puritan Poetry* (Berkeley: University of California Press, 1978), pp. 79–81.

22. Cf. Showalter, p. 191.

23. See the last paragraph of "Masculine Literature," and "Coming Changes in Literature," *Forerunner* 6 (September 1915), pp. 230–36. See also her comments on the novel with a "purpose," in "Detective Story," *Forerunner* 4 (September 1913), p. 252.

14

She in *Herland:* Feminism as Fantasy

Susan Gubar

I saw no Way—The Heavens were stitched—
I felt the Columns close—
The Earth reversed her Hemispheres—
I touched the Universe—

And back it slid—and I alone—
A speck upon a Ball—
Went out upon Circumference—
Beyond the Dip of Bell

Emily Dickinson

And when I ask how did we come to envision a world without
rape, I am asking about the shape of revolution because when
one dreams of a new world, this world immediately becomes
possible.

Susan Griffin (*Rape*)

What is the relationship between women and the fantastic? The epigraphs for my essay point to the crucial role played by amazing voyages in women's thinking about women: Emily Dickinson, knowing even the heavens to be stitched closed, imagines herself advancing through the sliding doors of the universe until she is poised, alone upon circumference; Susan Griffin reminds

This article originally appeared in *Coordinates: Placing Science Fiction and Fantasy,* eds. George E. Slusser, Eric S. Rabkin, and Robert Scholes (Carbondale: Southern Illinois University Press, 1983), pp. 139–49.

us that women abused by the probable refuse it by imagining the possible in a revolutionary rejection of patriarchal culture. What the subtitle of this essay—"Feminism as Fantasy"—means to point toward is the realization that women's fantasies have frequently been feminist in nature and that, concomitantly, feminism imagines an alternative reality that is truly fantastic.

We are, of course, much more accustomed to think about *male* fantasies, as any literary history of speculative fiction will prove, male fantasies not infrequently centered on women. Especially in the heyday of fantastic literature, the late Victorian period, the curious girl-child and the raging queen reign supreme. What exactly is the relationship between men's and women's fantasies in this period? Is it possible that one man's utopia may be one woman's dystopia? Or, do misogynist dystopias fuel feminist utopias of another Eden, a once and future queen, a somewhat different Paradise? If woman is dispossessed, a nobody, in the somewhere of patriarchy, is it possible that she might be somebody only in the nowhere of utopia? What Julia Kristeva calls intertextuality, the transposition of one system of signs into another,[1] can help us trace the dialectic between the father's curse and the mother's blessing in the relationship between H. Rider Haggard's *She* and Charlotte Perkins Gilman's *Herland*, because *She's* power and popularity transformed the colonized continents into the heart of female darkness that Charlotte Perkins Gilman would rename and reclaim in a utopian feminist revision of Haggard's romance.

It we take *She* (1886) as a touchstone for literature, painting, and philosophy of the *fin de siècle* femme fatale, as Sandra Gilbert has done, it becomes clear that Leo Vincey's trip into the savage origin of life and death, like Marlowe's trip in Conrad's *Heart of Darkness* to the more pretentiously evoked "inscrutable" and "ineffable" wilderness, is a voyage back not only to the infancy of the race but also to his own infancy with its feelings of rage at dependency on the will and whim of the inscrutable, omnipotent female. Certainly the image of Freud dissecting his own pelvis before the journey over the "cleft" into the "womb of the world" illuminates the male anxieties that initiate the colonial trip to an undiscovered country, be it the blank places on the map of Africa or the blank spaces Freud explicitly associates with the female genitals. Actually his dream implies that men experience themselves as haggard riders into the volcano of female transformation that still echoes the roaring inside her. If even Freud's dream of *She* implies that castration anxiety is a male response to female power, then we may find that feminists like Susan Lurie are right in interpreting psychoanalytic theories of female penis envy as a reaction formation to male womb envy.[2] Actually, this is exactly what the American feminist Charlotte Perkins Gilman implies.

By coming to terms with Haggard's *She,* Charlotte Perkins Gilman confronted the misogyny implicit in the imperialist romance. Gilman specified her critique by situating *Herland* on a "spur" of land "up where the maps had to be made,"[3] even in an extinct volcano: in fact, it is a volcanic blast that destroys all the men who are fighting a war and seals the women in a community of their own. As in *She* where the Amahaggar trace descent through the line of the mother, the society in Herland is matrilineal. As in Haggard's novel, moreover, this isolated community ruled by women worships a woman who has solved the riddle of life and death, for while Haggard's She is personally immortal, the inhabitants of Herland are an immortal species, each woman capable of parthenogenically reproducing herself: they gained this parthenogenic power, Gilman explains, 2,000 years ago, 2,000 being the approximate age of She. Just as three self-proclaimed misogynists penetrate into the caves of Kôr, *Herland* is told by one member of a three-man team of explorers whose misogyny is acutely analyzed by Gilman.

Gilman presents Terry Nicholson, Jeff Margrave, and the narrator, Vandyck Jennings, as three stereotypical and faintly ludicrous specimens of masculinity, each with his own all too predictable fantasy of what to expect in a country of no men. But, when they actually enter the no man's land of Herland, all three find their stereotypes of women disabused. Lo and behold, women do not bicker; they are well organized; they do not admire aggression in men; they can invent. As each of the sexist stereotypes of the men is discarded, we see the "flip-flop" or the "diametric reconfiguration" that Eric Rabkin considers so central to fantastic literature.[4]

> We had expected a dull submissive monotony, and found a daring social inventiveness. . . .
> We had expected pettiness, and found a social consciousness. . . .
> We had expected jealousy, and found a broad sisterly affection. (81)

The satiric critique generated from the utopian reconfiguration here means that the better Herland looks as a matriarchal culture, the worse patriarchal America seems in contrast.

Especially in the introductory chapters of Gilman's utopia, the men experience culture shock when they are treated like the minority they, in fact, are. Secondary creatures, they are herded in like cattle, bedded down like babies, and put on display as anatomical curiosities marketable only for matrimony. Considered inferior for their secondary sexual characteristics, they become petulant, irritable, jealous, vain of their physical appearance, in need of reassurance, rivalrous for approval, as Gilman humorously diagnoses the faults ascribed to her own sex as symptoms of a disease called "marginalization." While the three misogynists in *She* valiantly hold on to their masculine grace under pressure, the quarrelling men who are cooped up in a fortress of *Herland* try, like fairy tale princesses, to escape at night by tying together bedsheets and lowering themselves to a ledge so as to reach their airplane, only to find what they call their "machine" in the garden "swaddled," literally sewed up in a bag (42).

Part of what they must discover is that there is no central, secret interior place to penetrate, for there are no mines or caves in *Herland*. Bold and brave, the three men of Haggard's romance penetrate not only the womb/tomb but also to the single source, She, who is every woman, the essentially feminine. They will either possess her or be possessed by her, the plot implies. But the men in Gilman's utopia are "tamed and trained" (72, 73) into the realization that there is no She, but instead there are many Hers, some of whom are cautiously willing to welcome them as an experimental opportunity to restore "bisexuality." What Gilman seeks to call into question is the idea that there is or can be or should be a single definition of what constitutes the female. There is no Kôr in *Herland*. Historically such a core definition has fixated on the sex-function, and therefore Gilman gives us women with no sexual desire at all. Decentering definitions of the real woman, the total woman, the eternal feminine *is,* after all, the project of feminism.

What makes this project utopian is the imaginative leap it requires beyond empirical data to postulating the possibility of the primacy of the female. The contemporary anthropologist Sherry Ortner reminds us that "we find women subordinate to men in *every known society"* (emphasis mine).[5] Gilman would not have disagreed. Fifty-five years old when she wrote *Herland,* she had explained just this fact in such influential texts as *Women and Economics* (1898), *The Home* (1903), and *Human Work* (1904). For Gilman, the economic dependency of women means that female sexual arts become crucial for attracting and keeping a man: woman therefore identifies herself with the sexual function completely, while man is considered the human prototype. This is the reason why sexuality becomes highly exaggerated in women. As if writing about *She,* moreover, Gilman claims that economic dependency works "to make a race with one sex a million years behind the other":[6] "in her position of arrested development, she has maintained the virtues and the vices of the period of human evolution at which she was imprisoned" (*WE* 350). Haggard's denizen of the darkness with her massive lengths of hair, her gauzy veils, her turbulent desires, contrasts strikingly with the short-haired citizens of Herland who wear tunics quilted with functional pockets for greater freedom of movement in their work at creating and maintaining ethical and physical culture. Not merely a reflection of the dress reform movement, the desexualizing of women in *Herland* also shifts the emphasis onto the multiple "livings" open to women in a society that no longer opposes reproduction and production. Although Gilman could point to no matriarchal, or even egalitarian, culture in recorded history, her feminism consists in imagining a society in which the word "woman" conjures up the whole world of exploring and toiling that have made a two-thousand-year-old civilization, while the word "man" means only male, the sex (137). To imagine alternatives to patriarchy, to speculate on the consequences of female primacy, even if it may be damaging to men, is to engage in a strategy of role reversal that is central to the feminist rhetorical tradition from Anna Denton Cridge's *Man's Rights; or, How Would You Like It?* (1870) to the recent essay by Bette-Jane Raphael entitled "The Myth of the Male Orgasm."

Not content to reverse gender hierarchies, however, Gilman would replace the parasite-siren with the fruitful mother, for she believes that "Maternal energy is the force through which have come into the world both love and industry" (*WE* 126). The middle chapters of *Herland* portray motherhood completely transformed, divorced from heterosexuality, the private family, and economic dependency. Maternal feeling in Herland flows "out in a strong, wide current, unbroken through the generations, deepening and widening through the years, including every child in all the land" (95). Motherhood therefore serves as a paradigm of service so that labor and nursing become the model for work. Similarly all the evils of the private home—isolation of women, amateur un-healthy cooking, the waste of labor and products, improper upbringing of chil-dren, lack of individual privacy—are avoided not by destroying the idea of home but by extending it so the race is viewed as a family and the world as its home. Redefinitions of work, of the home, of motherhood itself confuse the male visitors who had initially insisted that in any "civilized" country there "must be men" (11). Eventually they are forced to renounce not only this assumption but the definition of "civilization" that makes it possible.

"Civilized and still arboreal—peculiar people" (17). This is how Van first comments on the unique culture of Herland. His first perspective of its inhabi-tants is a glimpse of three girls leaping, like wood nymphs, in the branches of a huge tree. With its forests that are cultivated like farms and gardens that look like parks, Gilman's Earthly Paradise banishes wilderness, replacing it with cultivation. From Frances Hodgson Burnett's to Nancy Friday's secret gardens, the landscapes of women's fantasies have mediated between the extremes of savagery and civility that have defined women to their own bewilderment.[7] In fact, the crucial difference between Herland and our land is the feeling Gilman strives to give us that culture there is no longer opposed to nature. This binary dualism, resulting in the domination of nature by culture, is presented in Gil-man's utopia as resolved more harmoniously, through the intercession of the female. Women, considered closer to nature because of their role in perpetuat-ing the species, break down the dichotomy between mind and matter. The architecture Gilman uses to signal art and nature thus allied includes airy gaze-bos, ceilingless temples, open-air theaters. Because the all-female Herlanders define the human as female, mother earth is no longer an antagonist. The implications of the mother as landscape are quite different for the two sexes, as the strong link between feminist and ecological movements suggests.[8]

Parthenogenesis functions symbolically, then, to represent the creativity and autonomy of women, mother-daughter reciprocity, and the interplay of nature and human nature. At the same time it releases women from the female

Oedipus complex, as defined by Freud: the daughter's rejection of the mother, her resulting sense of self-hatred, the extension of her desire for a phallus to desire for the man who possesses the penis. Haggard valorizes the phallic pillar of fire that strikes She dumb. Antithetically, by envisioning a race of woman born, Gilman valorizes the creativity of the womb which is and always has been, after all, the tangible workplace of production.[9] As the male visitors admit the greater power of the overmothers, two of them are converted to what they call "loving up," a phrase that evokes "the stirring" within them "of some ancient dim prehistoric consciousness . . . like—coming home to mother" (152). Analyzing the imperialist project in light of this regression, Gilman implies that the white man's burden is bound up with his not being a woman. The female, far from seeming castrated or mutilated or wounded or envious of the penis, derives her energy and her assurance from the fact that, having no penis, she cannot be castrated.[10] Gilman's radical rejection of Freud's identification of the penis with power is probably made clearest in her emphasis on the erotics of motherhood in *Herland;* "before a child comes," we are told, "there is a period of utter exaltation—the whole being is uplifted and filled with a concentrated desire" (70). Yet another consequence of Gilman's refusal of the phallic law of the fathers is her dream of a common language: linguistic activity in *Herland* is characterized by extreme lucidity, the simplicity that stimulates collectivity.

Gilman is understandably vague about how a mother tongue would constitute a different kind of linguistic activity from the father's law. Yet the very word "Herland" implies that this language, mirroring the two-in-one of mother-and-child, would allow for simultaneous expression of the self as self and the self as object. Certainly Gilman criticizes the closed revelation of the Word of God, contrasting it to the "Indwelling Spirit" of service that Herlanders' worship as the accumulated mother-love of the race. Haggard's She, you remember, is obsessed with obtaining eternal life for herself and for her lover Vincey. But while Haggard criticizes the barbaric vanity of this desire of every woman for personal physical immortality, Gilman claims that the Christian doctrine of personal spiritual immortality is no less egocentric on the part of every man, "a singularly foolish idea . . . And if true, most disagreeable" (116). Instead of desiring to go on growing on earth forever, her heroine wants her child, and her child's child, to go on forever. Identification with the species replaces personal identity, as Gilman insists on the importance of accepting death as an aspect of life. Therefore, while She reigns over a kingdom of perfectly preserved embalmed bodies, Gilman is careful to point out that Herlanders practice cremation. Replacing transcendent God the father with "Maternal Pantheism" (59), the Herlanders expose the narcissism of Christianity, as Gilman criticizes Western civilization for the faults ascribed by Haggard to the barbarism of savages.

Gilman's garden of parthenogenesis replaces the Judeo-Christian garden of Genesis, by claiming that the authority of the father—biological or spiritual—

is a myth fast degenerating to the status of a fiction. Writing at the turn of the century, Gilman implies that the disappearance of God reflects and perpetuates a weakening in patriarchal domination. But parthenogenesis, besides symbolizing the autonomous creativity of women, mother-daughter bonding, the secondariness of the male, and the disappearance of God, also effectively solves the problems of the pains and pressures produced from motherhood's status as a political institution in patriarchy: these include male dispensation of birth control and abortion, the economic dominance of the father and the usurpation of the birth process by a 'male medical establishment.[11] In her own time, women were becoming more vocal about the risks of venereal disease, unwanted conception, dangerous parturition, and abortion.[12] In her own life, Gilman had been profoundly afflicted by not a few of these factors. The painful experiences Gilman describes in her autobiography—of being deserted by her father at an early age, of being brought up by an economically and psychologically impoverished mother who denied her physical affection, of severe postpartum depression, shading into madness, following marriage and the birth of her daughter— are at least partially the result of the problem sexuality constituted for nineteenth-century women.[13] In *Herland,* she gives us this experience transmuted into an enabling fantasy celebrating mother-daughter bond and hinting at her desertion of the father who, in fact, deserted her.

Gilman's inability to nurture her daughter, as well as her difficulty sustaining concentration in her work, are brilliantly dramatized in "The Yellow Wallpaper," (1892) where a nameless woman, denied pen and paper by her physician-husband during a severe postpartum depression, can neither nurture her baby nor herself as she becomes obsessed with the yellowing wallpaper in the upstairs bedroom to which she is confined. Even in the midst of her despair at her confinement in the bedroom with the baroque wallpaper in which she reads the terrible script of women's lives in patriarchy, the narrator glimpses through her window a horde of women ranging freely outdoors where everything is green instead of yellow. Moving toward these "mysteriously deep-shaded arbors, the riotus old-fashioned flowers and gnarled trees,"[14] where can these women be fleeing if not toward the groves of *Herland* where Gilman, who begins her autobiography with a reference to her identification with Queen Victoria, radically revises Ruskin's Queen's Gardens.

Yet the contrast between the fantasy women crawling in the greenly growing country, and the narrator horrified by the patterns in the yellow book of her wallpaper also reminds us that Gilman's utopia has its Gothic shadows too. Certainly part of what drives the narrator of "The Yellow Wallpaper" mad is the bedroom she is made to share with her husband. In *Herland,* men are banished from the bedroom in a fantasy that goes so far as to eliminate both desire and difference. While tenderness and friendship characterize the relationships between women in *Herland,* as they did in Gilman's life, sexuality is fairly closely identified with heterosexuality, as it is in "The Yellow Wallpaper." Even as the climax of Gilman's utopia moves toward "bisexuality"—a word that implies optimistically that heterosexuality is as singular a choice as any other form of sexuality—in fact the plot works to reduce the three male visitors to women's tools or to banish them altogether. In the final chapters of *Herland,* Terry, Jeff, and Van must accept marriage in radically new terms: without a home, without a wife, without sex. For unregenerate Terry who attempts what constitutes marital rape, there can be nothing but anesthesia, confinement, and expulsion. Weir Mitchell's rest-cure treatment, which had caused Gilman the anguish documented in "The Yellow Wallpaper," is turned against the oppressor. The Herlanders' treatment of Terry is, moreover, similar to their response to all aberrant behavior; they use "preventive measures" instead of punishment: sometimes they "send the patient to bed" as part of the "treatment" (112). The sinister ring to their rest-cures reminds us that Gilman's strategy of reversal threatens to invalidate her feminism by defining it in precisely the terms set up by the misogynists it would repudiate.

Gilman's draining away of the erotic no doubt contributes to the boredom experienced by some readers, even as it perhaps unconsciously perpetuates the Victorian ideal of the chaste angel in the house. At first glance, "negative eugenics" (69)—women controlling the population by denying themselves motherhood—turns parthenogenesis into voluntary motherhood, an ideal form of birth control. On the other hand, Gilman describes how "the lowest types" of girls (those with sexual drives) are "bred out" (82). While eugenics empowers woman, it entraps her in the maternal role: she is important not for herself but as the Mother of a Race that is judged in terms of the racial purity of an Aryan stock. Presumably maternal in their respect for life, moreover, the women of *Herland* are presented as innately pacifist, yet their society originated out of war. Similarly this industrialized land, capable of producing motorized cars, seems magically unpolluted by the language, byproducts, labor alienation, or technology of industrialization.

While such contradictions are not uncommon in utopia fiction, their content here specifically points to tensions in feminist ideology at the turn of the century. Nineteenth-century social thinkers repeatedly associated men with war and women with peace, but the women's rights movement was born in the crucible of the Civil War. As Nina Auerbach argues, "Union among women . . . is one of the unacknowledged fruits of war."[15] Similarly, nineteenth-century feminists schooled in the abolition movement found themselves competing (often with racist arguments) against the claims of black men and generally insensitive to the double-bind of black women. Finally, nostalgia for the supposed power of women in preindustrial times and hostility toward the role of science in destructively controlling women's bodies combine in feminist thinking at the turn of the century to evade the hard issue of feminism arising in and having to address itself to a postindustrial world. The daughters of *Herland* are fittingly called "New Women" (56), then, not only because they embody Gilman's vision of a society of women born again, brand new, at the *fin de siècle,* the beginning of a female coming of age; not only because they represent Gilman's version of herself, now adequately nurtured and nurturing; but also because both the strengths and the contradictions of feminism at the turn of the century are reflected so clearly in the world she imagines.

Yet the very radicalism of Gilmans' biological solution in *Herland* pays tribute to the obdurate difficulty of altering patriarchy in a way that her other, supposedly more utilitarian plans did not. Utopian strategies have a special place in feminist intellectual history because they solve two problems: rather than attacking what women have been, they celebrate what women can yet become; instead of admitting that the political and economic strategies for creating a different world are unclear, they imagine them already having taken place in a different dimension, a world elsewhere. In America, we catch the tones of fantastic speculation in Elizabeth Cady Stanton's speech to the International Council of Women in 1888: comparing women to "the children of Israel . . . wandering in the wilderness of prejudice." Stanton explains that "Thus far women have been the mere echoes of men. . . . The true woman is as yet a dream of the future."[16] In England, at the turn of the century, we hear those same speculative notes sounded forcefully in Mary Elizabeth Coleridge's poem "The White Women."

> Where dwell the lovely, wild white women folk,
>   Mortal to man?
> They never bowed their necks beneath the yoke,
> They dwelt alone when the first morning broke
>   And Time began.[17]

Finally, in South Africa, the fantastic dreams and allegories of Olive Schreiner, as well as her *Woman and Labour,* explore the barren ground of female impoverishment with an eye toward a new "dream of a Garden" which "lies in a distant future" where men and women "shall together raise about them an Eden nobler than any the Chaldean dreamed of, an Eden created by their own labour and made beautiful by their fellowship."[18]

Not only does *Herland* uncover the utopian strain of feminist rhetoric; it also reveals the dispossession that valorized colonization as a metaphor of female socialization,[19] leading suffragists to proclaim punningly "No votes for women—no Home Rule." In *The Story of an African Farm* Olive Schreiner most clearly explicates the antiimperialist tradition in women's literary history. The colonies, which had been a dumping ground for redundant women in search of husbands, also served as a punishment for fictional female rebels like Moll

Flanders and Hetty Sorrel. There had actually been plans by men as sober as Gladstone to solve the prostitution problem in England by shipping prostitutes to outposts of the Empire.[20] Along with numerous nuns and nurses, such women might have turned transportation into transport. As if explaining why Mary Taylor, Gertrude Bell, Mary Kingsley, Winifred Holtby, Annie Besant, and the Pankhursts did travel to the colonies as a release from the constraints Victorian culture placed on women, the African explorer Elspeth Huxley wrote a book about Florence Nightingale's life-saving exertions in the Crimea. No wonder the idea of African farming quickens the imagination of women from Schreiner and Gilman to Isak Dinesen, Doris Lessing, Margaret Laurence, and Nadine Gordimer. Even more brutally colonized than these contemporaries, Alice Walker goes "In Search of Our Mothers' Gardens": reminding us of all the silenced black women of the past and present, Walker celebrates her mother's cultivation of the wildest and rockiest landscapes in her gardens resplendant with colorful blooms. Perhaps 200 years ago, she concludes, there was such a mother in Africa.[21]

The shift from *She* to *Herland,* from the caves of Kôr to the South American or African Farm, epitomizes the dialectic between turn of the century misogyny and feminism. For, even though no simple division of labor, no neat point counterpoint, no tidy conception contraception shapes the literary contributions of the two sexes in the twentieth century, an inheritance of double colonization did reveal to women writers the utopian dreams in which they revel, of transforming psychological, social, political, religious, and even biological secondariness and disease into speculations of primacy and health. From their white dresses and hunger fasts to their shattering of mirrors, paintings, and windows, the suffragists exploited fantastic images that empowered the rhetoric of their movement. It is hardly surprising that this dream of female supremacy, being enacted as well as written, in turn aggravated male anxiety, resulting in figures like Jack the Ripper, who haunted the poorer districts of London as if they were exotic climes, hunting down prostitutes whose contamination was punished and perpetuated by the law. He became famous, in 1888, the year after *She* was published, for cutting out their wombs.

Notes

1. Julia Kristeva, *Desire in Language: A Semiotic Approach to Literature and Art,* ed. Leon S. Roudiez, trans. Thomas Gora, Alice Jardine, and Leon S. Roudiez (New York: Columbia University Press, 1980), pp. 36–7.

2. Susan Lurie, "Pornography and the Dread of Women: The Male Sexual Dilemma," in *Take Back the Night,* ed. Laura Lederer (New York: William Morrow, 1980), pp. 159–73. Also see Susan Lurie, "The Construction of the 'Castrated Woman' in Psychoanalysis and Cinema, *Discourse* 4 (Winter 1981–82), pp. 52–74.

3. Charlotte Perkins Gilman, *Herland* (New York: Pantheon Books, 1979), pp. 2, 4. All subsequent quotations are from this edition. I am indebted to the excellent introduction by Ann J. Lane.

4. Eric Rabkin, *The Fantastic in Literature* (Princeton, N.J.: Princeton University Press, 1976), p. 8.

5. Sherry B. Ortner, "Is Female to Male as Nature Is to Culture?" in *Woman, Culture and Society,* eds. Michelle Zimbalist Rosaldo and Louise Lamphere (Stanford: Stanford University Press, 1974), p. 70.

6. Charlotte Perkins Gilman, *Women and Economics,* ed. Carl Degler (New York: Harper & Row, Torchbooks, 1966), p. 70. Subsequent quotations are from this edition.

7. Annette Kolodny has studied the relationship between women and the land in *The Lay of the Land: Metaphor as Experience and History in American Life and Letters* (Chapel Hill: University of North Carolina Press, 1975) and, more recently, in "Honing a Habitable Languagescape: Women's Images for the New World Frontiers," in *Women and Language in Literature and Society,* eds. Sally McConnell-Ginet, Ruth Broker, and Nelly Furman (New Yor: Praeger, 1980), pp. 188–204.

8. Susan Griffin, *Woman and Nature: The Roaring Inside Her* (New York: Harper & Row, Colophon Books, 1980).

9. See Gayatri C. Spivak's discussion of the womb in "Unmaking and Making in *To the Lighhouse,*" in *Women and Language in Literature and Society,* p. 326.

10. This is Susan Lurie's point about the male castration fear underlying the Freudian theory of female penis envy.

11. Adrienne Rich, "Motherhood in Bondage," in *On Lies, Secrets, and Silence: Selected Prose 1966–1978* (New York: W. W. Norton, 1979), p. 196.

12. Linda Gordon, *Woman's Body, Woman's Right: A Social History of Birth Control in America* (New York: Penguin Books, 1976).

13. *The Living of Charlotte Perkins Gilman* (New York: Harper & Row, 1975), p. 104.

14. Charlotte Perkins Gilman, *The Yellow Wallpaper* (Old Westbury, N.Y.: The Feminist Press, 1973), p. 15.

15. Nina Auerbach, *Communities of Women: An Idea in Fiction* (Cambridge: Harvard University Press, 1978), p. 161.

16. Elizabeth Cady Stanton's speech is reprinted in *Feminism: The Essential Historical Writings,* ed. Miriam Schneir (New York: Random House, 1972), p. vi.

17. Mary Elizabeth Coleridge, "The White Women," in *Poems by Mary E. Coleridge* (London: Elkin Mathews, 1908), p. 92.

18. Olive Shreiner, *Woman and Labour* (London: Virago Press, 1978), p. 282.

19. For a discussion of the relationship between woman and the colonized, see Barbara Charlesworth Gelpi, "A Common Language: The American Woman Poet," in *Shakespeare's Sisters: Feminist Essays on Women Poets* (Bloomington: Indiana University Press, 1979), pp. 269–79.

20. A. James Hammerton, "Feminism and Female Emigration, 1861–1886," and Judith Walkowitz, "The Making of an Outcast Group: Prostitutes and Working Women in Nineteenth-Century Plymouth and Southampton," in *A Widening Sphere: Changing Roles of Victorian Women,* ed. Martha Vicinus (Bloomington: Indiana University Press, 1980), pp. 52–71, 72–93.

21. Alice Walker, "In Search of Our Mothers' Gardens," in *Woman as Writer,* eds. Jeannette L. Webber and Joan Grumman (Boston: Houghton Mifflin, 1978), pp. 193–201.

Contributors

MARIA BRUNO teaches American literature, women's literature, and composition at Michigan State University. She has published short fiction in *Ms., Midway Review, Red Cedar Review, Women's Studies Newsletter,* and *The Burning World.* A book of her short stories is forthcoming from Wayne State University Press, edited by Susan Koppelman.

CATHY N. DAVIDSON is Professor of English at Michigan State University and Visiting Professor of English at Princeton University for 1988–1989. A Woodrow Wilson and a Guggenheim Fellow, she has published eight books, most recently *Revolution and the Word: The Rise of the Novel in America* (Oxford University Press, 1986). She has also written over forty essays and presented some fifty papers, keynote addresses, and invited lectures in the United States, Canada, and Japan.

CARL N. DEGLER is Margaret Byrne Professor of American History at Stanford University. He has published eight books, including *Neither Black nor White: Slavery and Race Relations in Brazil and the United States,* which won the Pulitzer Prize in History in 1972. He has been a Fellow of the American Council of Learned Societies, the John Guggenheim Foundation, the National Endowment for the Humanities, and the Center for Advanced Study in the Behavioral Sciences. He has also served on the editorial boards of eight scholarly journals.

JULIANN EVANS FLEENOR has been a freelance writer since 1983 and has published nonfiction extensively and two short mysteries, one in *Woman's World* and ;the other in *A Matter of Crime.* Her essay in this volume was originally published in *The Female Gothic,* an anthology of critical essays on the gothic form and women writers, which she edited.

SUSAN GUBAR teaches at Indiana University. Together with Sandra M. Gilbert, she has written *The Madwoman in the Attic, The War of the Words,* and *No*

Man's Land. Recently, they also co-edited the *Norton Anthology of Literature by Women: The Tradition in English*. In 1989, Ms. Gubar will publish a collection of essays on the dilemma of violent pornography, entitled *For Adult Users Only*.

K. GRAEHME HALL is an academic advisor at Michigan State University. Her poetry has appeared in *The Centennial Review* and in several other journals. She is currently engaged in research on rape in women's sexual fantasies, and on violence against women in modern American fiction.

JANICE HANEY-PERITZ is Associate Professor and Chair of the English Department at Beaver College in Glenside, Pennsylvania. Besides a number of review essays, she has published articles on romantic irony, allegorical indeterminacy, rhetorical politics, modernist aesthetics, the novelistic deployment of sexuality, and the teaching of writing. Currently she is working on two projects: the annual *Romantic Movement Bibliography* and a study of the sexual politics of Romantic discourse.

MARY A. HILL is Professor and Chair of the Department of History at Bucknell University. She has authored two books on Charlotte Perkins Gilman: *Charlotte Perkins Gilman: The Making of a Radical Feminist 1860–1896* (1980) and *Endure: The Diaries of Charles Walter Stetson* (1985). She is currently working on a third volume concerning the life and work of Gilman, focusing this time on the author's correspondence with Houghton Gilman (1896–1900).

JEAN E. KENNARD is Professor of English and Women's Studies at the University of New Hampshire. She is the author of *Number and Nightmare: Forms of Fantasy in Contemporary Fiction* (1975), *Victims of Convention* (1978), *A Working Partnership: Vera Brittain and Winifred Holtby* (forthcoming), and several essays on modern fiction and feminist literary theory.

CAROL FARLEY KESSLER, Associate Professor of English, American Studies, and Women's Studies at Penn State Delaware County Campus, has published *Elizabeth Stuart Phelps* (1982), *Daring to Dream: Utopian Stories by U.S. Women, 1836–1919* (1984), *The Story of Avis* by Elizabeth Stuart Phelps (1877, rpt. 1985). She is currently completing a study "Other Worlds: U.S. Women Envision Utopia, 1836 to the Present," supported by an NEH Fellowship for College Teachers.

JOANN P. KRIEG teaches American literature and American Studies at Hofstra University. She is President of the Walt Whitman Birthplace Association in Huntington, New York, and has published a number of articles on Whitman.

She is the editor of *Walt Whitman Here and Now* (1985), a collection of critical essays.

SHERYL L. MEYERING teaches American literature and composition at Southern Illinois University at Edwardsville. In addition to this volume, she is currently completing *Sylvia Plath: A Reference Guide,* to be published by G. K. Hall in 1989.

SHARON M. RAMBO holds a Ph.D. in medieval narrative and teaches American literature and Women's Studies at Michigan State University. In addition to her work on Gilman, she has published on Harriette Arnow, Caroline Kirkland, and Virginia Rich. Her current research interests include the Michigan novelist, Della T. Lutes, and a collaborative study of gender and intimacy.

CONRAD SHUMAKER is an Associate Professor at the University of Central Arkansas. He is currently completing a book on Nathaniel Hawthorne's response to the nineteenth-century view of women.

LINDA WAGNER-MARTIN is Hanes Professor of English at the University of North Carolina, Chapel Hill, where she teaches modern literature with an emphasis in women's and multiethnic texts. Recent books include *Sylvia Plath, A Biography; Sylvia Plath: The Critical Heritage;* and *The Modern American Novel, 1914–1945.* She has written widely on Hemingway, Faulkner, Glasgow, Levertov, Williams, Frost, Dos Passos, Morrison, Oates, Hellman, and many other twentieth-century writers.

CHRISTOPHER P. WILSON is Associate Professor of English and American Studies at Boston College, and the author of *The Labor of Words: Literary Professionalism in the Progressive Era* (1985). He has also published articles on Sinclair Lewis, John Reed, William Dean Howells, Stephen Crane, and others. Currently, he is working on a study of turn-of-the-century representations of the "new" middle class.

Index

This collection of essays, edited by Sheryl L. Meyering and with a foreword by Cathy N. Davidson, maps a way for readers to approach Charolotte Perkins Gilman's large body of fiction and poetry. In addition to providing biographical background they treat the fundamental ideas Gilman developed through her work: the need for women to do "meaningful work" outside the home, the conflict suffered by the woman artist, and the depression and breakdown frequently resulting from that conflict.

Sheryl L. Meyering is emerita professor of English at Southern Illinois University, Edwardsville.

Lightning Source UK Ltd.
Milton Keynes UK
UKHW042059270219
338152UK00001B/20/P